LIVE

YOUR

TRUE

ESSENCE

Learn 12 Secrets
That Will Empower Your Mind,
Balance Your Body,
and Enlighten Your Spirit

ROSE SANTIAGO

For information about special discounts available for bulk purchases, sales promotions, fund-raising and educational needs, contact www.LiveYourTrueEssence.com and www.RoseSantiago.com Printed in the U.S.A.

Visit the author's website at www.LiveYourTrueEssence.com and www.RoseSantiago.com

This manuscript and its content are for educational purposes and do not take the place of medical advice from your physician. Every effort has been made to ensure that the content provided in this manuscript is accurate and helpful for readers at publishing time. However, this is not an exhaustive treatment of the subjects. Although every precaution has been taken to verify the accuracy of the information contained herein, the author and publisher assume no responsibility for any errors or omissions. Pregnant women, elderly persons, children, people taking medications or facing surgery, or those with a compromised immune system must take special care for their health in conjunction with their healthcare providers. No liability is assumed for losses or damages due to the information provided. You are responsible for your own choices, actions, and results. Consult a trained medical professional for your specific healthcare needs.

Published by: Rosa Santiago, Somerset, New Jersey
Editing by: Christina Goebel, Livingston, Texas, www.linkedin.com/in/christina-chris-goebel

Santiago, Rosa, 2018 – *Live Your True Essence: Learn 12 Secrets that Will Empower Your Mind, Balance Your Body, and Enlighten Your Spirit*

ISBN: 978-0-578-40518-6
10 9 8 7 6 5 4 3 2 1

1. Self-improvement
First Edition

CONTENTS

Dedication vii

Preface ix

PART 1: THE MIND.. 1

Chapter 1:   Begin at the Beginning 3
Chapter 2:   Get to Know Yourself 18
Chapter 3:   What is Your Mindset? 40
Chapter 4:   An Attitude of Gratitude 53
Chapter 5:   Unharnessing the Power Within 67

PART 2: THE BODY 89

Chapter 6:   Welcome to the World of Essential Oils and
             Aromatherapy 91
Chapter 7:   My All-Time Favorite Essential Oils 105
Chapter 8:   Ingredients to Love 131
Chapter 9:   Ingredients to Love Not 154

PART 3: THE SPIRIT... 173

Chapter 10: The Spirit Essence That is You.................................... 175
Chapter 11: Step Into Your True Essence 197

Endnotes.. 215

DEDICATION

This book is dedicated to my mother, Teresa Santiago, an angel in my life, who has faithfully believed in me and has supported me every step of the way as I went through the process of writing my book. I also dedicate it to my best friend and great supporter, Dan Facchini, who has stood by me and dealt with my crazy moods when I couldn't get my thoughts out while writing a certain chapter. To my editor, Christina Goebel, whose experience and knowledge has contributed to the creation of this book, and whose confidence in me as a skilled writer has inspired me to work even harder to write. I am sincerely most grateful to God, and to all the people who have helped and believed in me while writing this book.

PREFACE

"Life isn't about finding yourself. Life is about creating yourself."
— George Bernard Shaw

Take a deep breath. Relax your mind and body and make yourself comfortable while we spend some time together learning about the wonderful benefits of effectively living a well-balanced lifestyle with true essence, starting today. Why not fix yourself a cup of hot herbal tea or a healthy cold beverage you enjoy and get in a state of mind for some great information that can transform your life?

You may think, "Can living your true essence really be achieved? Is it possible to live the life you want? Or is it just a pipe dream?" Well, I am here to tell you that YOU can learn how to live your most authentic and true self. It can be done. I did it! And you can do it too.

There was a time where my circumstances almost broke my spirit. I was married to a man that said he loved me, but his words and actions made me feel torn up inside and inferior. My self-esteem was virtually nonexistent. I was a total mess.

I remember when my son Gabriel was born, a precious baby boy that weighed seven pounds, eight ounces. I wanted my mother, Teresa, to stay with us for a while so she could help me care for my baby. What happened the day I spoke to my husband about it was the beginning of years of constant verbal and mental abuse.

My husband Lloyd's words hit me like a swift punch in the gut. "Your mother doesn't need to come," he said with some annoyance. "What for? My mother can help you with the baby."

"But I need my mother here," I said. "It's important to me. She should be here. You know that my mother is far away and it is not as easy for her to visit. She is my mother. I need her, and she has the right to spend time with her newborn grandson."

I desperately hoped he would capitulate, or, at the very least, that he could understand how having my mother there helping me with my baby meant a lot to me. Besides, I needed her to share those memorable moments of quality time with her grandson and her daughter who was now a new mother, and still was not familiar with all the responsibilities and care that an infant needed. None of that fazed him.

He knew that I had just undergone a C-section and was in terrible pain from the surgery. Yet, my voice fell on deaf ears. He ignored my pleas and made me feel like a spoiled child who was being scolded by her father.

"That's not possible," he said coldly. "It is not necessary. My mother can help you." Turning his back on me, he walked away, leaving me with my mouth agape at his insensitivity and unwillingness to be supportive or compassionate. No words could adequately explain the pain that shot through my body. The anguish of knowing that my husband cared nothing for my feelings or the feelings of my mother, who anxiously wanted to spend time with her daughter and grandson, left me speechless. The cruelty and absurdity of it made no sense.

Nonetheless, the tears of helplessness and anger spilled from my eyes like a burning flame. The piercing pain of knowing that my mother could not be with me at such a critical time swept over me like a thousand tiny pieces of broken glass that mercilessly cut through me. The worst part was that I had to submit to his final decision. I could do nothing to change his mind. His rigid behavior and cold disposition never really changed in our ten-year marriage before we separated.

The following weeks were filled with agony for me. I never felt so alone and abandoned. There were barely any words between my husband and me. Silence and the emptiness greeted me each morning when I awoke. The only solace I had was of caring and loving my baby. I spent hours feeding, changing, playing, bathing, and putting my young son down for naps. Those moments were filled with pleasure for me, despite the bitter and sometimes crude way my husband treated me. At times, I felt so exhausted and fervently wished my mother could have been by my side. Yet, I didn't expect my husband to change his mind, so I did my best to have a cheerful spirit when I was with my son. There were inevitable moments of sadness when I held my son in my arms as I rocked him to sleep, when the tears of helplessness and pain came.

This was my life, filled with rules and regulations. Submission was the order of the day. I had no opinions. No rights. Our religion imposed more rules and regulations. I felt like a prisoner, trapped in a world I could not control.

Those dark moments prepared me for what was to come. My husband, Lloyd, was my greatest teacher, for his hurtful words and unkind attitude toward me allowed me to come out of my shell. The relationship taught me to be strong, have confidence in myself, and have faith that I would be okay. It made me realize that I was the one allowing the verbal and mental abuse. Due to my fear of not acting in accordance with the Bible's principles on the wife's role in the family, I kept silent, believing at the time that the God I thought was outside of myself could punish me for my willful disobedience.

For years, I felt that nothing I did would please my husband. Many of the ideas, decisions, or opinions I had seemed irrelevant to him. If I wanted to visit with my immediate family, for example, it was not possible that weekend, or virtually any weekend. If I wanted to start my own business, he threatened me with no help or support. As my son grew, he said my opinions on child rearing were inadequate. It seemed that his mother knew all the answers to raising our child. In his way of viewing things, she was right and I was wrong.

However, when I dug deep within my spirit, I believed I could do what made me happy: having a business, rearing a child, and much more. I had to find that inner girl who loved living, despite the complicated events I was experiencing, and who had hidden dreams that were yet to be discovered. She was in there somewhere—the girl who dared to take chances, had so much to give, and was full of energy. That girl needed to make her appearance known again in a bigger and more powerful way.

I realized that my current life situations held me back from letting that inner girl shine through. I had settled for what I didn't want. The inner shego I had operated with for so long had to undergo some serious changes if I wanted to live my true essence.

The moment I decided to do something about the way I lived was when everything began to transform for me. I began to purposely plan my life. I made sacrifices, but I knew that if I stayed in that relationship, I would never have learned the secrets to living my true essence—the secrets that I am now sharing with you. So, I set out to create a more balanced and successful world for myself. Step by step, I learned new tools that I will share with you that changed my life forever. I will teach these same strategies to you.

Now, here's the catch. It is essential that you completely focus on what you are reading and your intention is set to learn and understand the topic at hand. This is important stuff you do not want to miss, so if you took the time to purchase this book, I know you want to get the best out of it.

Believe me, you can make time to learn something new that can create new possibilities for you. I promise you that if you spend some time with me and allow me to teach you how you can take the initiative to learn new rituals, work on training your mind to focus on the positive aspects of yourself, and experience natural methods that can enhance your mood and improve your health and well-being, I will make reading this book worthwhile. I will share proven secrets with you about how you can create and live your authentic essence physically, emotionally, mentally, and spiritually.

So, if you picked up this book, you must have a good reason for doing so. Is it because you want to take steps to more effectively have balance in your life? Or perhaps you would like to go beyond your present circumstances? To soar above the limits of your physical self? You know there is more to YOU and you wish to discover who YOU really are. Or, could it be that you desire to feel good and have more energy each day? Perhaps you simply wish to live a lifestyle that represents what you want to happen in your world as you dream about it? Those may be some great reasons for reading this book.

Or, maybe you are tired of taking over-the-counter or even prescription medications that don't work and are causing you more harm than good. Maybe you are exploring alternative solutions to personal care products that you heard are filled with thousands of chemicals that can have potentially dangerous side-effects on your body. Or perhaps you want to have great skin, fabulous hair, and put your best face forward without having to grab products off the shelves that contain shady ingredients that could harm your health and well-being.

These questions will be considered throughout this book. You will be well-equipped with the necessary tools to develop your true essence and create your inner world, which will allow you to go deep within yourself to discover that there is more to you than what you believe. You will have within your grasp secret tips and information that will help you better understand the importance of educating yourself on the behaviors, beliefs, and personality traits you were taught in the past that may not have always served any real purpose in your life. In addition, you will have access to the innumerable benefits found in the world of essential oils and aromatherapy. By immersing yourself in the study of this universe of essence, you too can significantly improve your overall health and well-being.

I have broken down this book into three parts, so that you can more easily follow what you are reading. The first part talks about the mind and how it can shape the way you think and live your life. In the second part, I will talk about the body, and how what you put in it can either make you feel healthy and full of energy, or feel physically weak and mentally drained. In the final part, I will discuss the spirit and what it means to fully express who you truly are within. The result of learning and applying these three factors is that living with completeness of mind, body, and spirit means that you will finally have the privilege of being formally introduced to your true and authentic essence.

Is this possible? Well, read on to find out. Relax, take a sip of your hot or cold beverage, and take a trip down discovery lane with me to see what lies ahead for you.

WHAT YOU WILL DISCOVER

Thank you for purchasing this book. In it, I hope you find gems of wisdom and new ideas that resonate with you and enlighten you. Throughout my life, I have scooped up these secret treasures and now want to share them with you. My intention is that you too can benefit from the transformative experiences as well as the new beliefs that have shaped me, and the lessons I have learned and grown from, which will be revealed to you through each chapter.

In the earlier chapters, I will share personal experiences with you about what I overcame in my life to get to know my true essence. There were moments that seemed insurmountable to me, but with a little recipe that included ingredients such as courage, determination, and a healthy scoop of love and faith, I met the challenges head-on, and in the interim, I discovered that there was more to me than what I believed to be true about myself.

The intention for writing this book is that you too can experience your own true essence and what that represents to you. It is my sincere hope that as you read through the chapters, you will ask yourself fundamental questions and look for genuine answers that come from your soul. By doing some simple exercises with me, you may discover that you are much more than you think.

Promise me that you will be committed to reading this book from cover to cover. I know it is tempting to go forward and peek to see what is up ahead in the later chapters, but believe me, you will want to read and cover the exercises in an orderly manner so that each step is clear and understandable to you as you progress and take the actions necessary to discover the secret to creating and fully living your most authentic self each day.

If you are in a noisy area, or if you are surrounded by every sort of electronical device that is beeping, ringing, and blurping, or if there are humans presently disturbing your concentration, then find a quiet place or shut off all the interruptions, and go where you can be alone and relax. Set your mind to learning what higher thinking is all about and how aromatherapy can significantly enhance your life when you incorporate the essential methods that I have provided for you that can be used to create many new opportunities and possibilities in every aspect of your world.

You will find great tips and ideas that you can incorporate daily to surround yourself with products that calm, energize, or stimulate your senses. I will show you meditation, visualization, and affirmation techniques you can start implementing right now to jump-start your path to living your true essence in mind, body and spirit, plus so much more!

Are you ready to transform from caterpillar to butterfly? Are you set to discover how you can live your unique and flavorful essence? Then, let's go!

You have control of only three
things in your life. The thoughts you
think, the images you visualize,
and the actions you take.

Jack Canfield

PART ONE

THE MIND

CHAPTER ONE

BEGIN AT THE BEGINNING

"You have control of only three things in your life. The thoughts you think, the images you visualize, and the actions you take."
— Jack Canfield

MY BEGINNING

I was born in San Sebastian, a municipality of Puerto Rico that is located on the northwest side of the island. About a year and a half after I was born, my parents, Teresa and Aracelio, moved our family to the United States and this became our new home. My father found us a small apartment in New Jersey for our party of six, and we settled there.

Shortly after my birth, when I was a few months old and still living on the island, my mother, Teresa, discovered that there was something terribly wrong with her fourth child. My elder siblings, Aracelio Jr., Luis, and Maritza, were born healthy, with no visible signs of complications, but there seemed to be a serious physical developmental issue with me.

It wasn't until I was three months old that one day my mother, lovingly and adoringly playing with me, noticed that I was not following her gaze anywhere. I would make the appropriate cooing baby noises and respond to her gentle touch and affectionate words, but my eyes didn't follow her as she moved about the room. Neither did I react to the toys she placed in front of me. It was only to her voice that I would respond to by turning my head toward the sound.

At that moment, my mother discovered that I was blind. Knowing that doctors in Puerto Rico could not prove conclusively that I had a visual impairment due to the lack of medical technology during that time, my mother had no choice but to wait until our family moved to the United States before a doctor could determine with absolute certainty that this was the case. After loads of tests, a doctor confirmed to my mother that I had optic nerve damage and incurable blindness.

The reaction my mother took must have surprised the doctors, her family, and the other people she was acquainted with then. The question of "Why do I have a daughter that cannot see?" may have momentarily crossed her mind, but my mother accepted the fact as a way of life. Even though her other children were healthy and physically intact (of course that is subject to opinion), there seemed to be nothing wrong with them.

Instead of feeling shocked and worried about how she would help and care for this special child, my mother decided that she would care for me the same way she would the rest of her rambunctious gang. Less than a year later, more rug rats were born. In total we were seven, with two children born blind, myself, and my younger brother, Eddie.

Questions must have plagued my mother's mind. Questions like, "Why did this happen to me? Why did this have to happen to my daughter?" but she never complained about having two kids without sight. I admire my mother for that. She never showed any signs of blame toward God or anyone else for the children she bore who had to grow up learning how to live in a world where their other senses needed to be heightened to compensate for their lack of sight.

Throughout my young life, my mother ensured that I was treated equally and had the same opportunities that my brothers and sisters as well as other children had. I attended public schools and joined many extracurricular activities, such as chorus (where I learned how to use my singing voice more effectively), cooking classes (where I learned to make simple dishes), and the out-door club (where I learned to rock climb, mountain climb, hike, camp, and participate in other outdoor adventurous activities I enjoyed). I also joined school plays, talent shows, even fashion shows (if you can believe it). I was never afraid to try new things. I loved taking chances, even though some things were challenging for me. I still tried nonetheless.

However, life wasn't always full of adventures for me. There was a time when I was a kid where I experienced a particularly dark moment that almost broke my spirit and caused me to abhor my blindness with every breath in my body.

A TARGET FOR BULLIES

When I was in elementary school, my blindness became a real problem for me. Never had I been self-conscious or noticed my lack of sight as a wall that separated me from the rest of the world. It wasn't until the sixth grade that things started changing. The dark years were ready to crush me like I never knew they could.

"You blind bat." That is what one of the male students in my seventh-grade class said one day to me. It was the first time I ever was referred to in that way. Sure, I knew I had little to no sight, but to be compared to a bat, now that gave it a different twist.

At that time, I didn't know bats were not blind. This fact was not known to me until years later. All I knew was that this mean kid was comparing me to a flying creature I considered dirty and stupid for supposedly not having sight. This was the beginning of my trip down Pity Party Lane.

Soon other supporters joined his little "hate the blind girl" gang, dishing out their cruel remarks toward me. Each day, they taunted me and played dumb tricks on me. They stuck out their foot so that I would trip. They followed me home from school threatening to beat me up. Yeah, it was a lot of fun . . . not.

Seriously though, those years changed me from an innocent girl who accepted herself as she was, to a bitter kid who now thought she was the worst person in the world. I developed a self-consciousness and insecurities about my blindness that I had never thought of before. Everything from how I ate to how I walked around in school affected me.

I didn't use a cane, because I hated it from day one. It's not like I didn't think it was useful. It's just that I felt that walking around with a white stick was a sure way to get much unneeded attention from my persecutors. So, I walked alone, using as much of my little sight as I could to get around.

Feelings of inadequacy crept up inside of me. Emotions of not being enough surrounded me daily. I felt helpless, constantly comparing myself to others and never feeling like I would ever be in their league. I felt like

I could never measure up. Who was I after all? I couldn't see, therefore, there was not much I could do, either. I just didn't belong.

Every day at school, the kids pointed out to me that the only thing I knew how to do was bump into walls. They thought it was funny that I was blind. They teased me mercilessly, but not once did I cry. I held all their ridiculing and crude remarks inside.

In time, however, I began to believe their words. I felt completely trapped in my dark world. I thought, "What good am I to others? What difference can I make in someone else's life if I can barely see in front of me? Why am I even here?" I went deeper into depression, to the point where I decided that the only answer I had was to simply not exist.

A STORM CLOUD OF DEATH APPROACHES

Careful that no one was around, one evening I silently crept into the bathroom of the apartment where we lived, which was in a low-income housing part of New Jersey, and listened intently to make sure my mother was still watching her soap operas in Spanish. Relieved that she didn't know that I had gone to the bathroom, probably thinking I went to play with my brothers and sisters who were downstairs in the living room watching TV, I soundlessly closed the door and hoped no one would pick that precise moment to call my name.

Moving toward the medicine cabinet, I quietly opened the glass door and grabbed the first bottle of pills I could find. I didn't know the name or didn't much care which bottle I took, so long as it did the job. Whatever they were, they were about to go down my throat. I only wanted the pain to end. Those were the thoughts that invaded my head.

When I opened the small bottle of pills, I hesitated briefly. The pause was simply a stab of regret that I would cause so much pain and sadness to my mother. However, existing in a world where I felt worthless and mistreated was not worth living if that was what I had to endure for the rest of my life. That's the way I saw it then.

Pouring several of the small pills onto my palm—I don't know how many they were exactly—I put them in my mouth and swallowed. I drank some sink water to get them down, but hated the bitter taste. As if that would matter in a few minutes.

The mental images that played in my mind was of the kids making fun of me because I was different. They made me feel worthless, unimportant, useless, and weird because I had little sight. Their taunts reverberated in my head like loud, untuned instruments whose incessant sounds I desperately wanted to drown out. The inner voice of reason in my head was practically nonexistent. She was almost completely overshadowed by the other negative voices that crowded my mind. The ones I wanted to silence forever.

Leaving the bathroom, I felt a little woozy, but showed nothing to set off alarm bells to my mother who was nearby still watching TV. I lay on the bed in her room, sure that if I fell asleep, at least she would be the one there next to me. The one person I knew had always accepted me for who I was, but it was not enough, because I wasn't enough.

Time passed, but nothing happened. Okay, what kind of pills were these, anyway? I thought with some annoyance. Why was I still here? Were they vitamins? They couldn't be, because I felt a bit dizzy and shaky.

These were the first thoughts that popped into my head the next morning when I awoke. I was actually pissed. For all I knew, they were probably cold pills or something. I should have known that the worst type of pills in the house would probably be Tylenol or cold medicine.

Just great, I thought angrily. I was attempting to take pills that should have done the job, and instead, I took pills that just put me to sleep. My brilliant attempt to end my existence turned out to be a big fail. When I woke up, I was somehow back in the bedroom I shared with my two sisters, Maritza and Madeline. Of course, they knew nothing of what had almost transpired just a few hours earlier.

FINALLY HEARING THE REAL VOICE WITHIN

I was alive and well. Nothing happened. My life was intact.

It was the dumbest thing I had ever done. It was great that I told no one of my brief encounter with insanity. It took a moment, but I reasoned, Really? Was I truly helpless? Was I incapable, or stupid? Did I bump into walls? Of course not.

Suddenly, I realized I was more than what my peers thought about me. There was much I had to offer despite my blindness. I possessed many attributes and, if anything, I had talents many people didn't have. I was my unique brand of person. I considered myself to be a decent singer and writer. So, I was not so bad after all.

That inner voice that was buried deep beneath the surface of my mind, began speaking words of wisdom in my ear. I heard her shout with relief that I had finally come to my senses. She knew she was almost drowned out, but when she came back, boy, did she come flying in with a vengeance. The good thing was that I paid attention.

AN EYE-OPENING EXPERIENCE

At that moment, something rose deep inside of me, something that I believe was greater than myself. It was the need to accept myself for who I was. If I believed all the lies and stories told by my peers, or anyone else for that matter, I would never have been able to live it up. It was up to me to change my thoughts about myself, the images I held about myself, and the actions I needed to take from that moment. So, I did.

Some time passed by, but I decided that I'd had enough of the crap my fellow students piled on top of me. They were still bullying me, yet I learned how to block the mean things they said. I had to find a way to stop their persistent taunts, but I still didn't know how to just yet. All I wanted was the strength to make them understand my blindness, which was of prime importance, and so I set out to show them that I was just like them. Even though in some ways we were different, in many ways we were the same. I wanted them to see that my blindness didn't change me from being a kid like them, that we could still share and learn from each other and that we could get along despite our differences. I wish I could say it worked, but it didn't.

My eighth-grade year of school was almost over, and the bullying still hadn't stopped. High school was right around the corner, and I knew that if I was tired of putting up with the kids in elementary school and wanted a normal teenage life, I had to do something to stop the treatment I was still enduring. I had to find a way to teach the kids that tormented me practically every day that their bullying was wrong and that it hurt me. If I wanted to survive high school, I had to stop the vicious three-year cycle of bullying in my life right away. But what was I going to do?

One day, I believe it was early spring, I had my first aha moment. I knew exactly what had to be done. The idea gave me hope, and if it didn't work, at least I would know that I gave it my best shot.

One thing I love to do is write poetry. So, I thought, what better way to express my feelings about not having sight? What better example to help my peers as well as others understand blindness, than with a poem?

That night, I concentrated with all my mind and thoughts on how I would develop what I hoped and prayed would shed a light of understanding about blindness to my eighth-grade class. I sat in silence, facing my typewriter, waiting for the words to come pouring out. Typewriter, ha ha, here I am giving my age away. Let it be our little secret. After all, isn't this a book of secrets?

Anyway, when the words finally tumbled out, I typed until I was satisfied with what I had written. I hoped my teacher and the students in my class could grasp the meaning behind the words of the poem. I would soon find out.

The next day, I arrived at school, ready to see how this would play out. I handed the poem to my eighth-grade teacher, Mrs. Perkins, and asked her if she could read it and let me know her thoughts. A few minutes later, she walked up to my desk and asked if she could read the poem aloud to the students in the class. I told her it was fine. After all, wasn't that the plan? Of course, she didn't know that.

When she read the poem aloud, nothing happened. Well, not exactly. The room was silent for what seemed an eternity. Mrs. Perkins hugged me and told me how proud of me she was for doing this very brave thing. She had an idea of how the kids had bullied me, but she didn't know the extent of it.

No one approached me in the classroom, yet I felt a change in the air. The kids that taunted me suddenly ceased their obnoxious taunts. Just like that. They stopped their bullying. Wow, I thought in surprise, I didn't know it was going to work that fast.

That wasn't the end of it, though. My teacher wanted to give the poem to the principal, Mr. Pane. After reading the poem, the principal asked me to write it in braille, a format developed where blind individuals who were print-challenged could read with their fingers. He wanted me to recite it over the school's loudspeaker the very next morning after the saluting of the flag.

Well, I didn't expect all of this, but it felt liberating to express my feelings to all the students and faculty through my poem. I felt emotionally uplifted that they could finally empathize with me as a blind person. The poem was written with the sincere intentions of my heart to make them understand how I lived as a person without sight.

I remember parts of the poem to this day. In detail, I explained how I wished I could watch the white, puffy clouds float high above the sky, how I longed to gaze at the stars that danced and twinkled across the heavens, and watch the moon as it followed me with its brilliant, glowing light. I remember that I talked about the beauty of the tall, lush green trees and all the colorful flowers I was unable to see. Yet, with my fingers, I read in part, I could explore their delicate petals and inhale their beautiful essences.

After reciting the poem over the loud speaker, I knew I had made some impact. Not just with the students, but I had also made a strong impression on my teachers. They really were never exposed to blindness, since I was the first and only blind student in the school.

The principal was so delighted with my poem that he asked me if I could recite it once more at my eighth-grade graduation. Wow, I thought, parents and other students will be there. This is turning out to be bigger than I first thought.

VOICES INVADE MY MIND ONCE AGAIN

The nerves started. I trembled with the thought of speaking in front of such a crowd. The voices in my head commenced their incessant chant once again. "How are you going to do this thing?" they began. "The truth is you are blind. What lesson do you think you can teach these people?"

Talk about being hard on myself. I was the queen of self-pity at the time. The voices got louder and louder, and I became more fearful of reading the poem aloud at my graduation ceremony.

Amid the pounding noise in my head, however, there my inner voice was again, screaming above the other voices, hoping to get my attention and kicking out in frustration when I ignored her. She was attempting with fruitless efforts to thwart the idea that I could find a way to enlighten my audience with the truth. Here I was, trying to bury her deep inside of myself again where she could not be heard.

Fear coursed through my body and for a moment, I believed I couldn't convince anyone that blindness was not the characteristic that defined me or made me who I was. That was the truth.

Yet, my inner voice whispered as softly as the touch of a gentle and fleeting breeze when the other voices finally calmed their negative chatter. She said, "You can recite that poem in front of parents and other students, and anyone else who wants to hear it. You are just like them. You are unique in your own way, but so are they. You are special, but so are they. You have talents and abilities, but so do they."

"Yes, you are right!" I said, and to her great relief. Why should I be afraid? If have come this far to deliver this poem to the students in my class, why not just read it to everyone else? It would help so many people come to understand my world and it could make things better for me.

Then and there, I decided that my poem had to be read one more time—this time in front of the entire graduation class, teachers, parents and other students. So, I listened to my inner voice and recited the poem once more for all to hear. I smiled broadly, for in my mind I saw my inner girl pump her fist in the air with pure joy. She did a little dance and shouted with ecstasy at her latest triumph.

Believe me, that was no small feat, though, but I had mustered the strength to do something about what I was feeling. Either I did it, or I died. There was no in-between. That was when I realized that this was the person I would eventually evolve into. With love, understanding, and putting myself in the shoes of my peers, I could comprehend that those kids didn't know blindness, and in a convoluted sort of way, they had teased me because of their ignorance about knowing what not seeing was like, and how weird that must feel. You could say it was another aha moment for me.

The real joy came for me when, after the graduation ceremony was over, each student who had played a part in bullying me for three years, one by one, stood up from their chair and walked up to me in front of the entire auditorium. They shook my hand, their voices trembling with deep sorrow as they sincerely apologized to me for all the pain they had caused me for so long. No standing ovation, no trophy, not even a Pulitzer Prize could have made me feel happier.

It felt so amazing to know that my plan had worked. Instead of ignoring the problem, pretending that it would go away—even going so far as to attempt to end my life to escape the world that I had come to live in—I faced it head on. I needed to find a way to win my peers by helping them to understand where I was coming from. And I did. It was indeed a proud and victorious day.

I shall never forget this eye-opening experience. The kind words and future actions of my peers were no longer rude or aggressive. From that moment, I was treated with dignity and respect from the students who had at one time bullied and taunted me with cruel words and deeds.

Yet, there was another important lesson I learned. When I flipped the switch of my negative thoughts to positive ones, everything changed. When I replaced the dismal images of how the kids taunted and bullied me every day, and painted a prettier picture of a happier outcome, that is what occurred. Finally, when I found a way to stop the malicious behavior toward me, there was a much better and more favorable result than if I hadn't taken any action. The problem was solved and even sweeter, the outcome was better than I had imagined.

Jack Canfield, the fellow I quoted at the outset, was onto something. I had learned how to flip the switch of my thoughts from a negative mindset to a positive one. We will discuss more about this mindset in chapter three. Simply put, I now understood that my thoughts had the power to hurt or heal me. The images in my head could spell doom or joy. And if I took no actions, then I would see no results. However, if I took decisive actions, believing that there must be a solution to any problem or crisis, then there would be the great possibility that the results would be in my favor.

THE JOURNEY HAS JUST BEGUN

The process of learning what was my true essence was in full swing. I am grateful that I went through those particularly difficult times, because through the pain and agony, I learned more about myself. Blindness only had the power to control my actions if I allowed it to. The limits of what

I could or could not do depended on me. I didn't know that then, but I was going to find out soon enough.

It would take a long time before I could understand that I was the only one in charge of my own happiness. There were more life-changing experiences that needed to occur in my life for me to finally figure that out, as well as to discover what my real purpose was for living. At the time, however, the negative voices in my head made it almost impossible for me to listen to the small voice in my head that desperately wished to be heard. I wasn't yet familiarized with my higher self, but when I was finally introduced to her, I at last understood the genuine power that connected me to the higher source, which had transformed my entire life forever.

Unbeknownst to us, we are born in situations we have no control over. We are also affected by the way we were raised by our parents, the type of information we were taught to believe as children by our teachers, and the ways we were treated by our siblings or peers that can positively or negatively impact the way we view the world. Their beliefs or actions can greatly affect the way we view ourselves.

The question is, will the undesired roadblocks created by others to accept that what they believe should be true for us inhibit us from living our true essence? Can we develop the ability to go deep within ourselves to find the genuine essence of who we are that can allow us to live an exceptional life in mind, body, and spirit, regardless of the experiences we have had in the past? This topic will be considered in the next chapter, so stop, stand up, and stretch. Now take a deep, fortifying breath and get yourself ready to tackle the important exercise I have prepared for you. Don't panic. It's a simple action step I am confident you can complete.

I have always made it my goal to strive to be the best of myself, and have sought through a variety of avenues to "live my true essence." Even though I have not always made the best choices in my attempts to discover who I truly was, each day I get better at this lifetime endeavor. This is the reason I know with absolute confidence that you to will begin living your true essence starting today. Is it possible?

A famous quote spoken by the former president of the United States, Ronald Reagan, really drives this point home. He said, "There are no constraints on the human mind, no walls around the human spirit, no barriers to our progress except those we ourselves erect." I believe those words wholeheartedly, and have made them my own.

Sure, there have been many challenges, bitter moments, and spiritually draining experiences along the way, yet, I believe the particularly difficult life situations that showed up in my world were there for a reason or as an opportunity to learn, grow, and expand in thought, knowledge, and ability.

The constraints, walls, and barriers I faced created in me an unstoppable spirit that today helped me breach those seemingly unbreakable walls, and allowed me to firmly understand the quoted words above.

All my life, I have been intrigued with the subject of the mind, body, and spirit. This yearning and deep fascination to know more about where we came from, why we are here, and where it is that we are going has caused me to research and study books on religion, psychology, philosophy, and health. This enabled me to better understand behaviors, rituals, and beliefs that may or may not hinder the progress of knowing the authentic essence of who we are.

For me, there have been many twists and turns on the path that led me to who I am at this junction of my life. At times, I have gotten lost, but somehow, these moments have been enlightening in curiously interesting ways.

ACTION EXERCISE FOR LIVING YOUR TRUE ESSENCE

FLIP THE SWITCH OF THE NEGATIVE THOUGHTS IN YOUR HEAD

Okay, here is an exercise for you. Are you ready? Don't worry, I know you can handle this and I am here to support you if you need to retrace your steps. We can do this!

This is what you're going to do starting tomorrow; mark it on your calendar if you must. You are going to only think positive and empowering thoughts. Starting tomorrow, you're going to have images in your head that will make you feel happy. You are going to take the necessary action that will totally change the outcome of your day. If even one negative thought pops up in to your head, you're going to wear a rubber band on your wrist, so go find a thick one. I'm dead serious.

As soon as a negative or disempowering thought comes to your mind, you are going to pull that rubber band. This is not meant to hurt you but it is going to sting a little. Take it like a champ. This exercise will remind you that negative thoughts are not allowed. At the end of the day, you are going to write down those thoughts that made you feel limited or powerless. Why not have a little journal so you can document your thoughts and feelings each day throughout this exercise?

If the first day, you see that your wrist is welted up from all the snaps and you have written an entire scroll, don't worry, the next day will be better. It will get easier as you progress. I promise. The point is that you realize how your thoughts have not been serving you at all until now. Believe me, this works. You will be surprised to see how many thoughts can come into your head during the day, and you will feel excited when you discover that you have the power to control them.

The main reason for this important exercise is to demonstrate that it is possible to control those annoying voices inside your head which incessantly play the same dispiriting song without let-up. Learning to completely shut out the negative voices that overcrowd the space in your mind is the beginning to finding the one single voice that speaks the truth to you and teaches you that you are more than what you may believe to be true about yourself and your thoughts. That you are enough. That no matter what your circumstances, you can rise above the scatterbrained talk those negative voices speak, and learn to listen to the inner voice that is wise and knowing. The true voice that will always guide you toward living the true essence that is the genuine you.

And don't worry about your wrist, it will heal in time, the same way your thoughts will give up their destructive litany as you move closer to discovering the real part of you that may have been buried deep beneath the myriad of negative thoughts that have controlled you up to this point. In time, you will realize that replacing your negative thoughts with positive thoughts will feel empowering. You will begin to look through the clear lenses of who you truly are inside, and this will push you toward manifesting what you really want. You will have the strength to start believing in yourself and in your true abilities.

So, I challenge you to complete this exercise, and remember, make sure you write all the negative thoughts that suddenly popped up during the day, many times without your notice. Get it all down in your journal. Then, at the end of the day, review the thoughts that didn't empower you and stop to ask important questions about these beliefs.

For example, answer the following questions about those thoughts:

- Do I believe that what I'm thinking about or telling myself is the truth?
- Do others around me believe it to be true?
- Is it something that I can change?
- Am I better or worse off because of it?

This exercise will help you search inside yourself for genuine answers that may surprise you. The more you practice this exercise, the better you will become at shutting out those negative voices whose goal it is to keep you from living your true essence and whose mission it is to stop you from reaching your real potential.

The longer you practice this exercise, the more you will see tremendous changes in your life. If the rubber band becomes too painful for you, then you know that your thoughts are not helping you at all. You need to try harder to focus on having more thoughts that make you feel good, and that may take some time and practice. The result should not be pain. It should help you succeed in eliminating, for the most part, a negative mindset that has rarely, if ever, encouraged you in any way.

After thirty days, you will probably not even be snapping the rubber band as much anymore. You will start to become used to having positive thoughts. You will feel proud to know that you are not your thoughts. You can control what is on your mind, and that knowledge is power.

If you honestly look at where your thoughts have led you, you will realize that you have allowed this to happen. Your wrist will be an indication of how far you've come. The good news is that most people prefer to back away from pain, so I am sure you will succeed in your efforts. Trust me, I know you can do this. It will get easier with each passing day, but you must stick to it or all the stinging would have been in vain. Your negative thoughts would win then, and you would lose. But that will not happen to you. You will be feeling great when you see the positive results in your life. You will come to understand that the thinker of thoughts is the one in control, and that you hold in your hands the power to change the thoughts in your head and the images you choose to see in your mind's eye. The actions you take right now will be the deciding factor in creating new and enlightening ideas and possibilities that will appear in your world as you work on this action step.

As you will learn in the following chapter, the You that is invisible, that cannot be seen by the naked eye, plays a very important role in determining the outcome of your life. Knowing how to change the way you think of yourself is a starting point to moving toward visualizing the life you really want, and as you take the necessary action steps to make it a reality, you will get closer to living your true essence in mind, body, and spirit.

Are you ready to learn more? Are you set to create the new YOU that will jump-start your life in a more exciting and positive direction?

Awesome! Then let's go on to the next chapter, shall we?

CHAPTER TWO

GET TO KNOW YOURSELF

**"The key to growth is the introduction of higher dimensions of
consciousness into our awareness."**
—Lao Tzu

How can you discover the true essence that makes you, you? The things you are sure about in your own mind? The experiences that resonate with and empower you? The true desires you hold inside your heart?

Do you desire to feel good physically, emotionally, mentally, and spiritually? Is there a way you can live from a higher part of yourself? Is it possible to live your truest and most authentic essence and feel that your life has definite purpose and true meaning? We will answer these questions in this chapter.

Maybe you are certain of the answers. Or maybe you're not. The difference can mean living a life experiencing love, peace, health, abundance, and freedom—or settling for having the leftovers of yourself. Learning information that can help propel you toward the opening of the eyes of your soul is critical to knowing who you are. The ability to turn inward can absolutely help push you toward discovering limitless possibilities that will show themselves in your outer world.

"But how can I have access to that part of myself that can take me from where I am now to where I want to be in the future?" you may wonder. (I already let you in on one little secret in the last chapter.) I will challenge you and let you in on the twelve proven secrets that will help you get acquainted with one person that matters, you. Perhaps there are things that you find difficult to believe about yourself, things that you aren't sure about or understand. However, when you dive beneath the surface, sift through all the layers within yourself, you may be surprised to discover that there is more to you than a person that lives and breathes and exists. To find answers to the questions about you, let's learn more about you, shall we?

THE TRUTH ABOUT YOU

Most people want to do, be, and have more than what they currently have today. Many would like to find ways to improve their circumstances to live a more enriched and fulfilling lifestyle. Yet, is that enough? Does this describe you?

Others find it sufficient to go through the motions and do the things they normally do each day without conscious thought. They go through daily, weekly or yearly routines that seem mechanical. Is that the life you choose because you believe that's what you deserve? Or do you believe that this is the life you were given and there is not much you can do about it? Is that you? Is that the truth about you?

Well, if you want to live your true essence in mind, body and spirit, you must first decide that you can do it! A famous quote by Henry Ford says, "If you think you can do a thing or think you can't do a thing, you're right." Despite what anyone may think or believe about you, to know yourself, you must embrace who you are right now. You must work with what you have at this present moment. If you want to do, be, and have more health and vitality, experience more joy and happiness, and enjoy more success and prosperity, then you need to decide that it is what you want. If you settle just because you think you can't for whatever reason, and you accept this as your legitimate excuse, then you are right too, and reading this book would be futile.

The challenge is that if you want or expect more from yourself, you will need to become your own best friend, partner, and confidant, even if that means accepting the undesirable or negative aspects of yourself that need constant work. Accept yourself as you are. Right now, you are enough.

On the other hand, if doing this is difficult for you due to the stressful or complicated life situations you are currently experiencing, then just breathe deeply. You will get through this storm. I promise.

Perhaps you are feeling unsatisfied with who you are, and where you currently are in your life. That is okay. Now you can take 100 percent responsibility for what has brought you to this point. The time has come to make a definite plan about where you want to be going forward, and to dare to imagine what kind of life you want.

Some people believe that if they had more money, they would feel great. They believe that money can buy love, happiness, fulfillment, and peace of mind. Is this the truth about you?

Some people live an exceedingly abundant lifestyle. They enjoy a life of luxury, fame and fortune, all they could ever ask for. Yet they are miserable. Take Robin Williams (one of my all-time favorite actors who has touched millions of lives with his humor and extraordinary talents), for example. He had it all. He was smart, funny and wealthy, yet perhaps the thought of the health conditions he was diagnosed with caused him to feel anxiety, stress, and maybe fear.

What was the result of striving after all that life could offer, to not be at peace with himself? What could have been his inner thoughts about himself? I'm sure you can guess the answer. He was probably overwhelmed by feelings of sadness, or his inability to purchase good health, that in certain instances, money cannot buy.

Robin Williams lived an extraordinary life from the outside. He achieved many accomplishments, acted in countless films, and won an Academy Award for Best Supporting Actor in 1998. He also received two Emmy Awards, six Golden Globes, two Screen Actors Guild Awards, and three Grammy Awards.[1] The reason I express all his successes is to demonstrate that someone like him should have been ecstatic about life and attaining all the prestige he could ever want. Yet, for all his wealth and fame, he was unhappy. You might say that his existence came from a part of himself that operated from the lower, or physical self.

Many people live from this part of themselves. Interestingly, no matter how much they acquire, they are not satisfied. Why is this? Because they believe that money is the key to happiness. When they reach a higher level of success, they realize that it is not enough. In Robin Williams' story, this seemingly brilliant actor and comedian may have thought this when he took his own life. Perhaps he too felt that he was no longer enough, despite his millions.

For others, food is the ticket to happiness. They eat to escape from the problems that weigh them down. They eat to fill a void that never seems to go away. Perhaps they broke up with their significant other, or had an argument with a friend. Maybe they are unhappy at their job or at home, so they eat to feel good. Food becomes their companion through the bad times. It temporarily fills the void they feel inside.

Still others turn to drugs and alcohol. They look for something that makes them feel good, that fills their souls, and for the moment, they escape from the pressures they face daily from family, friends, co-workers, or the dog. Drugs and alcohol may not have positive benefits, but they serve a purpose, and for a little while at least, people who use them seem content. They are still operating from the lower self. Is this the truth about you?

Whether it is money, food, drugs, or overindulgence of alcohol, many people seek what makes them feel happy, at peace, and content. Not to say that any of these things are bad, well, excluding the drugs and alcohol, however, when we believe that resorting to these things to feel good is the solution to any problem, then we are focused on the lower part of ourselves—the outside of ourselves instead of another part that operates from a higher place that exists within.

Pause and think. What would you be like if you operated from a higher part of yourself? What would the real you be like? Who would you be if you had limitless resources? Knowing the answers to these questions can mean the difference between living a mediocre and bland existence, to opening a new pathway for yourself that can lead you to begin learning how to live with purpose. I sincerely believe it is possible for you. So, allow me the privilege to formally introduce you to your truest and most authentic essence—what some call "the higher self.

WHAT IS THE HIGHER SELF?

Deepak Chopra, an author and M.D. who specializes in Internal Medicine and personal transformation says, "When you contact the Higher Self, the source of power within, you tap into a reservoir of infinite power."[2]

In the book, *Wishes Fulfilled: Mastering the Art of Manifesting*, written by bestselling author, father of motivation, psychologist, and educator Dr. Wayne W. Dyer, he said this about the higher self: "The initiates of old insisted on the importance of the knowledge of the higher self because this awareness opens up tremendous possibilities for growth, progress, and yep—the ability to have one's wishes fulfilled."[3] You don't need to search far and wide to find this power. You don't even need to ask anyone how you can find it. It resides in you, and the best part is that you can access it whenever you wish.

Getting in touch with your higher self allows you to tap into the source that knows everything and is connected to everything. Just so we're clear, I'm not referring to the self that some regard as the ego or shego, or to the self that believes that she is defined by what she possesses or owns, achieves or wins, or by her strengths or expertise. This self goes much deeper than failures or successes. I'm talking about the higher self that transcends beyond time and space. It is the thinker behind your thoughts, since you are not your thoughts. The higher self is universal and that is a bigger, better, and more powerful part of you.

The higher self is where your true essence lies. It is unchangeable, an infinite part of you that recognizes no passage of time or space. Even if your body goes through constant changes, replacing 100 percent of your cells each year, your higher self remains the same. When you get in touch with this divine part of yourself, usually through meditation and stillness, you come to truly know your genuine essence and fully understand why you have come in to this world. You will probably have an aha moment and realize what the true purpose of your life is. That's what happened to me, and that is the reason I am sharing it with you.

You may say, "But I don't even know how to begin to learn about my higher self. I still have trouble knowing myself as I am right now." Well, I say, why don't we begin at the beginning? Isn't that how everything starts?

INTRODUCTION TO YOUR HIGHER SELF

Getting to know your higher self requires no tremendous effort. The space between your thoughts is where infinite possibilities begin. You can easily find out what your deepest desires are when you get secret access to this timeless part of you.

Many people walk around mindlessly like robots, oblivious to their deepest hopes and desires. They start the day getting up, showering, having a hot cup of coffee, tea, or a preferred drink, and maybe having a quick breakfast. They go to work or school, work or study all day, come home, eat dinner, watch the tube, or surf the net and before you know it, it's bedtime. The next day, the cycle starts over again. Millions of people live like this, not realizing that within them there is an infinite self that can be accessed at any moment.

How many people do you know that have been introduced to a higher part of themselves that is infinitely wiser? Are they familiar with their better self that knows what's in the best interest for them? Most people don't ask themselves fundamental questions. What about you? Have you looked in the mirror with all sincerity and asked yourself soul-searching questions, such as, "Am I existing with a purpose? Have I come to this life to fulfill only a small part of me? Where am I right now in my life? Where have I been for the last few years?" and, more importantly, "Where am I going?" Or, have you found yourself making the same daily, repetitive actions without giving thought to anything else? Think about it, and please, for everybody's sake, tell yourself the truth. Stop kidding yourself. That is the real commencement to getting to know your true essence in mind.

Are you nodding your head to the latter? It's okay. Don't panic. That's the last thing you should do. No, seriously. The truth is, you are not alone. Many people live this way and don't think twice about it. Their minds and thoughts are trapped on the outside of their world, and they are not consciously aware that they have an unlimited ability to connect with another part of themselves that is endless and which holds the secret to having powerful ideas and creating amazing opportunities they may have never contemplated. Yet, now what you are learning how to do is unlike what many people in the world are doing, and once you grasp this ability, you will be impressed by all that you can do.

But is there more? Well, I will totally let you in on another little secret; it is possible to go beyond the mundane way you may have been living and discover the power you hold within—by looking deep inside yourself for the truth about you. At least that's the beginning.

DO YOU KNOW WHAT YOUR PURPOSE IS?

It is important that you know your purpose and what desires you hold true to your heart. Why are you here? There must be a reason, and your job is to find out what that reason is.

When that purpose is established, you must fervently and completely believe that it is so. The burning desire inside of you should be so strong that you will not doubt that what you want will be fulfilled. It is essential that you have a pulsating desire to make a lasting change in your life that will not allow for any excuses or buts.

"But how can I continuously motivate myself to realize all my desires?" you may ask. There goes that "but." It's okay though, I will let this one pass. Let me explain.

When you wanted a cup of hot tea or a drink, for example, you got up and made it. You acted. It is what you desired to drink. There was no mental struggle in accomplishing that task, was there? You did it. That's all. You didn't have to think about it. It was a small desire, but you wanted that tea or drink. If you listened to me earlier, right now, you're probably drinking a cup of hot tea, so I am sure you get my point. Simply put, you took the necessary actions to prepare a cup for you to enjoy. It was easy, right?

You can also attain bigger desires. It takes the power of the state of mind known as a burning desire to truly believe and know with certainty that you can make your dreams a reality. More than that, it is essential to take the initiative to create a definite plan of action to acquire the clear desire you have placed in front of you. You can also study others who are doing what you want to do.

That is what I did. I had learned that if I wanted to live my true essence and accomplish any goal, I had to look at others who were doing what I wanted to do. It was important that I studied the lives of others and found mentors that were already living their true essence.

I followed their example of how they became the success they are today. That helped me develop the deep desire and drive to create a definite plan that would allow me to live my own unique essence, to strive to achieve what I truly desired to happen in my own life.

Someone I consider a mentor is Tony Robbins, an author, life coach and transformational speaker. He had the burning desire when he was but a teenager to help many people live happier and more fulfilling lives. He grew up surrounded by challenging circumstances that could have resulted in a life of pain and discontentment, or could have broken his spirit if he would have allowed these circumstances to negatively shape his life.

Yet, Tony Robbins had a fervent desire to break through people's emotions, teaching them how to find their innermost, secret desires. Early on, he knew his life was more than his present circumstances, so he focused on his most outstanding qualities and strengths to create his own true essence, enabling him to touch thousands of people's lives by helping them to transform, regardless of the challenges they faced.

According to his website biography (www.tonyrobbins.com/biography/), Tony Robbins is known as a world authority on leadership psychology and has empowered more than 50 million people from 100 countries around the world. More than four million people have attended his powerful seminars and he has sold millions of copies of his six internationally bestselling books. He is a great example of someone who took massive action through a burning desire to learn what his true purpose, passions, and driving motivations were.

You can find out what your true essence is too. You can discover your desires. Really think about them and write them down. Read them every day as you go about your business. Give yourself a timeline. By when will these desires be fulfilled? What will you give in return for these desires? You can't get something for nothing. There are certain sacrifices you will need to make. In the end, you will be excited and jubilant that you did it! You will be proud that you never gave up on your wants.

FASTER ACCESS TO YOUR DESIRES

Is there a faster way to reach your desires? Yes, you can write them down and view them each day. You can have them on your mind all day long. You can dream about them during the night. But you can do more.

You can tap into the part of yourself where infinite possibilities lie.

When you can center yourself, or align with your higher source, that is where your real power will unfold. It is that easy. It can be done and has been done for millennia.

When you learn to get in a place of stillness, you can then allow your thoughts to float away like little clouds overhead. At this precise time, you can silence the noisy chatter of the myriad thoughts going around and around in your head. Tell your mind to relax and be quiet so that you can tap into the part of yourself that connects with the true being that is all-powerful. When you search for this extraordinary part of yourself that is aligned with the Creator of thoughts, you learn how to make better choices about where you would like the direction of your life to go. You also learn how to focus more readily on the positivity that will lead you to create limitless possibilities in your life that are at your fingertips. You can access this part of yourself anytime. Best of all, you don't have to pay a penny to tap into this amazing power.

No, this is not hocus-pocus or woo-woo stuff. This is an amazing ability you have within that you can tap into whenever and wherever you want. It is up to you.

The higher self, or what I call, "the true essence within," is a more powerful part of yourself, and is the eternal or infinite self that we all possess. It is where you can obtain higher power to achieve anything you want. When you learn to practice meditation, affirmations, and visualizations, which I will discuss in a later chapter, you will experience real magic. What you desire will show itself in your outer world. Do you know what those desires are yet?

What are your thoughts about life? Have you discovered what it should look like in the next year? In the next five years? Or are you still pondering the subject with no set goals in mind?

What about the bigger desires? If you want happiness, excellent health, spiritual awareness, financial stability, and freedom from the repetitive patterns you may or may not have inadvertently developed, then you will need to make a promise to yourself today that you will immediately start to live your deepest hopes and dreams. Think about what those true inner wishes are, and write them down where you can see them every day as a constant reminder of who and what you want to become, what you envision yourself doing, and the things you will have that will bring your desires to fruition. This honest commitment begins with you.

When I decided that the relationship with my husband Lloyd opposed my best and higher self, I planned everything I needed to do to move on. At that time, I had started a natural housekeeping business, which provided cleaning services to customers in the Hudson County area of New Jersey. I saved money to get an apartment, and planned my total independence as a single mom. I started this by filling out an application to get a Seeing Eye dog.

In two years, I had saved enough to get an apartment, train for my service dog (a dog that guides the blind), and settle into my new life.

What changed? I did. When I took control of my life, and purposely took it to where I wanted it to go, that was when things changed. If I would have remained that scared little girl who was nervous about confronting her husband, anxious about asking for permission to do the things she loved, and worried about not fulfilling her role as a submissive wife who questioned nothing, I would never have grown in knowledge and understanding of what my true inner self really is. I transformed my way of thinking to thoughts that positively impacted my life. And I didn't know much about this higher consciousness awareness that is invisible and is everywhere.

You, too, can take control of your world. Get in the driver's seat of your life and grab the steering wheel with both hands, making the conscious decision right now to turn your life in the direction of your chosen destination.

You don't have to wake up each morning repeating the same patterns and settle for that. You don't have to allow life to take you wherever it may, like a feather carried on the waves of the sea. You don't even need others to dictate to you where it is you should go. Where you want to go and how you want to get there is absolutely up to you. Start immediately to steer your life toward the location of your choice. You are in charge.

WHAT ABOUT THE PAST?

Let go of what has happened in the past. If you could turn back time, then you would. But you can't. So, the best thing to do is to take 100 percent responsibility of where you are now and move forward. If you continue in the same direction, and you haven't gotten any results, then that should indicate to you that what you have been doing is not working.

"If you always do what you've always done, you'll always get what you've always got," Henry Ford said. If you repeat the same patterns and get the same results, then you need to change the patterns to achieve different results. Does that make sense?

You can have a balanced lifestyle and live with true purpose by daring to explore the amazing and unique abilities you have within yourself. You can do this by centering yourself and finding a more powerful part of you that connects to a higher source that works side by side with you to create realities that you may never have dreamed possible. You possess the capacity to develop specific qualities that can shape your destiny. These qualities can be in the form of traits, talents, and the ability to make informed decisions that could lead you toward achieving the goals and dreams you have set out for yourself, but had put aside due to your lack of self-confidence and the fear of failure you felt in the past.

Yet, today, you will start defining the essence that is you! Begin by letting go of the fears that have set you back. It is up to you to reach deep within the recesses of your mind and spirit to find your higher self, where your true power lies. When you connect to the infinite source that resides in you, you can begin to co-create with that source. By centering yourself each day with this divine essence, you will bring about new possibilities and unforgettable experiences that will allow you to fulfill your desires and wants.

If you believe that, you can finally live your true essence and learn from your past mistakes, putting them behind you. You are not your past. Stop fooling yourself into believing that life will happen anyway, whether you like it or not. If you understand that you need to plan life and take control of it before it takes control of you, then I applaud you. You are on the right road to attaining the lifelong goal of knowing your true essence and what you can accomplish. However, if you are like most people, and are uncertain or undecided about yourself and where you are going, you will find the secrets to living your most authentic essence here. By following and applying the simple exercises and creative tools you will find throughout this book, you will indisputably live the best that your whole self offers.

ARE YOU READY FOR CHANGE?

How do you feel? Are you tired, stressed, or simply exhausted and clearly need the rest that you insist on ignoring? Are you physically or emotionally drained and feel as if you have temporarily lost your way? Perhaps you don't have the strength to try anymore because you feel that everything you have attempted has been a big fail. Don't worry, I have confidence in you and know that as you read and take seriously the action steps I have provided for you, you will be well on your way to developing the essential qualities that you need to become your best, most authentic self.

Now is the time to stop everything and give yourself some space to re-evaluate your life and the thoughts that have brought you to where you are. Maybe you're feeling as if you've gone far from being true to yourself. You work long hours, your kids need attention, you are swamped with tons of school assignments with deadlines, and it's showing on your skin and in your overall health. Maybe you're sleeping fitfully. Your eyes look tired, and it is obvious that you need some major TLC soon before you flat out give in to exhaustion or unmanaged stress that can lead to illness or disease. You're always in a rush—and even your hair has had better days.

Well, rev up your gears and learn how you can look and feel amazing in record time. You will understand how you can become at one with yourself by taking the time to analyze what it is you desire. The power to effect change lies deep inside of you. To achieve this, we must peel back the layers of negative emotions, mental blocks, and self-destructive behaviors that don't serve you.

There may be undesirable attitudes that you have allowed to be the driving force in your life up to this point. Perhaps certain negative personality traits you have developed tearing you down instead of building you up. You may identify former patterns that you were unaware of in your life, which now you realize have not always worked out to your advantage.

Decide right now that you want to be the unique person you know that deep within your spirit you can become. We all possess many outstanding qualities, some more pronounced than others; however, it is up to us to do all that we can to evolve into the flavorful and unique essence that makes us who we genuinely are. The amazing attributes that define you can be mentally created and will eventually take you where you want to go. You want to have the fervent desire to open your mind and spirit to many limitless possibilities so that you can live your true essence. When you learn how to develop a new way of thinking, a positive outlook, and a love for all that is good in your life right now, it will become easier to step into the best fitting shoes that make you, you.

THE INNER VOICES

We all have experienced many times that weren't all peaches and cream. Maybe, at this very moment, you are dragging along as if a large boulder has landed on your back. Ouch! Don't worry though, this is our little secret. I promise I won't divulge it to anyone. Although I hate to have to be the one to tell you, but I'm sure your loved ones and dear friends may have already whispered something of the sort in your ear, and maybe that's why you ran out and grabbed this title.

No . . . really. I commend you for committing to doing something about the way you feel and look, which is the first step in choosing a new path that can transform your world forever. You are ready to shake the cobwebs out of your life and are eager to start over with a different attitude and point of view. You have decided with conviction to connect with your inner voice.

No, not the voices in your head that do not know how to shut up. I am speaking of the distinct voice that lives deep inside of you. The one that implores you to listen attentively. The one that feels instinctual and that you believe you should follow, even if you dodge her words of wisdom most of the time.

You know, the one that is the picture-perfect person you long to be. She does flips and high fives you each time you accomplish a goal, and jumps up and down with glee when you triumph over a difficult situation. The same inner person shakes a fist at you when you do something stupid that you wish you could take back, and kicks out in frustration when you fail to do what you knew in your heart of hearts you could do. Guess what? You have ignored your inner voice for too long.

You've tuned out the inner person that speaks total sense. That is your higher self that lies dormant and is ready to wake up. She's a very powerful part of yourself that deserves your undivided attention.

Oh yeah. I know her well. She has pointed an accusing finger at me plenty of times when I have ignored her. She has kicked out in frustration at me too for some of the poor decisions I have made, because she knew I could do better. She has lashed out at me, using language I dare not mention, because she knew my fears had kept me away from many opportunities and possibilities, due to my insecurities. Opportunities had been within my grasp, but because of my lack of confidence, I let them go. Oh, believe me, she was not happy about that and gave me a lot of lip about it. But, I should have listened to her voice. She was right after all, as I learned at my eighth-grade graduation.

All of us have an inner voice, a smarter person, a higher self, whatever you want to call it. Sometimes, we ignore that voice because we think or believe it is wrong. It's a part of ourselves that gives us warning signs, clear direction, and intuitions that let us know (if we're paying close attention, of course) that we may be heading down a road that will lead us to inevitable pain and disappointment if we don't come to our senses.

At times, we shut that voice out, even when it speaks the truth. Some of us have ignored that voice so completely that we live each day going through a series of motions and unhealthy rituals, not realizing that the habits we have developed are not empowering or enabling us to see far ahead of ourselves.

Another secret to tapping into living your authentic essence is to learn about your higher self. This is the beginning to understanding the power of an inner voice that will manifest itself with new thoughts and Ideas you may have never even previously contemplated. Knowing and being clear about what lies inside of you is the starting point to helping you determine the real abilities you have that may not be fully evident until you look within yourself. What lies deep inside of you is the key to unlocking the true potential that will eventually show itself on the outside.

"As a being of power, intelligence and love, and the lord of his own thoughts," James Allen says in *As a Man Thinketh*, "man holds the key to every situation and contains within himself that transforming and generative agency by which he may make himself what he wills."[4] We hold the key to our present and future, and by our thoughts we proceed in the direction we choose to go. But can we trust that intelligent and universal inner voice, the Thinker of Thoughts? Can we tap into a higher self where that voice can become infinitely louder so that we can hear what it's whispering to us?

Yes, and yes! The decisions you make right now to deliberately channel your mind toward living your best and truest essence requires no real effort to call upon, yet will create lasting change in the one person who has the power to listen again to that inner voice that is not afraid to speak the truth . . . you. You can decide this moment to shut out or kick out (whichever you prefer) all those negative voices that keep playing the same obnoxious song over and over in your head. Yes, those voices that keep chanting about the impossibilities and limitations that you don't have. At times, you have allowed them to crowd your head with the lies they tell to keep you from your real destiny.

Give yourself permission to open the door of your mind and command all those voices that have been setting you back, restraining you from living your true essence and fulfilling what resonates deep inside of you, to get out. For some time, you've allowed those self-destructive voices to push you around at will. Tell them to go! You don't need or want to hear them anymore.

Now, close the door on the nonsense they told you for years, and open yourself up to the real inner voice that wants you to have a life full of meaning and truth that you know will make a major difference forever. Let go of the things that you believed you were incapable of achieving, and take control of where you want your life to take you going forward. Now, you can focus on the path you know for sure will lead you to places you never dreamed possible.

Don't shake your head at me. I never said it was going to be easy. This is a one-on-one conversation and, believe me, I know how you feel. I've been there many times before, so this isn't groundbreaking news. Would you rather continue the way you are going? Or would you rather try something new that has been tried and tested scientifically and neurologically by experts to work effectively? We will discuss this in future chapters. For now, set your mind to start thinking empowering thoughts that don't tear you down.

REVERSING THE CURRENT

In *The Science of Getting Rich,* Wallace D. Wattles says, "There are three motives for which we live. We live for the body, we live for the mind, and we live for the soul. No one of these is better or holier than the other . . . and no one of them, body, mind, or soul, can live fully if either of the others is cut short of full life and expression."[5] Clearly, it is our duty to find out how we can feel complete. By determining that we love ourselves in mind, body, and spirit, and finding out what purpose we have for being on this earth, we can discover what living our true essence means.

Have you allowed circumstances to take over your life, never considering that you have a choice in the matter? Perhaps you feel like the waves of the sea are tossing you this way and that with no real direction. Maybe you are feeling imbalanced and want to find physical, emotional, mental, and spiritual well-being, but just don't know how to go about it. Or maybe for the first time in your life, you want to make a lasting change that will take you to new heights you've never experienced before, but you want to better understand how this can be done.

Whatever the case, choose the path you feel is best for you. You don't have to allow the strong current of life to push you wherever it pleases. You have the choice to follow the river that will carry you upstream to better places. You can choose to live in a flow state where you will simply know where you are headed, because your goal is to live your true and authentic essence. This ultimately encompasses connecting with your higher self and is best done by taking a few minutes daily to be silent and meditate.

WHAT IS MEDITATION?

"Meditation? What is that?" you may ask. The word meditation, according to *The Free Dictionary by Farlex*[6], is a "Continuous and profound contemplation or musing on a subject or series of subjects of a deeper or abstruse nature." No, this is not weird. Meditation and reflection have been practiced for centuries, and it is the pathway that leads to reaching the part of you that is indefinite or eternal, and which has no end. It is the infinite time and space that lives on forever. It also connects you and me with everything that exists on earth and throughout the universe. It is your higher self. Some call it the higher source or God. In any case, we are gifted with the unique privilege of owning an infinitesimal fragment of this greatness and higher power that surrounds us and that is a part of us.

It is my opinion that the instinctual voice that speaks in the innermost sacred chamber of our spirit is the connection we have that allows us to love, grow, achieve, and succeed as individuals. It is the eternal force that takes us by the shoulders and steers us in the right direction if we would simply allow it to do so. Many times, we can be stubborn and must practically drown under the waves of turmoil or be in a frenzy before we realize that we are swimming against the current and that we need to turn around.

For me, it was through learning how to meditate and listen to that inner voice that I began the journey to discovering how to live my true essence. I learned about meditation several years ago when I started studying books written by Doctors Wayne Dyer and Deepak Chopra. At first, I would ask myself questions like, "Does this stuff really work? Can I really access a higher part of myself that can connect me to my higher source?"

Those were crucial questions for me and the answers, when they finally came, transformed my entire life and the thoughts that had brought me to where I was. They made me believe that I could indeed create limitless possibilities in my current reality, that I was more than my thoughts. I especially became convinced through the words I read in Deepak Chopra's book, *The Spontaneous Fulfillment of Desire*[7], where he says, "The most powerful tool we have for learning to live with synchrodestiny, to see the connective patterns of the universe, to make miracles out of our desires is meditation."

When I began the practice of meditation, I saw firsthand the real abilities I had within that I had allowed to lie dormant. One of those abilities was to write. This has always been a deep desire I kept hidden, believing this dream was somehow simply out of my reach.

Today, I am an author, and you are reading the stories and examples of how I dared to go within to find my true self. So, my friend, dreams can become a reality, and making those dreams come true is in your grasp.

You, too, can learn how to meditate daily. It is the key to opening many possibilities that you can tap into anytime you wish. Another key to realizing your desires is asking questions.

ASK CRUCIAL QUESTIONS

When uncertainty rules the day, ask yourself vital questions that deserve honest answers that will absolutely come to you in many forms. "How?" you say. It is simple. Answers come when you pay attention to everything around you: through a conversation you had or overheard, from a book you read like this one, via a program that you watched on TV, while taking a walk or exercising, while in deep meditation or contemplation, or during yoga practice.

Your questions have answers. The universe has your back and you can be confident that you will receive answers if you simply ask, ask, ask! Some people are afraid to ask questions, however, because they fear the answers that they may receive. What kind of questions scare people?

I am referring to internal questions. Questions you can put out there to your higher source. For example, "What can I do that will help me:

- Make better decisions that will allow me to stop repeating the same mistakes?
- Stop being afraid that I may keep failing again with whatever I try?
- Listen more closely to my intuition and stop relying on others to tell me what is the right thing to do?
- Know how I can stop the negative habits that are not serving any real purpose in my life?
- Find a better way to break free from the repetitive patterns that keep me from moving forward?"

The answers to many of these important questions can be revealed to you in a variety of ways and can be found all around you if you are paying close attention to the signs. A friend may give you advice. A co-worker may present some new ideas to you. You may receive an unexpected phone call from someone who you haven't heard from in years. On your way from work or school, you may hear a conversation and the subject is precisely the answer you seek.

Coincidence, you say? There is no such thing as coincidence. If you ask, the universe must respond. In some form, your answer must come. If you are meditating or contemplating a specific goal or if you need help with any matter that you are not sure how to pursue, you can find the answers simply by being in tune with everything around you. Seems simple, right?

When I no longer was part of a religion that I think had more laws than the Pharisees, I felt hurt that all my friends would not be around me. Once you are no longer part of this religion, you are basically shunned. I believed that God was far away from me, and that I had no spirit protection. These are the things taught to you in the religion that I was a part of for about fifteen years.

One day I prayed, even though I thought God was not listening. I asked, "Are you present in my life? Are you still with me?" The answer came a few weeks later while I was listening to a Joel Osteen sermon that my sister Maritza texted me. Joel Osteen is a bestselling author and pastor of his church in Houston, Texas.

The sermon was *You are Not Damaged Goods*[8]. I listened intently to his words. Then I heard, "I am with you. I will never abandon you." It was as if Joel Osteen were talking directly to me. Has that ever happened to you before?

Many people don't ask fundamental questions; therefore, they don't receive genuine answers. "Ask, and you shall receive," says the holy book. Answers to your questions can come from anywhere. If you think you are not good enough or that you don't deserve to ask for anything, think again. We are all creators, and were created by an infinite Creator who has made all things, including us. Why wouldn't the very Being that allowed us to live a human experience deny us or limit us from the things we truly want?

But what about the bigger questions? Questions such as, "What is the true purpose of my life? What do I want the outcome of my life to be? Is my life at this moment everything that I planned it to be? Am I completely satisfied with where my life has lead me?" These fundamental questions deserve genuine answers. Have you taken the time to reflect on questions like these? If you haven't, the time has come for you to consider them. Search deep within yourself, find the truth, and begin living understanding the reason for why you exist.

You can ride the life current that will guide you toward the true essence that makes you who you are inside and out. You can make better choices today that will greatly impact your life in a positive way, which will create limitless possibilities for you tomorrow. Can it be done?

Can those questions be answered? I say, "Absolutely!" The answers are found wherever you look. All it takes is for you to pay careful attention to everything around you. And, if you are willing to be honest with yourself, you will tell yourself the truth and act to change the answers you don't like. By taking the necessary steps outlined for you here, you can be on the way to improving your life exponentially and dramatically, bringing you closer to the essence you wish to exude in mind, body, and soul.

If you are reasoning, "I've heard it all before and nothing has worked," no one knows it all or has tried it all. Besides, you are here because you want to find better answers. And I promised you that I would provide them.

SOMETHING ABOUT MYSELF

Life hasn't always been that easy for me either. However, through my many experiences and challenges, I have learned to channel my energy in a more positive direction that allows me to grow and meet those challenges head-on. I didn't wake up one morning having supernatural powers to live my truest and most authentic essence. I didn't magically acquire knowledge and skills about what those deepest passions were. Not even close. It was through almost two decades of trial and error that I have discovered that there is more to me than what I previously believed, and I am proud to have experienced what living my true essence means to me today despite those difficult times.

The tests and trying circumstances I have traversed in my life have shaped me into the woman I am. Bitter moments along the way almost broke my spirit, but the process of being introduced to my higher self, and the different lifestyle changes I made allowed me to discover the path I now take, have made it worth the trip. I share my story with you so that you can see and believe that it is absolutely possible to learn how to live your truest and most authentic essence, starting right now.

The knowledge and experience of almost two decades of utilizing essential oils and aromatherapy in my organic businesses as well as in my personal life, and the more than twenty years of extensive study and practice of spiritual enlightenment have allowed me to show you that living your true essence is not only possible, but it is achievable. Through the power of the mind, the ability of the body to heal, and the reviving of the spirit, living your true essence can be within your reach.

By sharing with you the twelve secrets I have incorporated in my own life, and taking you through each step to begin using them, you can live your true essence in mind, body, and spirit. If these important steps worked for me, I know they will work for you.

If you don't follow me, that's okay. You will get the sense of it as you read on, so don't let your tea get cold. Sip some and stay with me. Relax. Take a deep breath and exhale slowly. This helps your mind focus more intensely on what you are learning. And what you will learn next is how important your mindset is. Trust me, this will be good.

ACTION EXERCISE FOR LIVING YOUR TRUE ESSENCE

FOCUS ON YOUR HIGHER SELF AND TRUE DESIRES

Have you found any secrets in this chapter? Come on, I know you can find them. think about it for a moment. I can wait.

Okay, I will help you out. I hope you're game. The most important step toward living your true essence is getting to know your infinite self. Taking some time each day, say about ten minutes before you get out of bed or ten minutes when you get into bed at night, is the perfect time to go deep within yourself to meditate.

You can do this in silence or listen to meditations you can find online. Motivational and transformational teachers such as Lisa Nichols; Bob Proctor, the owner of Mindvalley Academy; Vishen Lakhiani, and Deepak Chopra have professional meditation exercises you can listen to and follow if that is easier for you. Many of these experts on the mind, body, and spirit can be found on YouTube, and you can hear them over and over until the words you hear become part of your subconscious awareness. This is essential to tapping into the infinite power that is a part of you, and that you are a part of.

Here's another secret. What about your desires? Do you know what they are? Why not start with one or two desires?

Get a clean sheet of paper or a journal that you will keep for recording answers from this book. Yup, I mean right now. If you don't have one nearby, get on your computer and open a new Word document, or unlock your phone and go to your notes. You can do this, so let's get moving.

Now, think about what your true desires are. What do you want? It could be a new job, starting a new business, taking better care of your health, looking and feeling good about yourself, losing weight, improving your grades in school, overcoming the negativity in your life, or anything that you want to see change for the better or completely.

Write those desires down in big bold letters. Write them in any form that works for you, and put them where you can clearly see them every day, at least three times a day. These desires written by you will be a constant reminder of how much you want these desires to become a reality.

During your meditation sessions, focus on those desires, and after 30 to 90 days, you will see in different ways how the universe will conspire with you to make that desire a reality.

I challenge you, and when circumstances occur in your life that are taking you toward that desire, and new ideas take form in your mind, you will begin to understand the power you hold within that can make you feel excited and elated.

Believe me, when you connect with your higher source to help you with the questions you have asked about what your true inner desires are—questions you truly want answers to—the universe or God will conspire with you to create whatever it is you wish for. In time, it will become a living reality.

It's like having a genie in a bottle and wishing for anything you want. It's so much fun to do, and the best part is, you can start with simple things.

All you need to do is focus on your desires and in time, those desires will show up in your outer world. You can live life more fully and begin to trust in the capacity you have within yourself to create anything you want.

The first step is to believe it can be done. The rest is history.

CHAPTER THREE

WHAT IS YOUR MINDSET?

**"We are what we think. All that we are arises with our thoughts.
With our thoughts, we make our world."
—Buddha**

Remember how in Chapter Two I quoted Wallace Wattles? The gist of it was that our mind, body, and soul should be complete. One cannot work fully without the other. Well, if we want to live our best and most authentic self, we must first recognize and be aware of our mindset. What do you believe to be true about yourself? What do you believe to be true about your thoughts?

Our thoughts empower or disempower us. You saw this firsthand with the experience I shared with you in Chapter One. There is a difference between a positive and negative mindset. The thoughts we think can help us or harm us.

For example, when you wake up, what is your first thought? Is it, "Oh, I have got to go to work?" or "Wow, here goes another day of nonstop traffic, dealing with my miserable boss, working every day on tasks I hate, trying to complete homework assignments on subjects that are totally boring and irrelevant for the career path I am studying for, dealing with these unruly children, putting up with my husband's constant complaining, dreading my wife's unpredictable mood swings," and on and on it goes?

Stop . . . I mean it. Just stop.

The next secret to changing the essence you live and breathe is by changing your mindset. The way you feel each day determines the life you will experience and the scent you will evoke not just toward others, but more importantly, toward yourself.

If you begin each day by thinking of all the millions of ways your day will go sour, if you place thoughts in your head that make you feel sad, angry, worried, and discontent, then you are preparing a recipe that smells pretty funky. You are clogging your mind with things that detract from living your authentic essence. Your day will go according to your mindset.

A NEGATIVE MINDSET

Napoleon Hill, author of *Think and Grow Rich*, once said, "Whatever your mind can conceive and believe, that is what it will achieve."[9] The mind is powerful and can take you to fantastic places or lead you to the deepest dungeons, where you can be held captive without hope or desire for living out your true potential. It can play tricks on you if you're not watching or paying close attention.

On the other hand, once you understand what having a positive mindset means, this type of higher thinking can lead you to live an extraordinary life you probably never dreamed possible. A new and exciting path will open to you and you will attract the good that you deserve. Even if there are moments that seem bitter along the way. Even when you think you want to simply give up. There will be moments when you don't understand why things are happening to you that will seem to point you in the opposite direction. You feel like you keep failing—falling and getting back up, getting full of mud, but getting back up. You are still creating and learning your true essence. This mindset is good because it teaches you to stay strong and creates qualities in you such as confidence and steadfastness that will enable you to reach any goal you have set. These goals will help you become the person you desire to be.

During my teenage years, I wore a personality with a recipe that included hot temper, with a good dose of paranoia, and topped it off with the cold behavior of a rebellious bitch. I am sorry, but there isn't another way of putting that. I was figuratively smelling pretty funky back then.

You would think that my previous experiences as a younger child would have made me feel better about high school. Well, apparently, I still had a lot to learn. I was out to prove myself, going about it by wearing a tough exterior. At times, the voice in my head attempted without success to tell me that this was not the way to discover my true self. She spoke out her objections to the anger, frustration, resentment, and bitchy attitude that was only a cover-up for who I really was. And, in the end, she let me know with no uncertain terms, that it wouldn't make a bit of a difference. That deep, inner voice said that until I accepted myself fully and completely for who I truly was inside and out, nothing or no one would take me seriously. Not even me. Imagine that? The nerve of her.

Yet, I ignored that voice of reason, the voice that I would later learn was my higher self. It was confined to the recesses of my mind. She was almost stomped out of existence was more like it.

When I thought I had everything under control with the obstinate personality I projected to the world, inside, I still was that little girl who was afraid. I was still plagued by all the insecurities and doubts about all the things I couldn't do. I was too busy focusing on all the negative aspects of myself to consider paying attention to a voice that made no sense to me—a voice that whispered many possibilities in my ear. Unfortunately, I didn't want to listen to what she said.

A very important lesson in having this type of mindset is that the mind can guide you toward failure as easily as it can guide you toward success. It can guide you toward pain, or it can guide you toward pleasure. Difficult to imagine, but true. You're the boss of your life, so you must take full responsibility for your own actions.

For example, think of a farmer. One sows generously, planting a variety of vegetation to feed a kingdom. The other farmer plants just enough to get her through the winter. One farmer plants plenty of seeds with the intention of harvesting more than enough food, not only to feed her family, but to feed many families. The other farmer plants enough seeds for her family, but doesn't anticipate losing crops or planting enough for the entire season. During harvest time, what will each farmer reap? Exactly. You guessed it.

Both will reap what they have sown. Even the Bible states this when it says in 2 Corinthians 9:6, "But this I say, He which soweth sparingly shall reap also sparingly; and he which soweth bountifully shall reap also bountifully."[10]

Clearly, it is the same with our minds. Although the mind is more sophisticated and complex, the same principles apply. Whatever we sow in our thoughts, whatever intention we put in our minds, that is what will come about.

Easier said than done, don't you think? You're absolutely right! Why do we reach this conclusion though? That question begs to be answered.

When our problems don't have any immediate solutions, that is when we panic. When we feel that there is no answer that is forthcoming to our current crises, that is when we want to give up, throw in the towel, and tell ourselves that we are losers. Therefore, why should we expect anything to change? If anything, we believe it will get a lot worse. Yet, is that true?

We are all guilty of having thoughts in our heads about ourselves that made us believe we were failures (unless you came from another planet). Those of us that come from Earth, however, at some point have had a negative mindset that was conducive to horrible thoughts and actions that did not serve us in the least.

I can assure you, I have had plenty of experiences where my mindset was off kilter. One experience stands out for me and made me see the level of insecurity and vulnerability I still had about myself, and the misguided thoughts I had that prevented me from embracing who I was.

I want you to understand what I mean when I say that the mind can play tricks on us and make us believe that we are somehow not good enough, or it can make us lose out on what could otherwise be a wonderful and fulfilling experience.

AN OPPORTUNITY LOST

There was a time when I allowed what could have been a new and exciting relationship, a chance to sing and act, to become a lost opportunity that I wish I could have forgotten forever. But for the sake of showing you learning experiences that taught me either pain or pleasure, I will let you in on the secret of what happened to me in a high school play, *Bye-Bye Birdie*.

During my senior year of high school, I was a young seventeen-year-old active teen that loved getting involved in extracurricular activities. I auditioned for a play which I really wanted to be in, *Bye Bye Birdie*.[11] It was inspired by the singer, Elvis Presley. The main character in the musical was Conrad Birdie, a rock singer who travels to Ohio to make his final television performance and kiss his most beloved fan goodbye before he is drafted. The actor playing Conrad Birdie's part was a student I had a major crush on.

Since my vocal dynamics teacher was doing the auditioning and he believed in me as a talented student, I knew I pretty much had a part in the play. And, let's face it, he gave me the chance to show that I had a lot to offer despite my visual challenges. He understood I had to work harder to do what came more easily to the rest of the students, but he knew I had the potential to sing and act.

The determination my teacher saw in me let him know that I would do my best. So, when he called out the names of all the students that were going to be in the musical, I heard my name called and was not surprised, but I was happy that I was in! Yet, my true joy came from knowing that the guy I was crazy about was playing the lead!

My inner girl began doing flips and spinning around, hands in the air with a pumping action of pure glee. I knew that every time we met to go over lines in the play, he would be there and I could hear his sexy voice as he practiced his scenes.

The music teacher cast me as one of the fans. I had a small part, but I was elated to be near the boy everyone said was really cute, and who got to play the lead as Conrad Birdie.

Now, what I meant by the "lost opportunity" I spoke about earlier is what happened during one of the evenings when we practiced for the part where Conrad—the student that played the lead—went to sing for the last time to one of his beloved fans. Guess who he picked to be his beloved fan? Yes! You guessed it. He picked me!

I was shocked to say the least. You can imagine my joy. I bubbled over with delicious excitement. My disbelief that he picked *me* was overwhelming! My inner girl began doing flips in the air. She threw her hands up and shouted with joy at my luck.

Why did I think that I was so lucky? During that moment, I didn't know myself. I thought I didn't deserve the attention of a handsome young man who could possibly like a girl like me, who genuinely wanted me to be his beloved fan who would sing with him, and who chose me because he thought I was pretty and he knew I could sing very well.

I didn't doubt his enthusiasm for wanting to perform with me, since he ran toward me, putting his strong arms around me and saying with excitement, "Come on baby, sing with me please! Be my number one fan!" I was stunned, because I was still reeling from his words and the fact that his arms and body were crushing me. I really was his fan, but not Conrad's, his! Oh, how my head was spinning.

In that space and time, I imagined his lips coming down on mine. I imagined being locked in his embrace forever. I reveled in his sweet and persistent words telling me to please sing with him, because that's what he truly wanted. I imagined myself floating on air as I said, "Yes, yes, I will sing with you Conrad, or whoever you are. I will even dance with you, sway with you. If you like, I will even fly away with you to whatever paradise nest you have chosen for us to love in."

For a moment, my small body pressed against his, as his strong arms remained tightly locked around my waist. I played in my head what it would be like to sing with him on opening night when it was time to perform on stage. I imagined how he would look at me and how he would kiss me before the song was over. Remember, he chose me to be his number one fan in the musical, so a kiss with his most beloved fan was inevitable.

How romantic. What an incredible opportunity to sing in front of an entire audience. What a wonderful chance to sing with him. To be kissed by the guy I had a major crush on before there was even a play.

So, why did I turn him down? Why did I say no to a guy that I knew with absolute confidence wanted me to sing with him on opening night as his beloved fan, the number one fan Conrad Birdie was loath to part from?

I could not believe the words that came out of my mouth. I wanted to kick myself in the ass after denying myself this chance.

My thoughts and feelings led me to think that I wasn't good enough, that I would screw up somehow, forget the words to the song. I was too shy to perform in front of so many people, I thought, and I couldn't do my part in acting out the moves in the play. That mindset made me give up a great opportunity. Without even finding out exactly what I needed to do, I gave up.

If I would have thought highly of myself, had faith that everything would have worked out, and that the evening would be a smash, then I could have experienced something marvelous and very different from the mindset I had projected on myself.

I would have been kissed by a guy that I was head-over-heels about, and it would have been a beautiful memory I would have cherished for a long time. Perhaps, he would have considered being my boyfriend if I would have dared to be his number one fan.

Yet, it was a lost opportunity, due to my feelings of inadequacy and self-doubt. I thought that I didn't deserve attention from a handsome guy. Why did I think that? Why were my thoughts so negative when it came to the subject of me?

The inner girl in me kicked out in the air with frustration. "How could you possibly let this cute guy go? How could you give up the chance to perform in front of a great crowd?" I heard her voice in my head say.

I replied angrily, "You just don't understand."

Yet, I felt her deep sadness and it was almost palpable. It was because of the fear I felt. Inside, I knew I was brave and free, but outside, I trembled with uncertainty and felt trapped by my blindness. Inside, I believed I could do anything. I could dance, walk up to Conrad Birdie on stage, and dance with him. I could leap into his arms. Everything was possible in my imagination.

Yet the problem was that outside, I felt imprisoned in my own body. How could I dance if I couldn't see what was in front of me? How could I leap in to Conrad's arms and not miss? I felt denied the freedom I so much yearned for, and I missed out on the opportunity to experience what I believed I could not have. I hated myself for not being daring and believing enough in my abilities. I was angry for being born with a condition that made me feel so limited.

I did not realize that I limited myself by giving in to the negative thoughts in my head. I was too afraid to show my real potential and therefore, I lost out. I felt like a failure. I was not good enough.

Those were the cruel words I told myself. Yet, the inner me, the girl who was happy, spirited, confident, willing to try anything and wish for everything, was constantly ignored by me in those days. I only saw the condition. I only focused on the problem. I only listened to the negative voices that pounded hurting words in my head.

What would have happened if I would have listened to the inner voice inside, my higher self? What if I had inhaled the real essence that was there, but not yet exposed? I would have realized that I could do all those things and more, if I would not have allowed my fears and negative mindset to rule the day.

Sometimes, when we are afraid, that is when we must be the bravest. That is what I learned as time passed and I went from teenager to young adult. Little by little, I came to know that by listening to my inner voice more often, I accomplished much more than what I thought I could have done in the past.

When we fail, it is the perfect time to step back and analyze why, so that we don't repeat the same mistakes. A profoundly influential philosopher and author, Neville Goddard, once said about the mistakes we make, "Do not waste one moment in regret, for to think feelingly of the mistakes of the past is to re-infect yourself."[12] We must let go of the past and learn to embrace the present. There are times when we need to ignore the excuses our subconscious makes to stop us from moving forward and believing in ourselves. If we are honest with the person we face in the mirror each day, we can do much more than what we give ourselves credit for. We become our worst enemy and sincerely believe we can't, so we don't.

I regret what happened with the *Bye Bye Birdie* musical. Another girl took my place as Conrad Birdie's number one fan, and I lost out. Yet, it was not because I couldn't perform or dance with him, it was because of the fear I felt of failing. It was because of the great discomfort I felt. I was not comfortable in my own skin. I had to learn with time and experience that there was more to me that I didn't know about myself.

A CHANGE IN MINDSET

In *How to Completely Change Your Life in 30 Seconds*, author and transformational speaker, Earl Nightingale, says that a person's job is to learn who he is: "He will recognize and accept the things he cannot do as well as some other people, but he will also understand and appreciate those things it has been given him to do well. He will accept himself for what he really is—one of a kind, as different from every other person on earth as his fingerprints or his signature."[13]

Throughout my many experiences, both good and bad, I have learned how true these words were. I am unique in my own way, and appreciate the reasons why I am here and what I need to do to live a fulfilling life that makes me feel empowered and happy with the essence I exude each day. The world I had created in my past was limiting me from a positive and satisfying way of thinking. I finally decided to look at all the great qualities I possessed that not only helped me move forward with confidence and love, but also helped me to help others find it too.

So, what is your mindset? Are you willing to stop second-guessing yourself and start believing in your abilities to reach beyond the stars to get what you truly want? Are you ready to believe that you can and will achieve whatever you set your mind to? When you have a setback, are you going to let it determine the outcome of your future? Or are you going to learn from it and keep going until you get to the finish line?

Living your true essence means being willing to develop the mindset that you are in a place of self-acceptance. It means that, regardless of whatever you believe is setting you back, whether it is a disability, a difficult trauma, a bad experience, an illness, or anything that has caused you to momentarily lose your way, you will not allow these circumstances or difficulties to stop you from picking yourself up, dusting yourself off, and starting all over again to pursue the goals you have set aside for so long due to feelings of inadequacy.

However, to move forward to attract more greatness in to your life, more than a mindset is needed to achieve the end goal of living your true essence. The next chapter will help you see what else is needed.

ACTION EXERCISE FOR LIVING YOUR TRUE ESSENCE

FACE YOUR FEARS HEAD-ON

Before you move on, work with me through this simple exercise that can help you have a better and stronger mindset. An obstacle may be stopping you from getting you from where you are, to where you want to be. That is fear. Author and speaker Jack Canfield created an acronym to define fear as "Fantasized Experiences Appearing Real."[14]

You may have an active imagination. I know I did. You may imagine a terrible outcome from a difficult situation that you are not sure how to confront. You may ignore it and fervently wish that eventually it will go away. Problem is . . . it won't. Fear usually gets worse before it gets better. So, what do you do?

Try this exercise I learned that can help you face a fear you have of doing something that requires you to get out of your personal comfort zone. Not a fear of bugs or large animals. Nothing like that. No need to panic.

Get a piece of paper or the journal you're taking notes in for this book. If paper doesn't work, go to your computer and open a fresh document. Yes, I'm talking to you. If you want to live your true essence, start by being honest with yourself. You must be willing to meet your major challenges head-on to be, do, have, and give all the things that you want in your life. So, let's go. Get that piece of paper, journal, or open that document right now.

Write down a situation you are afraid of facing today that is particularly difficult for you and is standing in the way of taking you where you want to go. Even with your knees shaking, your heart pounding, and your palms sweating, embolden yourself and take a risk in challenging your fear head-on. Don't worry. I promise it is not that difficult. I am here to help you.

For me, it was getting past my blindness. Because of my fear of making a fool of myself, I held back from the opportunity of singing and acting, and missed a great chance to be with a guy I liked. Not only that, but I allowed for my blindness to make me lose out on other great opportunities I could have otherwise succeeded in overcoming. It was not until I decided to get out of my own way, step out of my comfort zone, and face my obstacles with complete conviction that no matter what happened I was going to do it anyway, that I began living and experiencing true happiness.

For you, it may be the fear of asking your boss for a raise, asking someone out on a date, or telling the person you are currently in a relationship with that you are no longer compatible. It may be that someone is treating you unkindly or unfairly and you want it to stop, but you resist confronting them because of how you think they may react.

Perhaps you have a disability and are afraid to ask for help. It may be that there are goals you want to reach badly, but you think your limitations won't allow you to—and you believe no one may want to help you. You have the desire and the mindset, but the fear of failure has put the brakes on pursuing your goals.

Whatever it is, my friend, write it down. When you relieve yourself from the pain that not confronting your challenges is causing you, you will be free from the constraints that your fear places on your life. You will breathe easier and feel more empowered when that monkey is off your back.

Okay, so now comes the important part. Read the statements below and fill in the blanks. Even if you have more than one fear, I want you to write the answer as truthfully as possible. You can do this! Write the answers to these following statements:

I am afraid to:

I want to:

But I'm scared that if I do, then:

Did you write what that number one fear is? I'm counting on it that you did. To be released from what's causing you anxiety, confront your obstacle and take the necessary steps to face that. It may be challenging, but once you have faced it, you will feel emboldened to overcome other fears that you may have and this will be the beginning of the journey to discovering how to live your true essence.

No, you cannot take a sedative. That is not allowed in my class. Seriously, really think about a fear and jot it down on paper, in your journal, or on the computer. I promise it will get better.

Here are some examples of what that fear may be:

I am afraid to: tell my friend that I don't feel comfortable with hearing her complaining all the time. I want to: tell her to please stop. It is not helping her or anyone else listening to her ranting and raving about whatever is bugging her. But I'm scared that if I do, then: she won't want to be my friend any more after I tell her how I feel.

Or, I am afraid to: tell my husband that I don't like the way he puts me down in front of my friends. I want to: tell him how that makes me feel. But I'm scared that if I do, then: he will get angry at me and tell me that I am acting like a child.

Another fear may be: I am afraid to: ask my friend's brother if he would like to go out for drinks after work. I want to: get to know him better. He is really a cute guy and I love his qualities. But I'm scared that if I do, then: he will turn me down flat and I won't live out the embarrassment.

These are genuine fears that can make us want to stay quiet and pray that somehow the situation will disappear. Or perhaps you think it's easier to let it go. You reason, "Well, maybe I'm better off just not saying anything."

But what if you painted this scenario? What if your friend appreciated your sincere words and stopped her daily complaining? What if your friendship improved and she was grateful for your honest advice?

What if your husband realized the pain he caused you by his crude words? He sees that you are important to him, and expressing how you feel has made him more sensitive and attentive to your feelings.

What if your brother's friend would be more than happy to go out for drinks with you after work?

Sometimes, we are the ones in the way of changing the outcome of any situation that could bring us happiness, because we allow fear to stop us from doing what we truly want. If your friend doesn't appreciate your honesty, then maybe you should reconsider if you want people in your life that have a negative mindset and can stifle your progress toward living your authentic essence.

If your husband continues to ignore your feelings, maybe it's time to think about taking further action to improve your marriage. Perhaps seeing a professional is something you could consider. If your marriage is important, then you will want to seek further assistance that could save it.

If your brother's friend says no to going out, maybe he is not the guy for you. Don't take it so personally. Someone will be interested in you if that is what you believe.

There is a saying that I heard which I often repeat aloud when I feel particularly afraid of facing a new challenge in my life. "If you keep on doing what you've always done, you will keep on getting what you already got." If I don't make a resolve to confront the fear I feel inside, I will continue to get the same old results. Again, I will lose out on new opportunities I would otherwise have experienced—if I only would have gotten passed the fear. Honestly, that is not a good place for me. It was discouraging and disheartening when I allowed fear to crush any possibility of moving forward or doing something that I loved because of my emotions. The pain is not worth surrendering to them.

Face your fears head-on and act! It is natural to be afraid when you have a situation you are uncomfortable with, or when contemplating a new goal that requires help from others. However, if you allow it to take control of your life, chances are that you will never get to where you want to be. They will hold you captive like a prisoner and you will only dream of what the real essence is that you could have been. You will feel regret. And trust me when I tell you, regret is a pain that is difficult to live with, all because you allow fear to be the ruler of your life.

Remember that no decision is already a decision. So, decide right now with absolute conviction, passion, resolve, and commitment that you will take the initiative to conquer your limiting emotions. Don't allow them to stop you from living your true essence. Don't allow them to be your master. Get out of your comfort zone and face your challenges. Stand up to your fear and do it anyway. You will feel freed from the constraints of it and will develop the confidence to face other challenges in your life with less hesitation. You will feel inspired and maybe, you will feel less threatened by the unknown.

The mindset we choose to have is key to unlocking the true results we will achieve if we persist in facing the challenges that stand right in front of us—even when we face fearful circumstances or troubling waters that are determined to set us backward. It is vital that we continue forward, filling ourselves with love, faith, and an unflinching resolve to be the best of ourselves. These outstanding fruits will inexorably keep us firmly on the path that will lead us to the true essence we wish to express.

But what about appreciation? Does possessing this simple quality matter when it comes to living our true essence in mind, body, and spirit?

Let's keep going and find out.

CHAPTER FOUR

AN ATTITUDE OF GRATITUDE

"Be thankful for what you have; you'll end up having more. If you concentrate on what you don't have, you will never, ever have enough."
—Oprah Winfrey

W hy should we feel gratitude each day? Does appreciation really matter? Can it change our lives ?

Appreciation and gratitude matter significantly. There are many ways you can be thankful each day. I found it in the most precious moment of my life when I held my newborn son, Gabriel, in my arms for the very first time. The immense gratitude I felt for the precious gift that had come into my life was overwhelming. The happiness and joy I felt had no words to describe how much love I felt for him.

I also felt gratitude the first time that I inhaled the beautiful essence of a delicate rose. It's no wonder I decided to study the world of essential oils and aromatherapy. The discovery of the many exquisite fragrances derived from nature that are abundant and found in many flowers, herbs, and trees absolutely fascinated me.

I delighted in the explosions of yummy flavors and the rich combinations of foods my mother cooked that made me lose count of my favorite dishes.

These delights seem small, but to me, they are invaluable treasures that I will always be grateful for. Today, I am happy and thankful to have my son in my life. I am grateful to have learned about the world of essential oils and aromatherapy. And, I enjoy my mom's delicious cooking, which still amazes me.

Being grateful each day is without question one of the most important attitudes we must practice that can help shape our lives, and can help create a world filled with meaning and fulfillment. The things you are most appreciative of help you feel happy and joyful for what you have right now. There is always something we can all feel grateful for today. Just think about it for a moment. I am positive you will come up with something.

When I felt more grateful for my life and the things I had in it, I developed a transformative way of thinking. I headed toward a new point where I grew in knowledge, and had bigger and stronger thoughts about myself. The inner and outer world I was creating was in full swing. I was also learning that showing appreciation each day was bringing more things into my life to appreciate. It was definitely a win-win for me, and I know it will be a win-win for you too.

I began to understand and appreciate my existence and why I came to be here, despite my blindness. I realized that the lack of sight I was born with would no longer inhibit me from reaching my true potential, and would not put an end to obtaining what I wanted to become, or how I really wanted to live my truth in every facet of my life.

What about you? You too can appreciate your world. You can start on the inside and work your way out. That is how I learned that appreciation is the one ritual you should make a regular habit of each day. Appreciation is one of the determining factors that decides our future outcomes. What do I mean?

APPRECIATE YOUR WORLD

When you open your eyes to a new and glorious day, do you look out the window and appreciate the sunshine that is adorning the sky and filling your room with its brilliant light? Do you marvel at how that same sun warms you? How it makes the plants grow so they can provide you with daily nourishment? How it gives you the vitamins your body needs so that it can function properly?

What about the radiant energy that increases the heat of the water? Are you grateful for this essential repeating cycle? If it weren't for these wonderful, natural cycles that re-occur every day, we would never experience life. These are things to be grateful for, don't you think?

It is up to you to decide how you perceive the world around you. By looking at it through a lens that reflects joy, peace, and love, you can create better outcomes each day. If you look at the sun, but are feeling unhappy, depressed, and full of sadness, then that same radiant sunlight will not bring any brightness to your day. You are in control of what you feel, what you believe about yourself, and how you choose to think about your inner and outer world.

Why not wake up each morning and extend your arms and legs as far as you can, feeling your bones settle? Take a moment to allow your body to stretch languorously, yawn, relax, and breathe deeply several times. This simple action is the fastest way to lower mental stress. Practicing this calming technique resets the brain, according to Dr. Mark Waldman, a neurological scientist and author.[15] He also said that when you have a negative thought, but intercede it with a positive thought, you shut down the part of the brain that can generate anxiety and depression.[16] So, when you open your eyes to a new day and negative thoughts crowd your brain, or internal and external stresses creep up into your mind and spirit, why not try to yawn several times? You will feel calmer and more relaxed, ready to begin your day with the right mindset and appreciative attitude.

I am not saying that you can't have a negative thought. We know that negative thoughts are bound to creep up on us. However, you can change your bad thoughts if you want to for better thoughts. You can control what you think about.

So, let's do a little experiment, shall we? Allow your mind to turn to all the blessings you have right now that you can sincerely be grateful for. I mean really think about it. It shouldn't be that hard.

For example, right now, think about all the things you love about your life and yourself. Sometimes, we are the ones in the way of changing the outcome of any situation that could bring us happiness, because we allow fear (Fantasized Experiences Appearing Real) to stop us from doing what we truly want. Sure, there are things you may not like about yourself or your life, but those things occupy too much energy that would be better spent thinking about the things that make you feel good and in time, could bring you many rewarding benefits.

Even if you have nine particularly difficult situations that make you feel oppressed and unhappy, but have one situation that is good and makes you feel hopeful, why not focus on that good situation instead of drowning yourself in the nine situations that bog your brain down and make you feel as if life is unfair or full of problems? Does that make sense?

So, now that you know this little trick, what did you come up with? This should be good. But if you insist and can't come up with anything, think about this, you can reframe the problems you are currently experiencing in your life with better or happier thoughts. How can you do this?

LEARN HOW TO REFRAME

First, "What is reframing?" you may ask. It is so easy for negative thoughts to fire out in our brain, and many times, it is automatic. According to Daniel G. Amen, MD, a physician, psychiatrist, and author, automatic negative thoughts, or ANTS, are basically patterns in the brain that talk to each other. Think of all those voices speaking to each other in your head. These voices want to communicate when you experience doubts, fears, or stresses. Those ANTS can disempower you.[17]

An example of ANTS would be thinking, "I'm in so much debt. How am I going to ever get out of this financial crisis?" Again, these thoughts can weigh you down, cause anxiety and stress, and take your joy away. Why not replace those negative thoughts by imagining positive ones?

How do you do this, you say? By turning your negative thoughts in to positive ones and reframing your thoughts to Automatic Positive Thinking™, or A.P.T.[18]

For example, if you have a fear of flying and are imagining all the horrible ways that your flight can go wrong, you can stop the thoughts by reframing them and thinking of your destination instead. Are you on vacation and going to a beautiful location? Is your family with you? What kinds of fun things will you be doing and planning? When you let go of the thoughts that are causing anxiety, and instead conjure up a picture in your mind's eye of how much fun you are having with your loved ones, A.P.T. will help you forget your fear and can make you feel better about flying.

Imagine what you would do if you were out of debt. Think of how you can save instead of spending your money so that you can enjoy it more with your family and friends. See yourself doing new and exciting things because you have learned how to properly invest and manage your money and have great ideas on how you can create new possibilities that will generate more income. Just think of how you can give more of your financial resources to provide help to others because you are grateful that you have more. That is the power of A.P.T., Automatic Positive Thinking™.

MORE EXAMPLES OF REFRAMING

So many times, we may have negative thoughts that intercede with our positive thoughts. Sometimes, the negative chatter in our heads can win the race. So how can we reframe these thoughts so that more often our true voice reaches the finish line?

Look at some examples of how you can reframe from negative patterns. Why not write your own disempowering thoughts, and do your best to respond with positive ones that will empower you instead? Remember that working on yourself is what will bring you to living your true essence each day. The goal is to aspire to feel amazing physically, emotionally, mentally, and spiritually.

There have been times when I have been hard on myself and have allowed very disempowering thoughts to control my mind. Check this out and tell me if this has been your experience. If it has, please note that you can change your negative thoughts, just as I did, to thoughts that will change your life for the better, the same way it did mine.

Here are some negative thoughts that may pop in your head, but you can immediately reframe them with thoughts that make you feel good:

- **How do I move forward with my life?** When in doubt, I'll just take the next small step.
- **I can't get over all the things that happened to me**. I must make peace with my past, so it won't screw up my present.
- **No one has problems like I do.** I must not compare my life to others'. I have no idea what their journey is all about.
- **I am blind. How can I make any difference in someone else's life?** Life is too short for long pity parties. I must get busy living, or get busy dying.

- **I can't accept what was done to me.** Life is too short to waste time hating anyone.
- **Other people can do better than I ever could.** Envy is a waste of time. I already have all I need.
- **I don't know if I have what it takes to do it.** I can't audit life. I must show up and make the most of it now.
- **I feel overwhelmed and not strong enough to cope.** Whatever doesn't kill me really does make me stronger.
- **Being a mother is harder than I thought.** My children get only one childhood. I must make it memorable.
- **It is impossible for me to really believe that I can get out of this hole I have dug for myself.** I must believe in miracles.
- **All I do is work, work, work!** My job won't take care of me when I am sick. My friends will. I need to stay in touch.
- **I lost my home. I lost my job. What could be worse than that?** Frame every so-called disaster with these words: "In five years, will this matter?"

When we reframe our thoughts from negative to positive, we will see change in our lives. When we focus on the things that matter to us and appreciate each day, we will see a significant difference in the way our days will go. But here's a question I would like to place in front of you, and that you should consider seriously. Will you begin today to show more appreciation in your life? I sincerely hope your answer was a resounding "YES!"

APPRECIATE AND CELEBRATE

You are grateful that you have a job that enables you to care for yourself and your family. You can deal with the bitchy boss, because you know that in the end you are more than what she gives you credit for. After all, she is not responsible for your happiness. You are.

You are fortunate to have children or grandchildren that bring you joy, and who are a gift from God, or your higher source. You are blessed that you have a considerate and loving wife or husband, despite their imperfections. You are happy that your parents provide you with what you need to live comfortably. You are relieved to live a life that is free and that you can decide for yourself what you would like to do with it.

Isn't that way of thinking better than listening to all those negative voices chattering in your head? They tell you that everything is terrible, nothing is working, your life sucks—and on and on they go. "Wherever your focus goes, your energy flows," says Tony Robbins, a transformational speaker, strategist, author and life coach. If your mind wanders to things that cause you sadness or brings you unhappiness, then you will allow the outcome of your day to have negative results.[19] However, if you decide each day to focus on the things that bring a genuine smile to your face and make you feel great and full of gratitude, then your day will have a positive outcome. You are the co-creator of your life, and have access to a higher source that is available to you at any time, so it is up to you to determine what you wish to do with it. This will result in more opportunities that will arrive where you can show more appreciation.

Each day, a new ritual you can develop is to spend ten minutes practicing gratitude. Mornings, right when you get up, are the perfect time. It is what I do. Applying this ritual in your daily routines can affect the way your day will turn out, and ultimately, even the way your entire life will turn out.

WHAT ABOUT COMPLAINING?

Complaining to others about how bad you have got it will not help you move forward. People who complain often do it because they may want others to feel sorry for their situation or want to find excuses to justify why they are where they are. I believe that if you do your best to get out of your comfort zone, then you will see that you have many possibilities. If you simply get out of your own way, you will find that there is much you can do to change your circumstances. If you don't like where you are, then do something about it. Change it. If you are not finding things to appreciate, then search for them. Chances are, you will be surprised to discover that there are many things you can feel genuine appreciation for right now!

When my son Gabriel started kindergarten, I decided to go back to work. I got a job as a personal assistant, taking care of scheduling appointments, answering the telephone, and completing clerical work. My boss was a small business owner and didn't have a large staff to manage.

The truth was that I wasn't too happy at this job. I didn't like the pay or answering phones all day. But, the experience I acquired opened a new world for me. I wanted something more. I wanted to be better valued for my abilities. So, instead of remaining in a job that I was unhappy with, or instead of complaining that I wasn't earning enough money, I started my own business.

The idea was born while I worked with a cleaning company run by my boss and his wife. I found a way to improve my finances because of what I had learned through my boss.

This couple came to this country legally and became United States' citizens. I admired their tenacity and hard work ethic to create a small company where they provided housekeeping services for our town. They had three young daughters to support and they did it through a company they established on their own. They decided not to work for someone else who would pay them a small salary that would not cover the expenses of caring for a family of five. Instead, they started their own business and made decent money that helped with all the family's needs and wants.

That really inspired me. I couldn't imagine how difficult it must have been to travel from another country and live in a strange one you don't know much about. All you know is that you are traveling to America and it is known throughout the world as the land of opportunity and however high the mountain is, you must climb it to get there. You will do it just to live a better and freer life.

That is what this family did and that is what my parents also did when they moved to the states from Puerto Rico. It is a big, scary step, but they overcame that fear and did it anyway. You must admire that.

If they could do it, I thought, then I could do it too. I have been in America since I was a toddler. What excuses did I have? That I was visually challenged? Well, my boss and his family were challenged by moving to a new country and leaving everything behind in the country they were traveling from. Surely, they had family and friends that they were leaving behind. It could not have been easy.

More than that, they left a country where they spoke a certain language to move to a country where they understood nothing. Yet, they went ahead and got out of their comfort zone, put aside their fears, and moved to a new location anyway.

They had no idea what challenges they would face. No exact map would guide them toward the right place. No manual could instruct them about which steps they should take to make their transition to a new home easier. They simply estimated the risks and had faith that everything would turn out fine.

I learned a lot from their story. It made me feel empowered, since I was fluent in two languages. I also had skills that could be developed to propel me into making my dreams a living reality. It also taught me a valuable lesson in appreciation. Everything I had then was quite a lot. I had to learn how to build on what I didn't have, which I immediately began doing while working in this small family business.

Even though I didn't know anything about reframing in those early days, I knew that thinking negative thoughts and complaining about answering phones all day would not help me in the long-run. I preferred not to waste any time dillydallying. I took advantage of the free time I had to read books on business and self-development. This helped me study the company more thoroughly and prepared me for a future launch of my own business.

I focused primarily on the training I received from my boss. Also, by learning through personal growth and self-development how to create and manage a business, I acquired much knowledge and experience. This, I was sure, would benefit me in carrying out the plans I had for embarking on the development of my own company. I understood the ins and outs of the family business, and I realized that I, too, could create a very successful business.

The salary he paid may have not been what I expected, but the learning experience was invaluable. What would have been the result if all I did was complain? If I would have done nothing to better myself?

It would have been a different outcome. Maybe, I wouldn't have thought of starting my own business. I wouldn't have cared about how my boss managed and ran his business. I would have never read all the books about business and self-development, and my life and mind would have been limited.

Now, I began understanding and appreciating my inner voice. I preferred not to focus on what I felt irritated or unhappy about, or what I couldn't do. Instead, I looked for genuine reasons to have appreciation for all the good I received throughout my life, no matter how bleak it looked.

Are you practicing the art of reframing, instead of complaining? This is how you can live your true essence. It begins with your thoughts. They are what creates your inner and outer world and the secret, driving force to discovering who you truly are inside and out.

Focus on what you can appreciate today. Every morning before you get out of bed, breathe deeply, yawn and stretch, and turn your mind over to the good things in your life. Appreciate them. Don't worry so much if you hate the job you're in or the situation you are facing now that is causing you anxiety. Try to focus your attention on what makes you feel good and brings you genuine joy.

Think about those moments where you can show deep appreciation. That moment when you hold your precious bundle in your arms and inhale the powdery scent that fills you with love and joy. Aren't you grateful for knowing that the beautiful baby that is happily cooing and nibbling on your finger is yours?

That moment when you find the person that you know you want to spend the rest of your life with. You are so grateful for this person that you can't wait to love and make him happy forever.

Those special moments when you spend time sipping hot coffee or tea with your mother, talking about love, life, and the bird. You wouldn't trade those precious moments for the world. Memories like this will always be with you even when she is no longer here to enjoy those many hours of conversation with you. However, you will always treasure those times as one of the keenest, most significant memories that you will cherish forever.

All the experiences you live while you are here should fill you with a deep desire to make this life the best it can be, despite the temporary hardships that may come up unexpectedly. When we appreciate the difficult situations that befall us, rough seas can teach us to thrive. Presently, the black clouds of despair and hopelessness may seem like a raging storm that never ceases its relentless, pounding rain and deafening thunder. The enormity of problems that surround you can make you feel lost and afraid. Yet, in time, the storm slowly abates, allowing for calmer seas and brighter skies. Hidden in every misfortune there is fortune. Hidden within the storms of your life is the piece that you yearn for. Life can be amazing again and you can ride the current downstream that will lead you to live in a flow state of love, joy, and prosperity.

Now here's another secret to learning how to live your true essence each day. Reframing is one of the keys to unlocking your power within.

When you learn how to counteract your negative thoughts by flipping on the positive switch in your mind, you will be freed by your own thoughts and escape from the internal prison in your head. By reframing negative thoughts with positive ones, you free yourself from personal bondage and begin to see the potential in everything you do. It may not be easy, but the point is that you start changing the thoughts that are keeping you from discovering your true essence.

LEARN TO SOLVE PROBLEMS MORE EFFECTIVELY THROUGH THE ART OF APPRECIATION

Instead of allowing yourself to be buried under problems that seem insurmountable, why not ask the right questions? Why do I say that? This is because problems are questions that beg to be answered.

To start with, attack the problem, not the person or people who we are having the difficulties or conflicts with. Some people pretend the problem doesn't exist and think it will disappear. As we discussed previously, that is where fear takes over and the problem gets buried under the rug with no real hope of being solved. Or, the problem gets worse.

Many problems can be resolved if we go to the drawing board and ask the right questions. If you feel unappreciated and taken advantage of at your job, overworked and underpaid, what do you do?

No, you don't pack up and move to another state. I'm serious here. Not true, I'm chuckling at my silly jokes.

Anyway, the problem is your job. The question should be: "What is great about this job?" Don't assume that you are forced to see some good in a job that you hate. Well, if you hate it that much, then maybe it's time to think about switching jobs or careers.

Now, you are faced with a question that will make you think. For some specific questions, you must search deep within to come up with answers that are genuine and true for the person that faces the mirror.

You will perhaps find a few good answers and realize that there are things you appreciate about your current job that you have the power to improve or change.

For instance, you have too many responsibilities in your current job that cause you a lot of stress that makes you feel overwhelmed and overworked. However, your job supports your family, pays the bills, allows you to buy cool stuff, has great benefits, has a schedule that works for you, etc., and overall, you shouldn't really complain. Yet, you feel that your job is not taking you to where you want to be. You are afraid to talk to your boss about new opportunities for growth within the company because you believe she will not consider you for the position.

It is natural for us to want to improve our circumstances. If we feel stagnant, as if our life is a repetition of the day before, then maybe it's time to change the patterns that have yielded the same results we have received until now. If you like the company where you're at, but don't like the area where you are, then change it. Find something great about the job you perform each week. Reframe the negative aspects of where you are currently. Try asking for a raise, or applying for a higher position in the company. These ideas can empower you and make you look forward to more possibilities.

So, instead of asking the wrong questions like "Why do I put up with this job that I hate? Why is this happening to me?" think differently. These questions lead nowhere. If you want real results, then ask better questions that will yield better answers. Believe me, you will get the answer, and it can come to you in several forms.

Other problems may have complicated solutions; however, if you look for them, you will find them.

Now, you are actively seeking reasonable answers to your questions. The universe will conspire with you to find the right answer somewhere. Isn't that way much better than living with pain? Asking no questions will result in no answers. Spend five percent of your time on a problem and ninety-five percent of it on the solution. Therefore, decide to have a positive mindset and the resolve to face each challenge by asking the best questions so that the universe can yield the best possible answers.

This, in turn, will create effective solutions for each problem by asking a question and figuring out at least three solutions for each one. Why at least three? Because one solution is no solution. Two solutions are a dilemma. Therefore, three solutions allow for more choices. Doesn't that make sense?

If your mind finds reasons to feel grateful and confident in your abilities to strategically solve your problems, then you will have gratitude and confidence. However, if your mind is set to feel out of spirits and gloomy, then your results will be out of spirits and gloomy. Your mind responds to what you think and feel. So, develop the feeling of deep appreciation.

Determine today with absolute certainty that you will have an attitude of gratitude. Have the conviction of mind that even though you may face situations that are difficult, you will find things to appreciate right now. Showing appreciation and gratitude each day will ultimately bring much more things to appreciate and be grateful for. Furthermore, the simple act of showing appreciation will create in you the ability to see past the problems and hardships in your life and will help you find solutions more readily and with an open mind.

ACTION EXERCISE FOR LIVING YOUR TRUE ESSENCE

DEMONSTRATE YOUR ATTITUDE OF GRATITUDE

So, now that you know the secret to feeling good, let's take it a step further. Get out that handy dandy piece of paper, or open your computer to a fresh document. Yup, I mean right now. Not tomorrow. Why do tomorrow what you can do today?

If you created a journal for this book, that's fantastic! Get that journal and open it up to an empty page.

Write down at least three things you are appreciative of today. What are those things? Come on, think. I know you can do this.

Are you grateful for being alive and well? Are you grateful that you live in a free country? Do you appreciate your spouse? Do you appreciate the children you have? Are you grateful for your parents? Are they an important part of your life? Do you appreciate all they have done and still do for you?

What about the things that many of us take for granted? For example, for many of us, clean water is available to us whenever we need it. The air we breathe gives us life. The food we eat sustains us every day. We have an ability to think and use our mind in the best way possible. Those are great reasons to be thankful. So, go ahead. Write them down.

Whatever reasons you have to be grateful each day, write them down. You can do this exercise each morning when you wake up. Find things during the day to be grateful for. I am absolutely positive you will find loads of reasons to give thanks.

If mornings don't work for you, or if you are an owl like me, then write your list of things to be appreciative for before you go to bed. It's the perfect time to reflect and to think about all you have accomplished throughout your day.

This exercise will help you see that life is not as bad as it may seem. You can take control of your life and include gratitude as part of your daily rituals. Learning to show gratitude and appreciation each day will get you closer to discovering your true essence. When you appreciate everything in your life right now, you will see more great things appear that you will be grateful for. Doing this will make a major difference in every aspect of your life. It is a secret and central quality you need in your arsenal to live your most authentic self.

This is great! You are making awesome progress. Why not reward yourself? Take a little break and do something that makes you feel good. Don't worry. I will be right here when you get back. Just don't take too long. I don't want you to forget what you have learned so far.

The next chapter is going to really rev up your gears. Get ready to learn the secret to unlocking the power you hold within. You will not want to miss this great and very important information.

CHAPTER FIVE

UNHARNESSING THE POWER WITHIN

**"Every human has four endowments—self-awareness,
conscience, independent will and creative imagination.
These give us the ultimate human freedom . . .
The power to choose, to respond, to change."
—Stephen Covey**

W hen you were born, you were already given this power. It comes
from an unlimited source. Whether you know it or not, you
possess this.

It is a power, that if used efficiently and strategically, can create
amazing possibilities in your life. How can you harness it? How can you
use it to your advantage? And what do you need to do to release this power
from within?

Please pay attention to what I'm about to tell you. I don't want you
to miss this little secret. Well, maybe not just one secret, but several.
This power that resides in you can be expressed in several forms. It can
be developed through practice, repetition, and a change in the way you
think about the world around you. It can even change the way you think
about yourself.

If you want to live your true essence starting right now, then you will
need keys to unlock five very important powers you need to take you to
the next level of your journey to opening the combination to a happier
and more fulfilling life that completes you and unites your mind, body,

and spirit. These powers give you that extra push to break the chains of disempowering thoughts that have bound you for so long.

Look at each of the five powers below and ask yourself if you are guilty of not following them throughout your life. I failed many times before I found the power I held inside of me to unlock the negative mindset and disempowering thoughts I had.

When reviewing the five upcoming powers, ask yourself if you are incorporating them into your life. If not, start implementing each one so that your dreams and desires become more attainable. Remember that unlocking these five major powers will give you access to reach your goals. You will live your true essence when you take the necessary action steps to create the essence that is the original self and the most authentic person you are. More than that, you can be that powerful person right now by putting yourself in the role you wish to become. This is done through a transformation that goes beyond your physical form, or what is humanly possible, which can be quite limiting, to living from a higher place within you that transcends all thought and is indefinite.

We will discuss this further in Chapter Ten. For now, let's discover your five powers, shall we? They are the:

- Power of Beliefs,
- Power of Decision,
- Power of Persistence,
- Power of Focus, and
- Power of Love.

THE POWER OF BELIEFS

Many of us, throughout our childhood and teenage years, developed beliefs about money, success, education, spirituality, sex, and other ideologies that do not serve us in the long run. Some of these beliefs disempower us. Many of them come from our parents, teachers, family members, friends, and maybe aliens (if they really exist). They give their opinions about their beliefs as the truth, since this is what they were taught as children. These opinions or beliefs, whether taught to us inadvertently or not, have become our core beliefs because that is what we heard for years. Yet, does that make the belief true?

For example, have you ever heard your mother say when you asked her for money, "I don't have any money. What do you think? That money grows on trees?" Boy, did I hear that a lot while growing up. Or, perhaps you were brought up in a Christian household and often heard, by either one of your parents, "Money is the root of all evil." These words were probably ingrained in your brain since you had the ability to remember. To them, people with money were considered evil. Their thoughts about the rich was that they could hurt others, that they were full of greed and selfishness, or that they possessed unloving qualities.

So, what view of money do you have? Perhaps that money is scarce, and very difficult to obtain. Or, that if you have a lot of it, you are contributing to the evil in the world. Is that true? Well, if you believe it, then yes, of course it is true from your point of view.

Yet, look at all the abundance around you. Can you deny or believe that abundance does not exist? Or that it is lacking in some way? Why not think of examples of what's plentiful on the planet and ask yourself, "How much of this is available to me?"

For example, how many varieties of seeds can you plant that produce vegetation? How many stars can you count in the heavens? How many flowers can you count that contain alluring essences that permeate all the world's gardens? How many grains of sand can you count near the sea?

Well, if your answer is like mine, the number is staggering, huh? In fact, it is innumerable. Money is also abundant. It is simply an idea. In ancient times, money wasn't even used to purchase anything. People exchange livestock, food, workers, etc. to obtain what they wanted. The concept of money was not created yet.

Later, it was introduced as a means of paying for goods. Is it possible that the money story you were taught when you were young is the reason behind the difficulties you may be facing today when it comes to money? If you were taught that money is scarce and evil, you unknowingly limit yourself from having more of it. These limiting beliefs hold many people back from creating ways to live abundantly.

If you believe that there is lack and limitation, or that money is not good to have due to what it represents in your mind, then that is a set belief based on what you were taught. It is what you saw or heard about money. It isn't your fault. It is what you experienced around the subject of money as a child, and later, as an adult.

Many of our behaviors are due to our upbringing. Certain thoughts and behaviors we have adopted, we have no control over until we realize that they are wrong, and decide that it is time to change them. What we see and hear around us is what we sometimes believe to be true.

If you have no good relationships, for instance, chances are that you didn't see many good relationships before. The core beliefs you had about marriage, friendship, or family relationships have taught you that most people never stay together long. You may think that most relationships don't work out. Most people can't be trusted. Is that a belief that empowers you?

Not at all. If you base your future relationships on the previous bad ones you have had, you will probably find yourself getting into another relationship that is bad for you again. The vicious cycle will continue until you decide to change your beliefs about love, trust, and friendship. If all you saw in your past were bad examples of people in horrible relationships, if you experienced friendships where you felt betrayed, then you will be apt to choose a partner that doesn't suit you, or find friends that will never forge strong bonds with you—unless you change your beliefs. Does that make sense?

When you develop empowering beliefs, you will understand that every relationship is different, and that you shouldn't base new relationships on past ones. Each person is different and unique. Not only that, but if you attract the same type of person, you may need to see if there is something you need to change about yourself that will attract the person you want. For example, if you're looking to find someone with great qualities, it is important that you also possess these same qualities.

Another belief could be that maybe because you live with a disability, whether you were born with it, or an accident or illness caused it later in life, you believe that you are now limited or inferior to others who have no visible challenges. You look at other people as normal and view yourself as less than normal. Does this belief empower you?

Absolutely not! Today, technology, science, and artificial intelligence make it possible for people who are blind to do more and live more independently than ever. The world is changing and blindness is no longer inhibiting many people with visual impairments from living the life they want, or from achieving their dreams, as it may have done many years ago before computers entered the world scene. Even then, individuals like Hellen Keller made a huge impact in the soundless and sightless world around her.

It is also important to avoid negative, disempowering emotions. They take you nowhere and allow others to steal your power. Giving attention to disempowering beliefs strips away positive emotions such as love, courage, strength, and confidence. Find enough strong reasons to change what you're doing right now to create the person you wish to become. You must have the leverage that will drive you to your desired end goal. Otherwise, you will sail through life like a ship without a paddle, with no clear direction or destination.

Beliefs, whether good or bad, can be powerful and can determine the life we ultimately lead.

As you can see, some beliefs are disempowering. Is that what you want? Or, do you want to learn new beliefs that will fill you with confidence and determination to face any challenges, despite the conditions/circumstances you may be confronting? Don't allow limiting beliefs to control your outcomes. Change your beliefs and look within to find abilities, talents, and creative ideas that can lead you to do, be, and have more than you ever thought possible, because that's what you deserve. Decide with conviction which beliefs you don't want to be your driving force, because you know they have not served any real purpose to this point. You must decide today that you will adopt new beliefs, because they can help you forge ahead with what you do want.

What are the beliefs you must change in your life? Put the book down and think about it a minute. Then, resolve today to change those beliefs.

THE POWER OF DECISION

Tony Robbins says, "It's in the moments of decision that your destiny is shaped."[20]

Do those words make sense to you? I absolutely believe they do. To shape our lives, we must take decisive action to let go of bad habits, attitudes, beliefs, or ideas that don't offer us happiness, health, and success.

We make decisions every day. Whether small ones or large, we must make them. Even decisions we don't make are decisions.

Some decisions that we make can screw us up no matter what we do. Yet, when we make bad decisions, should we beat ourselves into the ground because we didn't make the right one? Wouldn't it be better if we could learn something? Maybe there is a valuable lesson in that choice we made.

Perhaps we could ask ourselves questions such as, "What's good about this decision?" Something good could be a valuable lesson on how not to do something the same way because the results were not what we expected. Instead of placing our focus on the setbacks a decision has caused, why not put our energy into learning the lessons that can save us time, money, or pain? This ability can help us, or even save us from repeating the same mistakes in the future.

For example, when I started my first business, I made decisions about my company that set me back financially. I created a marketing campaign that was a complete fail. I selected a marketing company that promised me loads of clients, but realized too late that they didn't follow through on anything they said. They were only interested in the money I dished out and not in me, the customer. They were not dependable, did not offer great service to my business, and did not have competitive prices.

This experience taught me to be more alert to marketing companies like these, as well as to avoid them like the plague. I lost some money, and I can assure you, no new clients knocked on my door. However, I learned to create a detailed plan about exactly how I would market my services in future. The lesson was learned, thank you very much. That decision taught me to be more strategic and better informed about marketing my business. It taught me to do more thorough research about how to advertise more effectively with marketing agencies who have established a solid reputation, and who have the knowledge to find the types of customers that match my company's products and services.

When making any decision, remember to stay committed to that decision, but remain flexible in your approach.[21] The true power of making any decision is a tool you can use at any time to change your entire life. That was true for me. When I made the decision to absolutely do, not what I liked, but what I loved to do in my life, was when everything changed in my world.

Realize that the hardest step in achieving anything is making a commitment you will stick with no matter what—an intelligent decision that is quick, but very well thought out. Think about it, but don't wait months before you decide. Some decisions must be made quickly or the opportunity is gone and the decision is no longer an option. This can cause you to lose opportunities in your business and life.

If we want to take control of where we want our life to go, then we must decide what actions we should take to get there. We must think about our present actions and ask ourselves if those are going to move us to our real destiny, or are they going to push us back toward undesirable places that bring no joy or fulfillment? Each of us is responsible for the his or her decisions. Whether they are good or bad, they are the result of where we are right now.

Believe me, if you are feeling unhappy about that, don't worry, we have all been there and done that. The point is that you create change immediately to reverse your results. Don't waste any more time. Decide that against all odds, beyond a shadow of a doubt, you will make it your chief aim to do more to achieve what you want. You will be doing what many others have done before you, when they had nothing and decided with unwavering faith, that no matter what happens, they were going to create possibilities and move beyond their limitations to succeed and strive after what they most loved and desired. They transformed their lives to become the essence they wanted to live while on this earth.

THE POWER OF PERSISTENCE

In *Think and Grow Rich*, Napoleon Hill says that persistence is "the sustained effort to induce faith . . . Persistence is an essential factor in the procedure in transmuting desire into its monetary equivalent. The basis of persistence is the power of will. Will-power and desire, when properly combined, make an irresistible pair."[22]

Donald J. Trump and Steve Jobs never gave up on their desires. Yes, I believe they had a rather tough exterior, but they also had an important common denominator that allowed for them to accomplish many achievements that have benefited humanity. That superior quality is persistence.

Donald Trump, for example, when he was a real-estate tycoon, created thousands of jobs, homes, and business opportunities for many people. He is known for possessing the art of negotiating deals that made him a successful billionaire. Today, Trump is the 45th President of the United States, and uses these same talents to create favorable changes that can benefit America.

Trump is a "successful business magnate and television personality as well," according to Before It's News. The website further states that he is "an astute businessman and charismatic leader, [who] built and renovated numerous hotels, casinos, and office towers during his business career, accumulating a net worth of billions. He also owned several beauty pageants and ventured into reality television as well. Expanding the horizons of his ambitions, he entered national politics in the early 2000s and set his eyes on the presidential office."[23]

Apple's former CEO, Steve Jobs, when he was alive, provided jobs for thousands of people and created cutting-edge technology that enables us to have access to the latest music, movies, and the wonderful ability for people who are blind to navigate efficiently through an application called VoiceOver. This app comes already installed in the iPhone, iPad, Mac computer, and other devices created.[24]

Jobs worked tirelessly to create technology to make life easier, and expected the same dedication from those that worked with him. The world has greatly benefited from the genius mind of Steve Jobs. He also had a tough exterior, however, and expected those who worked by his side to be passionate about their work like he was.[25] Apple's accessibility programs give people with visual challenges more independence. This assistive technology has opened doors for more employment possibilities, and its online navigation enhances travel for people who are blind or partially sighted.

Another individual that I admire who has always been persistent and has triumphed over seemingly unsurmountable life situations is Oprah Winfrey. Despite a rocky upbringing, she knew that she was more than her present circumstances. Thus, she set out to live her true essence. She became a film actress, talk-show host, television producer, author, and philanthropist. Winfrey was America's first black woman to become a billionaire.[26]

According to *Biography*, Winfrey "launched the Oprah Winfrey Show in 1986 as a nationally syndicated program. With its placement on 120 channels and an audience of 10 million people, the show grossed $125 million by the end of its first year, of which Winfrey received $30 million."[27]

"Life magazine hailed her as the most influential woman of her generation. In 2005, Business Week named her the greatest Black philanthropist in American history. Oprah's Angel Network has raised more than $51,000,000 for charitable programs," according to the article.[28]

Oprah Winfrey said, "The whole point of being alive is to evolve into the complete person you were intended to be."[29] I believe that her words come from a person who lives and breathes from her higher self, the true essence that fully connects her to the spirit being that created everything. Her purpose was to serve humanity with love and persistence to create a better world. She believes that you can evolve into the essence you wish to be.

What about in the past? Henry Ford and Dale Carnegie had persistence and a definite plan of action that didn't stop until they achieved what they desired.

For example, Ford created the first engine for the automobile. It took him 10 years to succeed in making his first car. Ford never finished gradeschool, however, he surrounded himself with experts who assisted him in achieving enormous wealth and prosperity.[30]

Carnegie, who was a writer and lecturer, was known for his flexible leadership skills in influence and human relations. Carnegie developed self-improvement courses that ranged from public speaking to improving interpersonal skills.[31]

His persistence in helping others with his courses and writings made him an effective and successful leader. The books he authored, such as *How to Win Friends & Influence People* and *How to Stop Worrying and Start Living*, are still available and read by millions today who are in business and want to develop sharper business communication skills. Carnegie training courses have been taught to eight million people desiring to be great future leaders.[32]

Persistence pays off when the desire to succeed and become everything we wish for is made with absolute conviction and determination that we will reach the goal. If we give up at the first sign of failure, then we are not persistent. We are like the waves of the sea that toss us this way and that, with no clear destination now or in the foreseeable future. With persistence however, we have a map in front of us and solid steering skills to plow through the worst waves that may arise.

THE POWER OF FOCUS

Tony Robbins is famous for saying, "Wherever your focus goes, your energy flows."[33] I love that statement and do my best to live by that rule. Each time I notice that my thoughts deviate from the path I want to take that leads to health, happiness, and abundance, I remember that phrase and immediately kick out the negative voices that want to play their unrelenting out-of-tune symphony in my head. I cancel the thoughts that disempower me, and reset my mind to focusing on the goals I have set out to achieve.

Why is focus essential to living your true essence? When your mind and body are focused on the tasks you are attempting, your results will be positive, and the path you have chosen is closer to the outcome of what it is you want. When your mind is distracted or unfocused, your results will be poor and frustration may set in instead.

You have the power to change your focus. You can physiologically, emotionally, or mentally change your state. For example, you can change your facial expression from anger to joy just by changing the thoughts in your head and thinking of something that can make you laugh. You can control the physiological storms of emotions that may invade your mind. It can be done. Why not try it?

You can feel absolutely empowered and impassioned, or feel dead. The choice is yours. Certainly, food, lack of sleep, life situations, and pain can influence your focus. However, what you pay attention to can also change your focus. Your state of mind has a lot to do with where you are going. Whether it is achieving great success, or settling for whatever life dishes out to you. It is important to have the right focus.

Before, my focus on my blindness was very painful and stressful. Instead of focusing on all the great things I could do and the talents I had, I focused on the things I thought I couldn't do. It changed the state of my body. I felt unhappy, uncomfortable in my own skin, I looked sad and miserable, and this radical change in my facial features was noticed by many. They asked me what was wrong, but I could never give them a real answer. The shame of being blind and stuck in a body that felt powerless was too complicated to explain to someone who would probably never experience such a challenge. This focus made me feel emotionally drained, and helpless at times. It did not make me feel empowered.

I remember a day when I felt that my blindness was a curse. It was a sunny summer day in July. I wanted to go to the mall and asked my ten-year-old son Gabriel if he wanted to go. He was happy to accompany me (of course there had to be something in it for him. You know, like a video game, an electronic car, or some money, that sort of thing.).

So, grabbing my cane, we set out to the mall. We spent quality time together. I was shopping for toiletries and my son was bargaining with me for toys. We went to the food court and ate cheesesteaks. My son played with his new car. We left the mall. When we arrived at the train station, the train was already coming in. Taking my son's hand, we walked faster to catch the train before we heard the ding-dong sound of the closing doors, which meant we were too late, and would have to wait for the next train.

I went inside, momentarily letting go of Gabriel's hand to hold the side of the door, then waited for my son to quickly get in right behind me. Before he could step in to the train, however, the doors closed and the train began to pull away from the station.

Hot panic shot through my body. My heart pounded in my chest, and my hands grew clammy with sweat. I trembled violently and cried hysterically. "No," I said in a helpless wail. "Please God, no!"

A woman approached me and asked if I needed help. I told her what happened, and she immediately went to the conductor to tell him about my son being left at the station. The conductor contacted the station where my son was left, and a few policemen stayed with him. The woman then got my son and brought him to me.

The tears of agony and feelings of helplessness filled me with so much pain because I couldn't see my son to ensure that he was on the train with me. I was overcome with rage because I failed him and couldn't protect him at that moment. I called out to him, but the doors closed on him before he could get on. That day, I blamed my blindness. If I could see, I said, this would have never happened. A caring and compassionate friend helped me to see that I was not the first one to experience losing a child for a few minutes. She pointed out mothers had lost their kids in stores, in amusement parks, or during travels. They focus on something else for a quick second, and when they look back, boom, the child is gone.

That scary experience temporarily made me believe that my blindness was a horrible joke from God. The kind words of a friend were what made me turn my focus to feeling blessed and ecstatic that my son was okay. It could have been a lot worse.

When I changed the focus from what had kept me locked away in a dark world that I had created for myself to a more positive way of thinking where I could do much more than I gave myself credit for, that was when the state of my mind and body changed. Interestingly, it is absolutely true that wherever our focus goes, our energy flows. If we concentrate on what's bad in our life—our inability to lose weight, physical pain in our body like back pain, the way we look that doesn't please us, a physical challenge such as blindness, deafness, or other mental or emotional challenges that you feel limit you, the financial struggles—all that negative focus makes us feel lousy. Yet, when we purposely bring our focus to what we can do to feel good, suddenly our thoughts change to what is possible. We stand up straighter, have a smile on our face, exude more confidence in ourselves. What happened? Our focus changed just like that, from feeling dejected and powerless, to feeling amazing and powerful. That is the power of focus in action.

THE POWER OF LOVE

Why did I leave this key power for last? Because I always save the best for last. In my way of thinking, love is the deepest possible motivation that moves us to do anything. Love is why we're here. Love is why the universe operates with such exact precision. If we have set an intention where love is the fundamental quality and activating force that propels us toward fulfilling any purpose we may have set our minds to, then I am betting high stakes that we will reach that end goal that we have proposed. In the meantime, why not enjoy the ride as you get there?

Although I am not a religious person, I hold very strongly to the

Spirit that lives inside of me. I am in awe of everything that exists in the heavens above and the earth below, and the Source that created it all. That powerful and infinite Source has created me in a fear and inspiring way— the Source that I personally call God. Because of that powerful Source that is the actual personification of love, I can say that I am love as well. We are all connected to that infinite Source and share an infinitesimal part of the immense power that is emitted by that incredible Source. Love allows me to want to share what I know and have experienced.

There is a beautiful verse from the holy book that I truly appreciate and do my best to live by. This verse really resonates with me and I would like to share it with you. With the old use of the word, "charity," meant love, and you may be familiar with this scripture talking about love never failing or being boastful.

1 Corinthians 13:4-8 (KJV)

4 Charity (love) suffereth long, and is kind; charity (love) envieth not; charity vaunteth not itself, is not puffed up, Doth not behave itself unseemly, seeketh not her own, is not easily provoked, thinketh no evil; Rejoiceth not in iniquity, but rejoiceth in the truth; Beareth all things, believeth all things, hopeth all things, endureth all things. Charity never faileth.

To live your true essence, love must be an inherent part of everything you are and everything you do. It is the fundamental quality that pushes you toward all that you wish to accomplish. Love must be the spiritual force behind your intentions, your motivations, and the power behind them.

Love is patient. When you go through difficult moments and feel that your dreams are at arm's length, when your relationships are not where they should be, patience is the quality that will help you remain focused and calm. Patience helps you to see the problems in front of you and allows you to figure out the best way to proceed. It allows you to let go and wait for the answers to your questions about how to solve any problem or crisis. This quality builds confidence to continue moving forward toward the place you want to go, despite the obstacles that may be standing in your way.

Love is kind. No matter the person, whether it is family, friends, business associates, employees, or the cat, kindness toward anyone you know or meet along the way will always make a difference in someone else's day. As a kind word expressed, or a sweet smile in greeting, kindness can help others feel good when they are having a rough day. Kindness can be an investment. It will return to you many times over.

One of my employees was having a difficult time with her daughter in middle school. Her daughter was afraid of some boys that were bullying her and making her feel insecure. One day, she told me that her daughter was failing in school because of this situation. Naturally, my employee felt anxiety and pain over her daughter, even taking her to therapy to see what could be done to eliminate the horrible fear she was experiencing when she went to school each day.

I could empathize with her child, since I had experienced bullying in school when I was her age. I knew how hard it could be to concentrate on studies and be myself in a hostile environment. One day, I sat with my employee and her daughter, and with kindness, I shared my story of childhood bullies. I told her that there was nothing wrong with her. Those kids simply did not understand or know her, so their way of dealing with the situation was to make fun of or tease her. I explained that she was enough, and that she could face them with confidence—and surely, they would get tired of picking on her and would back off. A few months later, I was happy to learn from my employee's daughter that the kids did back off and that my kind words playing over and over in her head were what gave her the courage to stand up to them. Always remember to show much generosity when it comes to kindness. It will go a long way.

Love does not envy or boast. You don't need to envy what others have. Each one of us possesses unique qualities that makes us special. Be yourself. You are good enough. Envy is a waste of time. Focus on your personal goals and work on them until you achieve them.

Showing off isn't really loving. When you boast about your extraordinary qualities, achievements, possessions, or abilities, others may find your conversation boring or irritating. Wouldn't it be better to speak with pride of your accomplishments that in turn can help others? It is more loving to share your experiences and challenges that brought you to where you are today that can inspire others to want to do, be, and have more because of your encouraging words. Doesn't that make sense?

Love does not dishonor and does not self-seek. Whatever we do in life, we always want to bring honor to others, especially when they have been there for us or have stood by us through a particularly difficult stage. We shouldn't take all the credit for achieving many of our goals when there have been others who have helped us. Are we being loving when we have an elevated position and act as if we did it without help? Is that true?

In most cases, it is not. Chances are that if we have overcome a crisis, or have reached a level of success, it was because we have had friends, family, and others who have been there through each step, pushing us forward, encouraging us, and being a support when we believed we wouldn't make it. Through the most grueling moments when we thought we would fall apart, there was always someone there to lift us up, helping us to pick ourselves up, dust ourselves off, and start the process all over again—until the dreams we had set out for ourselves became a living reality.

The rest of these verses teach us that we should not be easily angered or keep record of wrong. Instead, we should be forgiving. When we learn to let go of what has hurt us or made us unhappy in the past, we will understand what living your true essence means.

Showing evil to others is equivalent to bringing it back to yourself. Instead, it is better to delight in what is true. Seeking to live these beautiful qualities will allow you to live the most authentic expression of who you are. You will find that you will attract others with similar qualities.

Finally, love always protects, always trusts, always hopes, always perseveres. When these outstanding qualities become a part of our personality, we will never cease in creating new possibilities, establishing lasting relationships, looking forward to the future, and striving to live the best essence we can in mind, body, and spirit right now. When we live in harmony with our higher source, share the best of ourselves with others to help them want to live a better life, and give lovingly of ourselves, we can say along with what the good book says, that love never fails.

EXERCISE FOR LIVING YOUR TRUE ESSENCE

Find your Inner Power

Get that lovely journal out again and let's try some cool exercises. This will help you plan each day with a clear view of the steps you will take to use the inner power you were given since birth to exercise your free will. This power that is all-knowing, omnipotent, and exists everywhere is in you and it is up to you to want to access it so that you can create miracles in your world. I want you to seriously think about changing the thoughts that are driving you backward. Begin to project better outcomes to the powers that follow.

Power of Beliefs

Change the beliefs that disempower you and create new beliefs that empower you. In your journal, create two columns. At the top of the column, entitle it "Beliefs that disempower me." Write down those beliefs.

Examples of these beliefs can be: I am unattractive and don't know what I can do to look better. Or, I can't let go of these habits in my life that I hate and don't know how to quit them.

Now, on the right of the top of the column, write this question: "What will I now believe instead that will empower me so that I can live my authentic essence?" For example, "I believe that I will always be overweight and have unhealthy eating habits. It's the genes. Hey, what can I say?" That is a disempowering belief because your genes have little to do with your weight issues.

What can you believe instead? How about, "I believe that if I eat healthy, exercise, and sleep sufficiently, I can not only lose weight, but I can avoid most diseases, maintain high levels of energy, and feel really good about myself."

If your beliefs have not positively impacted your life for the good, then change them. Decide what you really want and what's preventing you from having it now.

Decide what you do want to happen. The more specific you can be about the things you would like to see manifested, the more clarity you will have, and the more power you will make known to the universe to help you achieve what you want faster. At the same time, you need to learn what's stopping you from having what you really want. These are the disempowering beliefs that you will write in this exercise.

When you realize that some of your beliefs are in the way of your progress and intention, you will know that it is time to make a change. If your beliefs remain the same and you haven't gotten anywhere with them, this will invariably prevent you from making the changes that you link more pain to and prevent you from making the change to new, empowering beliefs. In that case, you will remain where you are, and where you have been. You will need to kick out the voices in your head that play a song that you don't wish to hear any more. Knock the supports out from under these beliefs that don't serve you.

Use the list that you have written identifying these negative beliefs you have accepted in the past. Question them and know with absolute certainty if they empower or disempower you, and when you understand that they have caused you more pain than pleasure, then you need to take swift action steps to change them.

Power of Decision

Use the powerful tool of decision to transform your life. When you take decisive action to commit to any decision you make, you will feel empowered. The more decisions you make and stick to, the better you become at making them. Just like your body muscles are trained to be strong when you exercise them, you are working out your decision muscles that in time will also be strong.

In your fabulous journal, I want you to open a fresh page and write all the decisions that you have been putting off until now. They may be a hundred or just one. Write it down, if you please.

For example, is it that book you never wrote, that song you never sang, or that beautiful poem you never wrote? Is it that painting that you can never get right, the new business you never thought you would get the money to build, or that recipe that never comes out the way you want it to? You have put off the decision to marry again, or let go of a relationship that has you feeling stagnant. Maybe you have put off changing a career you don't want because you believe it's too late to switch, or perhaps you are practicing rituals that for a long time you have questioned or felt unsure about, but practice them anyway because you feel that you will be letting down your family, friends, and (if they are religious rituals) you will be letting your Creator down if you decide to no longer follow them?

What are those decisions that you put on the backburner of your mind to rot away because you don't think you can create that vision for yourself? You think it's out of your league. Think again, intelligent essence. You can create anything you want. We'll cover more about how I am certain this is possible in the section covering the spirit.

After you write down those decisions, ask yourself, "Can I really decide right now to no longer put off the decisions that I used to believe would never happen for me, and, just do it?" Oprah Winfrey said, "Every right decision I have ever made has come from my gut. And every wrong decision I've made was a result of me not listening to the greater voice of myself."[34] You will find the combination of deciding with conviction and determination to be powerful. Decide today to listen to that inner voice and stop putting off what you know in your gut you want to see become a reality in your own life.

Power of Persistence

Think of people in your life who are persistent. What has been their driving force? Chances are it is a fierce desire to see their dreams realized.

Persistence is the key to attaining any goal. The opposite of persistence is failure. Most people give up at the first sign of failure, or procrastinate and never get around to pursuing what they truly want. They may believe it's too hard, thus, give up before they're even half way up the ladder.

Think of the desire to reach that goal you wish to achieve. How do you feel about it on a scale of one to ten? Are you indifferent or excited? When the going gets rough, do you get going? Are you persistent in the face of discouragement, or do you simply give up when things don't seem to go your way?

The answers to these questions will determine the level of persistence you have, which will either push you forward to reach your desires, or hold you back from reaching them. The power of persistence resides within you. If this power is dormant, wake it up by cultivating it through self-reliance and by creating a definite plan of action that will take you step-by-step to attain that desire .

Power of Focus

What is your level of focus if you had to measure it on a scale from zero to ten? Ten being completely empowered and on fire, and zero being totally dead? If you were on a level of eight or above, how consistent would you be at attaining what you wanted?

Here is a test of your level of focus. Have you ever had a bad headache that wouldn't go away, then someone asked you to do something, or asked for your opinion about something, and bam, your headache was gone? Just like that. You completely forgot about it, didn't you? No, it wasn't because you took a Tylenol. Your focus shifted to the situation at hand, and without even knowing how, your headache disappeared.

How did you do that? Because you changed your power of focus. You were no longer focused on the pain you were feeling, but now your focus was centered on the immediate task in front of you. You have the power within you to change your focus at any time.

Why not test your ability to focus? You can choose the pictures you wish to see in your head. If you want to feel good or if you want something badly enough, you will put your entire focus on that until you achieve it. Know that whatever you focus on has the power to upset you or excite you. It can make you feel pain or pleasure. The question then becomes, what do you prefer to focus on?

Start today to focus on what you consistently pay attention to. Notice how it makes you feel. If it makes you feel angry, sad, or depressed, then you know it is time to change your focus. You will see transformation when you change your focus from low energy emotions to high energy emotions that will positively change your physical state. "Three things clog your soul: negativity, judgement, and imbalance," said Wayne Dyer, father of motivation.[35]

When you hold your head up high, stand up straight, put your shoulders back, push your chest forward, and change your thoughts to something that puts a smile on your face, your focus has changed, thus the state of your body language changes. Now, you feel alive, happy, and have a pep to your step instead of feeling sorry for yourself by focusing on negative thoughts that disempower you.

Ask yourself when negative feelings arise, "What am I focusing on that is making me feel this way?" Or when you feel out of spirits when situations pop up that you don't like, why not attempt to change your focus to thoughts that have the power to change your state to reflect a positive attitude? When you fully understand that life happens for you, not to you, then pain and suffering disappear. It becomes an opportunity to learn and grow into the true essence that makes you, you.

Power of Love

Love is the motivating force and very essence of your being. You don't need to seek for it outside of yourself or from others to experience it. You are love; therefore, you can give love freely the same way your higher source gives love freely. The more you give, the more you receive.

When you feel the gentle touch of a breeze, when you feel the warmth of the sun on your skin, when you gaze heavenward to the display of luminous stars that are lighting the sky like brilliant jewels, this demonstrates to you that your higher source is all-loving.

However, if you seek love in an imbalanced way, such as through blame, which temporarily feels good, but is not loving, then you waste precious time and energy. You must align yourself with your creator who is the very manifestation of love, just like you are. D. H. Lawrence puts it this way, "Those that go searching for love only make manifest their own lovelessness, and the loveless never find love, only the loving find love, and they never have to seek for it."[36]

Think about this. We all desire love. We all want to be the recipient of an endless flow of love. Yet, if we put ourselves down, tell ourselves that we are not enough, or blame others and the world for not receiving the love that we desire, then we are like those that D. H. Lawrence mentioned.

Ask yourself these crucial questions: "Am I loving? Or do I expect others to show me love first? Do I go out of my way to find opportunities to be loving, or do I need to find it from outside sources? Do I practice the habit of being loving each day, or do I always find it difficult to express love?"

What you think about is what you bring about. So, if you have aligned your thoughts and behaviors with lovelessness, then that is what the universe will give back to you. If you are loving and not getting much love, then you will need to re-examine this. Are you angry at the world?

At yourself? At others? Then this is a recipe for disaster and you are relinquishing your power to someone else. Are you waiting for a shift in the world or in others so that you can be loving? Then you are not aligned with your thoughts and behaviors. Take one hundred percent responsibility for having this powerful quality, and give love in abundance so that you are aligned with the source that is the essence of love.

Unharness these five powers you have to create and manifest anything you want. Change the beliefs that disempower you to beliefs that have transformative power. Make decisions with determination and conviction, and don't allow for indecision or no decision to cause you to lose out on attaining your desires. Persist in doing all that is necessary to become the very essence of who the real you truly is. Focus on those things that bring you real joy and happiness, knowing that wherever your focus goes, your energy flows. And finally, it is important that you be the loving being that is aligned with the powerful source that is love, and who created all things, including you.

If each day you set yourself up to live from your authentic self, have a positive mindset, possess a grateful attitude, and utilize the five powers you hold to reverse the disempowering traits, undesirable qualities, and limiting behaviors that you struggle with, then you are on your way to discovering the true essence you were meant to live. But there is more!

The next section will help you to learn how you can know what is best for your body. Knowing this can enlighten you about how you may have been treating your body and your health up to this point, and what you can do immediately to change how you think of your body going forward.

So, stand and stretch for a few minutes. Take several deep breaths, and maybe go and fetch yourself a healthy snack so that you will have your mind set for what's coming when you return. I will be here, excited to share more secrets with you about how you can live your true essence. So, go ahead, but try not to keep me waiting too long. I don't want you to miss out on lots of great information still to come.

I invite you to drink in the divine nectar of aromatic love and let it penetrate you in the deepest, most profound ways. Trust that the oils are working side-by-side to heal, regenerate, and teach you. The more you use them, the more they'll reveal their secrets to you.

Elana Millman

PART TWO

THE BODY

CHAPTER SIX

WELCOME TO THE WORLD OF ESSENTIAL OILS AND AROMATHERAPY

"I invite you to drink in the divine nectar of aromatic love and let it penetrate you in the deepest, most profound ways. Trust that the oils are working side-by-side to heal, regenerate, and teach you. The more you use them, the more they'll reveal their secrets to you."
—Elana Millman

Remember when you were a young child, how your grandma took care of you when you weren't feeling well? Did she prepare medicinal teas for you that contained herbs and spices? My grandma would make a concoction of ginger, lemon, honey, and cinnamon to create a tea blend that helped with colds and coughs. When I or my sisters were sick, my grandma would fill the bathtub with very warm water and would use Alcoholado, a rubbing alcohol that was infused with natural plants and other essential oils, primarily bay rum, eucalyptus, marigold pepper, patchouli, ginger, southern fogfruit, yellow sage, sweet scent, peppermint, and camphor, which helped with infections and congestion. It was amazing to see how quickly we would heal.

Both my grandmother and mother used this remedy with us, for bug bites to fevers and beyond. It relieved many symptoms we had and made us feel better in record time. Alcoholado is still widely used in the Caribbean, and many find this natural remedy to be more useful than traditional medicines for easing a variety of symptoms.

Several generations ago, the average population didn't seek out a doctor who could remedy their illnesses unless it was a real emergency that required immediate attention. Most would turn to holistic or alternative medicines to treat many ailments that plagued them, including ingredients from nature's pharmacy, such as herbs, roots, trees, and other natural plants that have been used for centuries.

For some people, living a healthy lifestyle is an important factor in considering the choices they make about what they put on or in their bodies. Some strive to look for better alternatives when it comes to the foods they eat each day, the choice of skincare they prefer, and the medicinal treatments they use for pain and inflammation, as well as for other symptoms they experience.

Most people do not consider that the food they consume, the products they put on their skin, or the medicines they choose to take may have artificial ingredients that are accepted as normal. They do not question the safety or adverse effects that these unnatural ingredients may cause, and assume that food, personal care, and pharmaceutical companies know what they're doing and are ethical when they create products and medicines. In fact, consumers assume that these companies should know what's safe and what's not, and believe they would not deliberately put ingredients or chemicals in their products or medications that could be potentially dangerous for humans. Is that true? For example, are over-thecounter and prescription drugs free from harmful substances? Are people aware of the negative effects that continued use of these medications can have on their health and well-being?

OVER-THE-COUNTER AND PRESCRIPTION DRUGS: ARE THERE ANY HIDDEN DANGERS?

Ask yourself: do I know if these drugs are safe for me, or should I be worried about the potentially harmful side effects they can have on my mind and body with continued use? Are there alternative solutions to these medications, and where can I go to find them? Studies indicate that many drugs can have serious side effects, which many people may not be aware of when taking them. Furthermore, some drugs do not help to heal the body in the most effective or natural way.

Let's take, for example, medications that are used for stress, a major factor today. It has caused many to turn to antidepressants and prescription drugs to cope with life's physical and emotional imbalances. This has in many cases made matters worse. Why? Because these drugs, which are frequently prescribed by physicians today, and which are easily accessible, can have harmful side effects and be addictive. Some are used to relieve symptoms that can range from sadness to pain, or from fatigue to anxiety. However, is this the right course to take?

Have these drugs benefited consumers? Have these prescribed medications permanently relieved the symptoms of those being treated, or are they simply masking the underlying problems without any real cures? These are important questions that you should ask yourself. Ask your doctor how long you will need to take the prescribed medication, and if it is for the rest of your life, study the side effects of that drug, because you will become more likely to have those side effects as the years progress.

Ask yourself: Do I know if these drugs are safe for me, or should I be worried about the potentially harmful side effects they can have with continued use? Are there alternatives to these medications, and where can I go to find better solutions for my health? The answers may surprise you.

Today, many people turn to over-the-counter drugs and prescriptions to relieve their symptoms. Research shows that "81% of adults use over-thecounter, or OTC, medicines as a first response to minor ailments," according to the Consumer Healthcare Products Association.[37] The National Institute on Drug Abuse states that "nearly seven in ten parents have given their child an OTC medicine late at night to help treat a sudden medical symptom." Unfortunately, some of those medications are addictive. Examples of commonly used drugs that can be addictive are "cough and cold remedies containing dextromethorphan."[38]

What about prescription drugs? NIDA reports that prescription drugs that contain addictive chemicals are "opioid pain relievers, such as Vicodin® or Oxycontin®; stimulants for treating Attention Deficit Hyperactivity Disorder (ADHD), such as Adderall®, Concerta®, or Ritalin®; and central nervous system (CNS) depressants for relieving anxiety, such as Valium® or Xanax®." They also state that "stimulants such as Ritalin® achieve their effects by acting on the same neurotransmitter systems as cocaine. Opioid pain relievers such as OxyContin® attach to the same cell receptors targeted by illegal opioids like heroin. Prescription depressants produce sedating or calming effects in the same manner as the club drugs GHB and Rohypnol®. And when taken in very high doses, dextromethorphan acts on the same cell receptors as PCP or ketamine, producing similar out-of-body experiences." More information can be found at the National Institute of Drug Abuse's website.[39]

These drugs can be downright dangerous, and people can become dependent on them if not strictly monitored by a physician. They can also cause many adverse health effects with minimal use.

WHAT ABOUT HOLISTIC AND ALTERNATIVE MEDICINES?

First, what is holistic medicine? According to the WebMD, holistic health or medicine is "a form of healing that considers the whole person—body, mind, spirit, and emotions—in the quest for optimal health and wellness. According to the holistic medicine philosophy, one can achieve optimal health—the primary goal of holistic medicine practice—by gaining proper balance in life."[40]

Some prefer to turn to alternative solutions for ailments ranging from headaches, back pain, colds, coughs, and infections, along with imbalances in the body, rather than turning to traditional methods they consider to be unhealthy. They choose options such as healthier nutrition, exercise, detoxification, herbs, essential oils, and other natural remedies in their daily routines to relieve symptoms or diseases. Is it possible? Can we believe in or trust in a holistic approach to living a more natural lifestyle, rather than solely choosing the traditional treatments discussed above?

Absolutely! There are ways to holistically support your body from numerous physical illnesses, aches and pains, emotional imbalances, mental blocks, and spiritual weaknesses that allow for the mind, body and spirit to live in harmony as one, without needing to completely rely on over-the-counter or prescription medications to feel better.

Of course, like anything that we try for the first time, consult with a qualified health practitioner before using herbal products, especially if you are pregnant, nursing, taking any medications, or if you are currently under a doctor's care.

Holistic methods focus more on the root cause of the disease or illness. The goal is to encourage a person to develop healthier choices that can assist in bringing back overall balance and eliminating disease out of the body. This includes adopting practices such as relaxation exercises, yoga, and meditation to help relieve pain, anxiety, depression, and stress. Living a more holistic lifestyle improves overall health and balance—without depending primarily on drugs with major side effects. Understanding holistic methods can open a new pathway toward healing that can transform your life, and allow for you to feel rejuvenated, vibrant, and full of health.

We will primarily focus on essential oils and aromatherapy, and how aromatic essences can help you physically, emotionally, mentally, and spiritually. Today, essential oils are gaining popularity worldwide, due to their healing benefits and how they can provide balance to the mind, body, and spirit. In fact, they can help with the number one cause of debilitating diseases today, and that is stress.

WHAT ABOUT STRESS?

According to Dr. Eric Lartey in *Matters of Life Magazine*, "Stress is a normal part of life. But if left unmanaged, it can lead to emotional, psychological, and even physical problems, including coronary artery disease, high blood pressure, chest pains, or irregular heartbeats."[41] Have you experienced any of these symptoms?

Current statistics indicate that a large percentage of people in the United States experience high levels of stress. "The Stress in America survey results show that adults continue to report high levels of stress and many report that their stress has increased over the past year," according to the Global Organization for Stress. "75 percent of adults reported experiencing moderate to high levels of stress in the past month and nearly half reported that their stress has increased in the past year."[42]

The statistics should impress upon you the importance of taking time out for yourself each day to relax and allow the tension in your body to slip away. Take the initiative to care for your physical, emotional, mental, and spiritual well-being. You must take 100 percent responsibility for yourself. Why not set a goal to make a sincere effort to achieve optimal health, overall balance, and a sense of feeling great every day, despite the negative stresses you may be presently experiencing?

There are several ways you can alleviate the stress, simple ways you can help yourself feel better, healthier, and happier, despite daily challenges.

Understanding the many benefits essential oils can have on your mind, body, and spirit is a starting point to unlocking the powerful and healing effects that you can experience by incorporating these therapeutic and aromatic essences into your life. When these natural oils are added to skin care products, oil and diffuser blends, candles, mists, or other methods of inhalation or absorption through the skin, you will appreciate how introducing aromatherapy into your daily routines can have a tremendous and positive impact on the way you view your overall health.

Consult with a qualified health practitioner or certified aromatherapist before attempting to use essential oils and the use of aromatherapy, especially if you are pregnant, nursing, have any allergies, are taking any medications, or are under a doctor's care.

WHAT'S ALL THE FUSS ABOUT ESSENTIAL OILS AND AROMATHERAPY?

What is all the hubbub about essential oils and aromatherapy? For one thing, there has been extensive medical research and scientific studies made about essential oils and the role they play on our overall balance and well-being. For years, the use of important properties found in these aromatic essences have been scrutinized and tested for their beneficial and healing chemical components. Yet, for all the studies conducted by medical researchers and scientists, many in the world are unaware of how powerful and effective essential oils can be on our mind, body, and on our spirit.

Essential oils are known to naturally relieve symptoms with little or no side effects (if used properly) and work to provide overall balance to the body. They contribute to lowering blood pressure, managing sugar and insulin levels, lowering cholesterol, reducing pain and inflammation, and supporting the healing of a host of other abnormalities in the mind and body.

There are a few ways you can help alleviate the stress in your life, ways that you can help yourself feel better, healthier, and happier, despite daily physical and emotional challenges. When you learn about the benefits associated with essential oils, you will discover that by being introduced to the world of aromatherapy and essential oils, and by acquiring knowledge about how these natural and organic, plant-derived essences can help with your daily routines, you will be well on your way to learning the powerful and positive impact they can have on your overall health and well-being. You will better comprehend healing and therapeutic benefits that can pave the way to greater health, inside and out, as you learn how essential oils can enhance your mood, alleviate pain and inflammation, significantly reduce minor or major stress, and assist in improving and restoring physical, emotional, mental, and spiritual balance.

Yet, you may still wonder, "What exactly are essential oils? And how does aromatherapy work?" Those are good questions that we will consider in the following pages.

WHAT ARE ESSENTIAL OILS
AND AROMATHERAPY ?

What are essential oils? How can aromatherapy help to improve the quality of your life? The answers to these questions will change the way you think about plants and the typical way you may view them.

You may associate plants as a food source, and they are. You may also see them as looking pretty on your windowsill, or outside in the garden. They are great for that, too. However, did you know that some plants can be used medicinally to support your health? They are also valued for their exceptional cosmetic qualities.

Unlike fragrances that may contain a cocktail of dangerous chemicals that through continual use can lead to numerous harmful effects to your health and the environment, essential oils are highly concentrated plant extracts that are derived solely from whole plants or plant parts. These may include, seeds, stems, leaves, flowers, roots, resins, or wood. They possess highly beneficial properties and carry the actual fragrance, essence, or life force from the plants they are extracted from. Thus, essential oils possess powerful components that are effective in supporting your health for many types of physical, emotional, mental, and spiritual imbalances.

One way essential oils work is through aromatherapy. In fact, when an essential oil is used in conjunction with other essential oils, the result is a therapeutic blend that assists in improving common symptoms currently being experienced in the body.

What is aromatherapy, though? According to the National Association for Holistic Aromatherapy, "Aromatherapy, also referred to as Essential Oil therapy, can be defined as the art and science of utilizing naturally extracted aromatic essences from plants to balance, harmonize, and promote the health of body, mind, and spirit. It seeks to unify physiological, psychological, and spiritual processes to enhance an individual's innate healing process."[43]

INDULGE YOUR SENSES

How many beneficial uses do essential oils have? Let me count the ways. As you inhale the essences of aromatic oils, such as Lavender, Frankincense, Rose, or a citrus oil such as Grapefruit, you can receive innumerable benefits that can range from relaxation, to stimulation of the senses, or from stress relief, to pain relief. For example, when I have a long day of studying, researching, or writing, I unwind by preparing a bath with very warm water and using a calming blend of Geranium, Lavender, and Bergamot, which I have formulated to help me relax and ease the tension from my body.

During times of meditation, I use an essential oil like Frankincense, which assists in helping me feel calm and centered during stillness. Essential oil of Frankincense is one of the most ancient oils and possesses many physical, medicinal, and spiritual uses. It is one of my favorite oils, due to its ability to maintain youthful looking skin that appears to slow down aging, relieve stress, promote peaceful feelings during meditation, and so much more. This oil will be discussed in more detail in the following chapter.

There are so many ways to incorporate essential oils and aromatherapy into your daily life. Use them while relaxing in a bath. Diffuse them while you study or prepare for a meeting, interview, speaking engagement, school exam, or anything that requires your concentration or full attention. You can create formulations to soothe, calm, or energize your senses.

Place a few drops of Lavender or Eucalyptus on a tissue and inhale to help you sleep, or ease a stuffy nose. Mix them in water or hydrosols to create a mist using Lemongrass, Orange, and Grapefruit that you can use to refresh your home or office, or mist around yourself to uplift your mood. Blend them in carrier oils such as Almond, Olive oil, Jojoba, or a blend of these oils along with an essential oil formulation to use as a body or bath oil to relax or stimulate your senses. You can use them during a luxurious bathing experience, or after soaking in a warm shower. Blend oils, such as Hempseed, Evening Primrose, and Safflower, to soothe sore muscles, ease aches and pains, or to help with dry or cracked skin.

You can even blend essential oils with ingredients such as clays, salts, sugars, waxes, and butters to cleanse, exfoliate, and moisturize your skin, giving it a youthful and healthy appearance. Essential oils can also help your tresses look fabulous. They can strengthen your roots, promote hair growth, moisturize, nourish, and give shine to dull or dry locks. Add to that, the beautiful essences that they evoke, and, voila, you will give your senses a treat, and feel and look amazing at the same time.

PRECAUTIONS WHEN USING ESSENTIAL OILS

Essential oils should be diluted for the most part in carrier oils, water, or ingredients such as waxes, butters, sugars, or salts, since these aromatic essences in their pure form can irritate the skin or cause adverse reactions. Any essential oil used for the first time should be diluted and tested inside the elbow to ensure that your body does not have any allergic response to the chosen oil. Women who are pregnant or nursing should consult with a certified aromatherapist or medical practitioner before trying any essential oil. This also applies to individuals with asthma, epilepsy, or other health conditions.

If using essential oils on children, much care is required prior to use. It is not recommended that little ones under six months have any essential oils applied to their bodies. Since babies have an immature immune system and thin skin, avoid any essential oil on or around them. After six months, essential oils should be used only topically, however, even when using this way, these oils should only be used for a specific purpose, and should be of short duration. After the age of two, essential oils such as Lavender (which is said to be one of the gentlest of oils) may be used topically in a very low dilution. Note that little ones are very sensitive to aromas, thus, it is important to educate yourself on the uses of essential oils on children.[44] Lea Harris is a Certified Clinical Aromatherapist who provides a long list of precautions to take regarding essential oils for children and yourself. She also provides information about how to dilute essential oils, which requires a certain amount of a carrier oil blended with the essential oil to reduce its potency and any allergic response.[45]

Your furry friends can have adverse reactions to essential oils if not applied correctly. Because essential oils contain powerful compounds, these substances in small amounts can have strong biological effects. According to an article in *Dogs Naturally Magazine* by Dana Scott, "Animals have sensitive senses of smell, so in most cases it is best to use oils that are diluted and always provide an escape route. If a pet does not like an oil, do not enforce its use."[46]

Certain essential oils can be used on your pet or service animal, however, always test and dilute prior to use to ensure that your furry buddy feels great with the oil you choose. Citrus oils are not advisable. Some citrus essential oils are not tolerated by cats or dogs. Chikita, who is a black Labrador Retriever and my service dog, enjoys a rub-down after being groomed with a blend of Lavender, Cedarwood, Citronella, and Eucalyptus mixed in a carrier oil blend of Almond, Jojoba, and vitamin E. She happily wags her tail and nuzzles my face with contentment.

Some citrus oils can cause photosensitivity, which can result in adverse skin reactions like an allergy when exposed to the sun. Bergamot, Grapefruit, Orange, Lime, and Lemon are examples of essential oils that can be phototoxic. Some citrus oils are okay to use in the sun. However, it is extremely important that you know how these oils are distilled. Do your research and know with absolute certainty that what you are putting on your body is safe for you. Always err on the side of caution to avoid serious burns from exposure to the sun when applying any citrus essential oil to your skin.[47]

Utilizing essential oils and aromatherapy is very beneficial and can help to support a wide range of physiological, psychological, and spiritual imbalances. As with anything we incorporate into our lives, it is essential that we educate ourselves on their use. Respecting essential oils and understanding how to properly use them should absolutely be considered when trying them for the first time. Knowledge is power, so before using these beautiful essences, research the safety precautions of using them topically or internally. When in doubt, consult your physician, certified and trained aromatherapist, or health care practitioner. Remember that essential oils are powerful liquid plant substances that can promote and support healing of the mind, body, and spirit, but caution should be taken when using any single or blended essential oil.

I personally use Aroma Web, which is founded by Certified Aromatherapist Wendy Robbins, to learn about oil profiles, which include the properties, uses, method of extraction, safety information, benefits, and aromatic description that will assist you in learning more about the proper way to effectively use these therapeutic oils. This will help you feel confident when purchasing them, and will allow you to have peace of mind when using them. For best results, always ensure that essential oils are organic and of therapeutic quality. Some oils on the market today may be diluted, grown with pesticides, or adulterated, thus making them ineffective for supporting health and well-being. In fact, I do not recommend using oils that are not certified organic and for use in therapeutic applications. You can learn more from Aroma Web at www.aromaweb.com/articles/howtobuyessentialoils.asp.

Now, you may be wondering, "Where did essential oils come from? And how long have they been around?" Well, those are great questions, and knowing the answers to them can help you better understand and value their exceptional uses today.

HISTORY OF ESSENTIAL OILS
AND AROMATHERAPY

In ancient times, people used essential oils as a normal part of their lives. For thousands of years, they have been used for religious ceremonies, sacred rituals, and for healing purposes. In Biblical times, for example, essential oils were used by the Israelites. Moses was told by God to create a sacred anointing oil blend that included Myrrh, Cinnamon, fragrant

Calamus and Cassia blended with olive oil. This holy formulation was used to anoint the heads of leaders and the Ark of the Covenant. According to Dr. Josh Axe in *The King's Medicine Cabinet,* "Essential oils are also mentioned 264 times in the Bible and about 33 different essential oils are referred to throughout its pages."[48]

In the New Testament, kings brought Jesus, the future king of Israel (who was a small child of about two years old), gifts that included Myrrh and Frankincense. Even then, essential oils were highly valued for their exceptional and healing qualities.

Going back further, Egyptians were among the first to use essential oils. According to blogger Dr. Ashley Mayer (known as Dr. Green Mom), a naturopathic medical doctor and expert in nutrition and detoxification as it relates to pediatrics and families, aromatic oils were an integral part of their daily lives as early as 4500 B.C.E. These oils were prized and often purchased with gold.[49]

Ancient Egyptians believed that essential oils were sacred and that only royalty and high priests had the authority to use them. During that time, each deity was assigned a signature essential oil blend, and on frequent occasions, images of gods and goddesses were anointed with precious oils during religious ceremonies.

Ancient pharaohs also used essential oil blends for meditation as well as intimacy, and in preparation for war. Cleopatra, who was said to be one of the most beautiful women at that time, used essential oils in her lavish beauty rituals. The secret behind her mysterious beauty and youthful skin came from the fermented milk baths infused with the therapeutic essence of Rose, Jasmine, and Myrrh, which she frequently indulged in. According to an ABC News article, Cleopatra traveled from Egypt to the Dead Sea, where she bathed in the salty waters that naturally contained clay and minerals.[50]

These powerful aromatic oils were valued in Biblical times and for the ancient Egyptians, and they were also valued by the ancient Greeks. Socrates, an ancient physician and philosopher in Greece, used aromatherapy for enhancing massage techniques. In addition, according to *The Healing Art of Essential Oils,* by Kac Young, PhD, "when King Tut's tomb was opened in 1922, 350 liters of essential oils were impeccably preserved in alabaster jars."[51]

All in all, essential oils and aromatherapy have been used in a variety of ways to balance and improve the lives of people who have come and gone throughout time. But what about today? Are they still as potent and valued as they were then ?

ESSENTIAL OILS IN THE MODERN WORLD

The answer is a resounding *yes!* If anything, essential oils today are more readily available to just about everyone. There are many places where we can purchase them, and using them daily can significantly improve our overall health and well-being.

Yet, it is vitally important to note that not all essential oils are created equally. Again, if they are going to be used for their therapeutic properties, ensure that the essential oils you purchase are certified organic, and great for use in therapeutic applications. Why? Because more than 70 percent of essential oils sold on the market today are adulterated in some form. Some are made in laboratories using synthetic materials that alter their beneficial properties. Some are overly processed, or overly diluted with carrier oils. Many, although they are said to be of therapeutic grade (which is a term that is loosely used by some companies) are grown using plants that are liberally sprayed with pesticides, making them potentially toxic, and therefore, not appropriate for use in attaining their healing benefits.

Essential oils were useful in times past for their powerful medicinal qualities, and are still beneficial today. They can be used topically, such as in creams, soaps, shampoos, or conditioners for the skin and hair. They can also be diluted in carrier oils for massage, or for supporting health against certain pains or ailments. They are also great for cleansing and supporting the body's natural healing against wounds, or you can add them to poultices or compresses to help ease aches, pains, and inflammation. You can diffuse them in the air, and they can be inhaled for their cleansing and moodenhancing abilities. Lastly, they can be ingested, but this must be done under the strict supervision of an experienced certified aromatherapist or healing practitioner.

However they are used, essential oils can significantly improve your health and even transform your life. By studying their healing properties, you will realize that when traditional medicines are not as effective, you can incorporate the profoundly beneficial and practical advantages of essential oils into your beauty regimens and daily rituals. The benefits will be evident through the regular practice of using them in your personal, medical, psychological, and spiritual daily needs.

In the following pages, I have compiled for you twelve of my favorite essential oils that have amazing healing properties and effectiveness. I use them depending on my mood or ailment. I also use them in daily rituals such as meditation, for chakra balancing, and for visualization and affirmation practices. We will discuss more in depth about these practices in the last section that deals with the spirit.

The essential oils I have compiled for you are categorized by common name, Latin translation, note classification, description, and benefits to the mind, body, and spirit. When you begin using essential oil blends, you, too, will wonder as I did, why didn't you learn about their incredible beauty benefits and healing properties before?

With research and practice, you can experiment with formulating your own unique aroma blends to create beautiful scents more to your liking. You will find that the difference between using fragrances that contain dangerous and toxic chemicals, such as phthalates that can disrupt your hormones, don't come close to the powerful and cleansing qualities found in essential oils. There is really no comparison. Take the time to explore the world of essential oils and aromatherapy, and discover the wonderful and natural essences that come directly from nature to you. You will never want to live without these truly holistic little doctors that can cater to many of your needs at any given moment.

You will learn how to effectively use essential oils to enhance your mood, enjoy younger and healthier looking skin, reduce pain and inflammation, and everything in between—even ways you probably never thought of. Just be patient, and stick with me. For now, look at my favorite essential oils up ahead. Enjoy.

CHAPTER SEVEN

MY ALL-TIME FAVORITE ESSENTIAL OILS

**"The precious essence you breathe, that which has
been created from the earth, may very well be the true
healing you have been waiting for."
—Rose Santiago**

The essential oils you will read about on the following pages are
my absolute favorites. Not only do they smell beautiful, but their
innumerable uses in my life have been amazing. Whether I am feeling a bit
tired, gloomy, under-the-weather, or spiritually imbalanced, these essential
oils have always come to my rescue.

Lavender, for example, has been my little savior whenever I felt like
a cold was coming on and my body felt weak. A few drops applied to
my neck, forehead, and lung area did the trick. At night, I use it to relax
and get a good night sleep, or on my abdomen whenever I have an upset
stomach. You must use caution when using Lavender in its pure form, or
neat.

Although it is one of the gentlest essential oils, any oil you start using
on your body should be diluted in a carrier oil. Every individual responds
differently, so it is important to conduct a patch test of any oil you are
using for the first time.

Geranium is my faithful companion during relaxing baths. She smells
beautiful and helps me during times when I feel stressed. A few diluted

drops in the bath, and the entire bathroom is filled with her tantalizing aroma.

Frankincense is my queen of spiritual enlightenment and beauty. I use this incredible oil during meditation or while working on my chakras. In addition, I use Frankincense with other essential oils in my daily beauty regimens to maintain balanced and youthful skin. She also calms my spirit, and I love her warm and woodsy essence.

Remember, a little goes a long way. Essential oils are precious, and every drop matters. Each oil that I use has a purpose, and I sincerely hope you, too, will find a purpose for incorporating these powerful little helpers in your life to balance your mind, body, and spirit. And, here's a little secret, when you add essential oils to your everyday rituals and regimens, you will benefit from the tremendous power found in these lovely and aromatic essences. You won't need to always resort to traditional medicines that can have undesired side effects on your body.

It is with true faith and love that I say to you that inviting nature's gift of plants into your life is more closely connecting you to the energy source that created all things. This connection is from all that is found on earth, and connects with the universe that is part of you. Discovering the healing and supportive benefits found in these aromatic plant oils is one of the secrets that can make it possible for you to live your true essence.

Are you ready to begin creating your own aromatherapy formulations? Be sure that when beginning your experimentations with new blends, you will follow all the safety guidelines to make your journey into the world of essential oils and aromatherapy a safe and pleasant one. I use the safety guidelines at Artisan Essential Oils: www.artisanessentialoils.com/msds-essential-oil-safety/.

With continued use, you may find that they can help you feel physically, emotionally, mentally, and spiritually uplifted. When they are used properly, you will experience a revived and balanced life. When trying single oils or combining blends that can calm, invigorate, and stimulate your senses, you will discover that it was worth investing the time you spent learning about them. They have been an integral part of my life for a very long time, and I hope that you, too, will welcome these little treasures into yours.

FRANKINCENSE

Boswellia carterii
Base Note

Frankincense is a powerful and sacred essential oil that has been around for thousands of years. She goes as far back as Biblical times, and has been used in religious ceremonies, for burning incense, and in ancient medicines to promote healing. Throughout the centuries, Frankincense has been an essential part in the lives of kings and queens for enhancing sensuality, for anointing gods and goddesses, and to create beauty tinctures to protect and rejuvenate the skin.

Frankincense has a fresh, spicy, woody, and balsamic essence with citrus top notes. It readily assists with inflammation in the body, supports health against asthma, and acts as an immune system booster. It helps generate healthy cell production, which can reduce age spots and wrinkles on the skin. It can also help to tighten the skin and even out skin tone, allowing it to look and feel younger.

Essential oil of Frankincense is great for pain. Inflammatory problems such as arthritis, colitis, muscle, or joint pain can be significantly reduced by using it in combination with a carrier oil, such as jojoba oil. It even works to ease depression, mental fatigue, or improve spiritual awareness. Simply place a few drops of Frankincense on your forehead to help with focus, a drop or two on the crown of your head for spiritual enlightenment, or several drops on any area where there is pain or inflammation.[52]

More recently, research on Frankincense shows that this essential oil can fight abnormal cell growth and treat certain cancers. The chemical compounds found in this incredible essential oil can help to affectively help reduce swelling in the brain and target cancer cells in ovarian cancer.

According to H.K. Lin, Ph.D., "In 2011, a clinical trial evaluating 44 individuals monitored high doses of frankincense resin as a remedy for cerebral edema. In 60% of the patients, the swelling was reduced by 75% or more."[53]

Other interesting research done on the study of Frankincense stated that, "According to their press release, the Omani government-funded research has (for the first time) uncovered that frankincense has the ability to target cancer cells in late-stage ovarian cancer patients. And this all appeared to be due to AKBA (acetyl-11-keto-beta-boswellic acid)." According to lead researcher Kamla Al-Salmani, "After a year of studying the AKBA compound with ovarian cancer cell lines in vitro, we have been able to show it is effective at killing the cancer cells.[54]

Frankincense is taken by many people with no known side effects. This finding has enormous potential to be taken to a clinical trial in the future and developed into an additional treatment for ovarian cancer.[55]

In my opinion, Frankincense is the queen of essential oils. Her power to heal the body from physiological, psychological, and spiritual imbalances makes her life-saving qualities grand indeed. When you explore her depth, healing abilities, and amazing skin-rejuvenating properties, you will discover that it will be virtually impossible to live without her healing essence.

GERANIUM

Pelargonium odorantissimum
Middle Note

Essential oil of Geranium is extracted through steam distillation of the leaves and stems from the Geranium plant. She has a thin consistency and ranges in color from clear to light amber. She has a lovely fresh and floral essence, with a touch of fruit. This oil is considered a middle note in aromatherapy concoctions, and originates in countries like Egypt, France, Italy, and Spain.

Essential oil of Geranium contains many beneficial healing properties. It can help support dental health, and skincare to reduce wrinkles. The oil is wonderful for baths and promotes healthy skin. It can also support hormone balance and may relieve some symptoms related to depression, anxiety, and stress.

According to Dr. Josh Axe's website, Geranium oil is nontoxic, nonirritant and generally non-sensitizing—and the therapeutic properties of Geranium include being an antidepressant, an antiseptic, and woundhealing . It may also be one of the best oils for such diverse dermatological problems as oily or congested skin, eczema, and dermatitis."[56]

It appears that Geranium helps reduce inflammation, which speeds up healing. In aromatherapy, it assists in stabilizing emotions and may be helpful in relieving menopausal symptoms.

Geranium can be applied to bruises, burns, and minor wounds. It improves circulation, boosts kidney health, and may support a healthy blood pressure. It also helps reduce wrinkles by tightening facial skin, and prevents skin and muscles from sagging.

This powerful oil may help fade scars or spots from acne, age spots, pox, fat-cracks, surgeries, boils, and other scarring on the skin. Many people spend a fortune on cosmetic solutions with no real results. Geranium facilitates blood circulation below the skin, so this supports skin healing with less expense.[57]

As you can see, having this oil on hand can help with skin issues, calm the mind, and alleviate physical symptoms. It can be a great companion that provides many health benefits to your mind and body, something good to have nearby when you need a boost.

GRAPEFRUIT

Citrus paradisi
Top Note

I love the yummy scent of Grapefruit. She is my energy booster girlfriend and partner in getting things clean and smelling fresh. This essential oil has a delightful citrus, sweet, and tangy aroma with a thin consistency. She is considered a top note in aromatherapy and is widely used in the food and fragrance industry. She is cold pressed or expressed, and the fruit peel is used to extract the essential oil.

Essential oil of Grapefruit is made in the United States and the West Indies. It contains many health supporting properties. It can provide support with ailments that include: headaches, depression, anxiety, Alzheimer's symptoms, cellulite, obesity, water retention, puffy skin, sluggish liver, kidney, lymph, and vascular systems. It also boosts energy, and can be diffused, directly inhaled, ingested, or used topically in massage oils, lotions, shampoos and conditioners, and other body products.[58]

There are other great benefits to Grapefruit. This oil when diluted can be used to repel insects, particularly fleas, and if you care for horses, it can help repel flies. It can be diluted and topically applied to dogs to help with skin problems and keeps insects at bay. However, it should be kept away from cats, since if ingested, this essential oil can be toxic.[59]

Grapefruit is also added to nontoxic cleaning products and is great for disinfecting countertops, sinks, toilets, and other hard surfaces. During my fourteen-year housekeeping business, I created my own cleaning and disinfecting solutions for my customers. The housekeepers utilized these solutions, which included ingredients such as vinegar, baking soda, soap suds (like Dr. Bronner or Castile soap), and Lavender, Tea Tree, Orange, Lemongrass, and Grapefruit essential oils. The housekeepers mentioned during one of our team-meets that they had received many benefits from the essential oils they used during their cleanings, which according to them, made them less sick with colds and the flu.

I loved experimenting with different recipes to create earth friendly cleaners to effectively clean homes, buildings, and offices. With the oils, I created a natural glass solution, a bath room scrub, an all-purpose solution, and a cleaner and degreaser. Grapefruit is fantastic for removing grease, bacteria, and unwanted odors. Not only that, but this oil smells so yummy and makes me feel energized and ready to tackle any task of the day.

Essential oil of Grapefruit is a powerful essential oil that contains antiviral and antimicrobial properties that can assist in protecting the body from the harm done by a variety of toxins. According to Organic Facts, "This oil is effective in protecting the body from all harm done by various oxidants and toxins, including premature aging, degeneration of tissues, macular degeneration, loss of hearing, mental and physical sluggishness, disorders and other related problems."[60]

Dr. Joseph Mercola, a board-certified osteopathic physician who specializes in family medicine, and in treating the whole person approach, unlike medical doctors who only treat the symptoms, says that Grapefruit, "can help prevent oxidation-related damage, such as premature aging, vision problems like macular degeneration, poor hearing, nervous system problems, and many others."[61]

When used in meditation, it aids in clearing mental chatter, eases confusion, and helps relieve feelings of sadness or tension. If ingested, adding one to two drops of Grapefruit to a glass of water or herbal tea can help naturally detoxify the body, but consult a certified aromatherapist before ingesting any oils.

Grapefruit is phototoxic, so direct sunlight should be avoided when this oil is applied to the skin.[62] It may interact with the same medications for which you can't eat grapefruit and if you are not certain about whether you can use this oil while you take a medication, ask your doctor. This oil has a short shelf-life and should be used within six months from purchase. Grapefruit should be considered an important oil to add to your collection because she is useful in a variety of applications.

LAVENDER

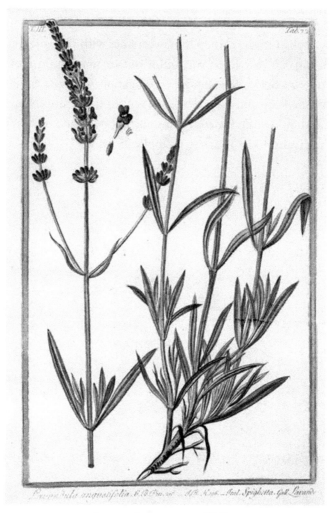

Lavandula angustifolia
Middle Note

Lavender comes from the Latin word Lavare, which means "to wash." There are so many wonderful benefits to the essential oil of Lavender. She is effective against many toxins, which can apply to a variety of ailments.

Lavender oil has been around for more than 3,000 years. Both Greeks and Romans used Lavender to perfume their bathwater and burned Lavender incense to appease their wrathful gods. It is said that Cleopatra, queen of ancient Egypt, anointed her entire body with Lavender oil to entice and seduce Mark Anthony and Julius Caesar.[63] Apparently, it was an aphrodisiac, in addition to many of its other uses.

Lavender is effective in calming the mind and spirit when feeling anxious or stressed. Its sweet, herbaceous essence relaxes, soothes, and restores overall balance to the mind, body, and spirit. It is also effective against burns and when applied on the skin, it allows the skin to improve. According to Dr. Mercola, "Lavender oil can help ward off mosquitoes and moths. It is actually used as an ingredient in some mosquito repellents." He also says that Lavender is "known for its anti-inflammatory, antifungal, antidepressant, antiseptic, antibacterial, and antimicrobial properties. It also has antispasmodic, analgesic, detoxifying, hypotensive and sedative effects. Lavender oil is one of the most well-known essential oils in aromatherapy."[64]

The natural antibiotic and antiseptic properties found in Lavender make this essential oil quite versatile. Not only can it be used to wash and clean scrapes, cuts, and bruises, but it can also be used for wiping down and cleaning appliances, tiles, countertops, and as a deodorizer.

It helps keep your pet calm, and her skin and fur clean and healthy.

Blended with a great carrier oil, such as almond or jojoba, Lavender helps your pet's fur and skin remain moisturized throughout the day. It will also help maintain pesky critters at bay and away from your pet, which I am sure she will demonstrate with much appreciation by merrily wagging her tail with joy as you show your love and care for her health and well-being.

Remember to always exercise caution when using essential oils on or around your pets or service animals. According to Organic Aromas blog, "If you have cats, you also need to be wary about certain oils. Cats are particularly sensitive to essential oils that contain polyphenolic compounds because they interfere with their liver detoxification process. So, if you have cats, use extra caution around essential oils like Cinnamon, Tea Tree, Thyme, Birch, Wintergreen, Clove, and Oregano."[65] Although Lavender is not mentioned here, if you decide to use this oil on your cat, it is important that you pay close attention to any signs of adverse effects it may have that can be potentially harmful to her health.

Lavender oil is my queen of calmness, relaxation, and taking it down a notch. She makes it simple to ease my nerves and allows for a comfortable and pleasant night's sleep. Her antidepressant properties assist in enhancing my mood, while her astringent properties help to cleanse and detoxify the body.

If you must choose one essential oil, I would say let Lavender be the one you purchase before introducing any other oils into your daily rituals or practices. Due to her versatility in tackling different imbalances that may stem from burns to depression, from sedative to antibiotic, and from pain to meditation, taking advantage of the incredible healing and antibacterial properties found in Lavender will truly make this oil a musthave that you can experiment with first. It can start you on the path to the discovery and the innumerable benefits of holistic healing. You should begin your journey with Lavender and work your way up to incorporating other fabulous aromatic essences into your daily routines; you will see how a lifestyle that includes using essential oils each day can transform your life.

LEMON

Citrus limon
Top Note

Essential oil of Lemon has a sugary citrus or zesty essence, much like fresh lemons. She is pale to deep yellow in color and has a thin consistency. Lemon is considered a top note and is used as a cleaning agent around the house, especially in the bathroom and kitchen. She also gives wood and silver a natural shine. A fiber cloth soaked in Lemon oil will help seal woods and spruce up your tarnished silver and jewelry!

Essential oil of Lemon originates from Italy, Spain, and the United States. The fruit peel is the part used to extract the essential oil. This oil contains healing properties which are antibacterial, antimicrobial, antiseptic, antifungal, astringent, and carminative (preventing gas formation).

Lemon has many applications. You can diffuse or directly inhale it with a carrier oil like Jojoba to help uplift your mood. You can also use it topically to help tone oily skin, smooth the appearance of wrinkles, and ingesting this essential oil can help with stomach upsets and weight loss. If distilled instead of cold pressed, this oil can be phototoxic, so direct sunlight should be avoided when it is applied to the skin. As I've stated before, prior to ingesting any essential oil, consult with a certified aromatherapist.

Lemon oil can repel insects. It can support the liver, and can also help improve circulation. Applying it diluted in a carrier oil such as almond or jojoba can soothe insect bites and makes an insect repellent for dogs. The next chapter will provide dilution guidelines when beginning your journey into creating your own unique oil blends, depending on what the oils are being used for. Before applying any treatment to your dog, consult with a veterinarian who is knowledgeable on natural methods that include essential oils for caring for your pet or service animal.[66]

During times of meditation or in aromatherapy, Lemon can assist with concentration. It energizes the mind, lifts the spirit, and promotes a sense of joy. You can diffuse this oil while studying for an exam, when feeling a bit gloomy, when waking up in the morning, for boosting energy, or for cleansing and purifying your spirit.[67]

Dr. Josh Axe reports that assistant professor Dr. J.V. Hebbar, Alva's Ayurveda Medical College assistant, describes some of the benefits of Lemon oil. It can help with digestion, provide cough relief, calm the stomach, relieve nausea, support oral health, and provide a remedy for halitosis (bad breath). It is also a thirst quencher that helps to nourish the skin and promotes weight loss.[68]

Lemon may provide support for healthy cholesterol levels and heart health. What has also made this oil quite successful is d-limonene. Lemon has a powerful cancer-fighting antioxidant, d-limonene, and some reports speculate that it may contain about 70 percent d-limonene![69] Scientists are quickly catching up with the healthy properties that come from many ancient therapeutic essential oils which can change the future of medicine.

I consider essential oil of Lemon to be my booster buddy when I need a pick-me-up. If you love the essence of lemon and want to experiment with an oil that will bring sunshine to your home and surround you with her truly cleansing properties, then you will enjoy welcoming her into your life. Make space in your medicine cabinet or personal care shelf for this energizing and fun essential oil.

LEMONGRASS

Cymbopogon flexuosus
Top Note

Lemongrass is a perennial that grows in large grass clumps. She is a tropical and subtropical plant that grows in South Asia, Southeast Asia, India, Egypt, and Sri Lanka. When this herb is steam distilled from the fresh and partially dried leaves, she reaps a pungent essential oil that has a thin consistency and is amber, yellow, or reddish-brown in color.

For hundreds of years in India, the leaves of Lemongrass were used in traditional medicine as an analgesic, carminative, antibacterial, stimulant, and antifungal agent. It has been combined with other herbs for tea remedies, and as an oil it has been used for many different ailments.

According to *Herbalpedia*, "Lemongrass was being distilled for export in the Philippines as early as the 17th century." It was a "popular herb in Brazil and in the Caribbean for nervous and digestive problems."[70]

What are the aromatherapy benefits of Lemongrass? She smells amazing with her earthy, fresh, and lemon essence! She helps clear the mind, lift the spirit, and promote feelings of optimism, hope, and courage. But of course, there's more!

Lemongrass is an exceptional oil for cleaning, since it contains antifungal, antibacterial, and anti- microbial properties. It can be diffused, and helps clean the air, since it also contains antiviral properties. If you have trouble waking up in the morning, Lemongrass will help you rise and shine, since she is emotionally uplifting and helps to stimulate the senses so you can get moving. Why not diffuse Lemongrass before brewing that hot cup of coffee?

Lemongrass is also great for repelling insects. It is used in tonics, and adds a great flavor to culinary preparations. In addition, Lemongrass is widely used for coughs and other respiratory conditions. The Chinese use Lemongrass for help in treating headaches, rheumatic pains, stomach upsets, and colds. It can also be effective with fevers in children. (Use caution with any essential oil before using or applying on children for any ailment. Always consult a doctor and an aromatherapist before attempting to treat children with essential oils.)[71]

Without a doubt, Lemongrass oil can be very useful in aiding with many health concerns. When using her as an herb, you can enjoy many delicious teas, meats, soups, and use her in a bath to energize your mind and lift your spirits. I highly favor Lemongrass for her wonderful energizing and antibacterial properties. I diffuse her a lot in my home, and she always uplifts and energizes me, especially in the mornings. She is my high energy queen when I am cleaning my home, or using her in my body butter summer recipes. You, too, should experience the benefits of Lemongrass and make this oil part of your collection.

MYRRH

Commiphora myrrha
Base Note

Essential oil of Myrrh is yellowish-orange in color with a thick consistency. She possesses a sap-like substance or resin that comes from a tree commonly found in Africa or in the Middle East. Prior to harvest, the trunks are cut into, releasing the resin, which is then dried along the tree trunk, and later this sap is steam distilled to create a healing essential oil.

Myrrh is an ancient and sacred oil going back as far as Biblical times. She has tons of benefits in modern times, as it did in times past. Myrrh was used as incense; her smoky, sweet, and woody odor bringing much pleasure to the God of Israel, who commanded that his people regularly burn incense as part of their sacred worship.

Essential oil of Myrrh was widely used in religious ceremonies and for anointing. It was also used by Egyptians in the mummification process. Myrrh was highly valued in Chinese and Ayurvedic medicine and this precious oil was utilized as a spice, and as a natural remedy for various ailments such as in treating hay fever, as a paste to help stop bleeding, as an antiseptic to clean and heal wounds, and as a flavoring agent for culinary dishes.[72]

Thousands of years later, Myrrh is still widely used and has many healing benefits. It is a valued oil in the perfume industry, and is also used during times of meditation to help ease the spirit.

When you're feeling sick with a cold, cough, or even bronchitis, the aromatic essence of Myrrh can be diffused or steamed to help ease symptoms. A few drops in a diffuser can help soothe stress or anxiety, and can assist in relieving fear or negativity. Myrrh is also great for soothing the mind and uplifting the spirit.

Myrrh is wonderful for the skin. You can receive a real treat by adding a few drops of it to a carrier oil blend, such as evening primrose, almond, or jojoba, to create a beautiful massage oil. The antioxidant properties of Myrrh help to rejuvenate the skin and are great for anti-aging or stretch marks. Use this diluted blend on your face to help reduce the appearance of wrinkles or sagging skin. Avoid your eye area, because your eyes are sensitive to essential oils and you should avoid getting essential oils in your eyes.

This oil contains many healing properties that make it antibacterial, antifungal, antiviral, and antispasmodic. It assists in reducing inflammation or swelling, and putting a few drops in a cold compress and applying it to any area that is infected or inflamed can help relieve pain or discomfort. Myrrh can also help with reducing phlegm or congestion from colds, and can support the relief of breathing problems related to upper respiratory conditions. Due to the many therapeutic properties found in this oil, it can be very beneficial in preventing infections, help with digestive problems, heal wounds, and reduce incidence of ulcers.[73]

The powerful antioxidants found in Myrrh help to protect against liver damage, according to a 2010 study in the "Journal of Food and Chemical Toxicology." Researchers also found that Myrrh inhibited growth in eight types of cancer cells, specifically gynecological cancers, which means that Myrrh may contain anticancer benefits.[74]

Essential oil of Myrrh is worth considering as a powerful force in your collection of aromatic essences. She is my rock star in beauty recipes that I create for the face, during meditation or while working on my chakras, for diffusing when I am writing, or in my bath salts for a luxurious bathing experience.

With all the therapeutic benefits found in Myrrh, you will certainly make use of all the wonderful properties that support healing which this oil offers. Feel alive and sensual with this rock star goddess.

PEPPERMINT

Mentha piperita
Top Note

Essential oil of Peppermint has a fresh, very minty, hot, and somewhat herbaceous essence. She is made in Hungary, Egypt, India, and the United States. Peppermint is easily cultivated and is not as expensive as other essential oils. She is typically steam distilled and is considered a top note with a thin consistency.

Peppermint contains health supporting properties that are useful for a variety of ailments. It is an analgesic, which means that it assists in healing pain. This essential oil is also antibacterial, anti-inflammatory, anti-parasitic, anti-spasmodic, anti-viral, and digestive. Peppermint can be used in topical applications, as well as in ingestion. Since this is more powerful than peppermint oil you buy for cooking, use caution with it.

Essential oil of Peppermint is a fantastic oil that helps to relieve pain in the muscles and joints, and because of its anti-inflammatory properties, it is used to assist with rheumatism and arthritis. Peppermint blended with a carrier oil such as Jojoba can be massaged on the skin after an intensive workout or yoga session to ease muscle tension, or use the blend to cool and soothe the skin.

Ancient Egyptians, Chinese, and American Indian cultures used Peppermint for many applications. Perhaps it was a favored essential oil for its extreme health-promoting properties. Its benefits and uses have been documented as early as 1000 B.C., "and have been found in Egyptian pyramids."[75]

Today, Peppermint is commonly used in many aromatherapy applications to heal the mind, body, and soul. Just one drop of Peppermint in a glass of water can soothe digestive issues or tummy aches. It also helps with headache pain, or to relieve strained muscles. It can be used to freshen breath, and to stimulate the senses, boost energy, and improve mental focus and concentration. It also has the capacity to relieve stress, recharge your internal battery, and refresh the spirit.

This oil can be used for support against pain. It soothes sore muscles, back pain, and literally melts away tension headaches. A study shows that when applying Peppermint oil topically, this oil has pain relieving benefits that are associated with Fibromyalgia, a syndrome that includes chronic or widespread pain in the muscles and connective tissues.[76]

Peppermint is an expectorant that can support the treatment of coughs, colds, sinusitis, bronchitis, and even asthma. It can assist in reducing hunger when inhaled through diffusion. It also energizes, so instead of grabbing that potentially dangerous energy drink to fuel your system, why not choose a nontoxic alternative, and take a few whiffs of Peppermint oil?[77]

I love Peppermint in my tea. In a cup of hot water, I place about a drop of Peppermint essential oil and add my tea bag. This helps me feel energized and able to concentrate more fully on any given task that I need to tackle during the day. I also purchase bars of natural soap with essential oil of peppermint and love showering with this oil during those scorching hot summer days. Peppermint feels so refreshing on my skin. She is absolutely my queen of comfort, and soothes me when I feel pain or restlessness.

Have caution when using essential oil of Peppermint. This oil may interact with certain medications, so research this oil prior to application and discuss your plans to use it with your doctor. Dilute any essential oil you are using, and it is a good idea to wash your hands after use. Because Peppermint oil is hot and minty, it can sting eyes if accidentally touched with unwashed hands. Avoid using it on or near any area where a burning sensation would not be pleasant.

Peppermint is great to have in your medicine cabinet. With all the healing properties in this energy-boosting oil, it is no wonder that it has been around for centuries and is widely available today. Experiment with Peppermint and discover how this refreshing and soothing essential oil can assist you with pain or discomfort that you may be experiencing .

PATCHOULI

Pogostemon cablin
Base Note

Essential oil of Patchouli is my sensual goddess. I use this oil frequently when creating exotic perfume formulations. She is a very aromatic oil, so I love using her provocative essence in blends such as lotions, body and massage oils, and shampoos and conditioners.

Essential oil of Patchouli also helps with burns, stings, minor wounds, and insect bites. Inhaling Patchouli has a powerful impact on the hormones, and on the mind and body. It stimulates the release of chemicals in the body, such as serotonin and dopamine, causing negative emotions to disappear.[78]

Patchouli also helps rid your hair of dandruff. If you add it to your body oils, it makes dry skin feel moisturized, and if using it on the delicate skin on your face, it can help to reduce the appearance of wrinkles, open pores, thoroughly cleanse the skin, and assist in relieving oily skin and hair.

It may help to relieve fevers. It can help with internal inflammation, such as with arthritis and gout. One of the most important benefits found in Patchouli is its antiseptic properties. It supports clean wounds so that they hopefully won't become septic. Small wounds can become infected and can lead to much more serious complications like tetanus, if the wound was exposed to rusty iron. Taking proper care of yourself before an infection can occur is important.[79]

During meditation and aromatherapy, Patchouli helps to alleviate nervous exhaustion, is grounding, and may relieve stress. It helps to quiet the mind, increases focus, and eliminate feelings of insecurity.[80]

A great reason for using this essential oil is for its aphrodisiac properties. It is wonderful for treating sexual imbalances, including: loss of libido, impotency, decrease in sexuality, sexual anxiety, erectile dysfunctions, and frigidity. It is great for couples who want to bring sparks back to the bedroom by stimulating sexual hormones, such as estrogen and testosterone, which boost sex drive.[81]

This wonderfully aromatic essential oil has been useful for centuries in ancient Egypt and has been used as an aphrodisiac for royal lovers. Well,

I must say that royals weren't the only ones who enjoyed the scintillating effects of Patchouli. I remember the first time I experimented with this oil through diffusion. My body and senses reacted strongly to its sensual properties. Luckily, my boyfriend at the time was nearby to satisfy all those urges (I am totally laughing aloud about that crazy experience with Patchouli). After that, I used Patchouli in my bath water, in perfume concoctions, colognes for men, and am still creating products with this stimulating oil.

Patchouli is an essential oil that will captivate your senses and put the oomph back into your sex drive. Blending her with citrus essential oils, such as Lemon and Bergamot (which may be phototoxic, so do not use it in the sun), Tangerine, Frankincense, or Geranium can really create an aphrodisiac that will keep you stimulated all night long. It's truly a treasure to keep around. Although her scent is intense, when combined with softer essential oils, she can be quite the aromatic sensual goddess that you will reach out to, just as I have many times when I wanted her intoxicating and heady essence in my life.

ROSEMARY

T. 5. Nº 44.

ROSMARINUS officinalis.

ROMARIN officinal

Rosmarinus officinalis
Middle Note

Essential oil of Rosemary is a versatile oil capable of supporting your health with numerous ailments. She's very useful in aromatherapy, and can assist during times of meditation. Although Rosemary is an evergreen, her essence is not overly woody. She is quite herbaceous, fresh, and sweet, with medicinal undertones. Rosemary is steam distilled with a thin consistency.

In aromatherapy, Rosemary is considered a middle note. It originates in France, Spain, and Tunisia. Some of the properties contained in the essential oil of Rosemary are analgesic, antarthritic, antibacterial, antifungal, aphrodisiac, astringent, decongestant, digestive, diuretic, hypertensive, restorative, stimulant, and tonic. For topical use, it should be diluted very well, with half essential oil and half carrier oil. It can be used in diffusion, in topical applications, and through inhalation.

It can help ease pain from arthritis, rheumatism, and muscle cramps. It improves circulation, eases respiratory discomfort, helps with colds and congestion, and repels insects. On the hair and skin, Rosemary helps to combat dandruff, hair loss, reduce acne, oily skin, and dull skin.[82]

Rosemary was often used in wedding ceremonies during ancient times. Sprigs of the herb were tied with beautifully colored ribbon and often presented to guests at the wedding ceremony as a symbol of love. Since Rosemary is also considered by some to be a harbinger of wealth, when the herb is placed in the entrance of a home or business, it is said to increase income.[83]

Essential oil of Rosemary can be used to create formulations that include nontoxic cleaning products and air fresheners. It can be diffused in the air, and blended in massage oils, shampoos, conditioners, lotions, soaps, and in other products that can be used in topical applications. It is very stimulating to the mind and helps with focus and memory, especially when working on school assignments, studying for an exam, or preparing for a job interview. It can assist with meditation by providing relief due to stress and anxiety, and can also promote clarity of mind and increase intuition.

Another amazing benefit of Rosemary is that it has an antioxidant ORAC value of 3300, which is equal to goji berries. The chemical responsible for this in Rosemary is carnosol, which the medical journal *Cancer Letters* credits with having anti-cancer properties.[84]

According to Dr. Axe, the "chemical carnosol found in Rosemary acts like a military sniper who only takes out his enemy target and doesn't damage neighboring cells like the chemotherapy nuclear-bomb approach, which kills everything in its path."[85]

Essential oil of Rosemary can offer you many beneficial healing experiences. She is my healing queen. As an herb, she is quite delicious in my meat and soup recipes. As an essential oil, she has been by my side during a long bath, and in a diffuser to help during times of writing where my focus and concentration are key. I also use Rosemary in my sports massage blend to help ease sore muscles after exercise.

Use her when in pain. Apply her to your skin or hair, along with other nutrient ingredients to help keep your skin looking clean and clear, and your locks strong and healthy. Trust her chemical components that can help with hair growth and with your doctor's support for serious conditions, such as cancer. Whatever the case, Rosemary will be there for you whenever you need her assistance to support healing, help improve your mood, or to maintain overall balance and well-being.

TUBEROSE

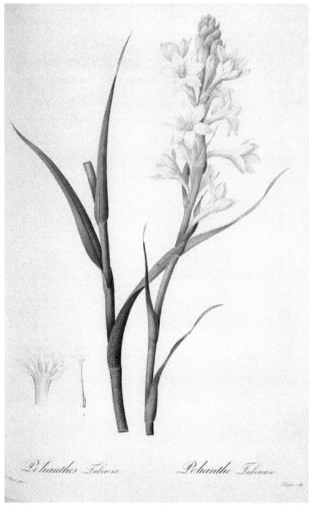

Polianthes Tuberosa
Base Note

Tuberose is a beautiful and exotic flower with an intoxicating and heady fragrance that only blooms at night. She is an accepted aphrodisiac with narcotic properties. Romantic names of the night have been given to this sensually erotic flower, such as "Queen of the Night" or "Mistress of the Night," and she is very popular with perfume manufacturers.[86]

In aromatherapy, this exquisite flower is mainly used for its aphrodisiac properties. However, there are other great health benefits from the essential oil extracted from this alluring flower. For example, essential oil of Tuberose is great as a deodorizer, for relaxing, as a sedative, and as a warming substance.

The Tuberose flower is grown in Mexico, India, and South America; however, it is not certain where it originated. It is in high demand for perfumes in Africa, the Middle East, and in India. The process of extracting the precious essential oil from the flowers is done through *enfleurage* (with oil and alcohol and without solvents)[87] or by a solvent extraction method.[88]

Essential oil of Tuberose should never be taken internally. Because steam distillation does not capture the full essence of Tuberose, it is thus obtained through other means, enabling more of the molecules of the flower to be present, and the flower itself is toxic.

The intense, heady, and powerful floral essence of Tuberose is effective in dealing with difficulties with libido, impotence, erectile dysfunction, and for treating rigidity. It's seductive, warm, deep, honey-like fragrance helps to create a romantic and loving atmosphere that promotes sensuality during intimacy between couples. There are also certain components found in this essential oil which work to stimulate a part of the brain that are responsible for arousal, sexual desire, and libido.[89]

In Ayurvedic medicine, this aromatic flower has been used in making attars that are held in high regard for their ability to enhance emotional stability and strengthen the mind. It has been utilized in the primordial times for helping to open the heart and crown chakras.[90]

There are many stories and legends told about this sensually fragrant flower. In France, for example, unmarried girls were warned to not inhale the essence of Tuberose after dark. Its sensual and intoxicating essence was not appropriate for them to inhale, since they were not yet acquainted with the arts of seduction. During the Italian Renaissance, it was also forbidden for young, unmarried ladies to walk through the gardens at night where the scent of Tuberose permeated the air. It was said that the alluring and intense aphrodisiac essence could evoke sexual desires that were inappropriate for young girls who were not yet married.[91] It was said a woman who exuded the bewitching scent of Tuberose could cause mimicry recalling orgasms.[92]

Another story tells the seductive tale of how women would place fresh

Tuberose under their skirts to attract men they desired to seduce. The ancient Victorians attributed the aroma of Tuberose flowers to sensual and voluptuous qualities.[93] Like butterflies, we are seduced by the floral mystery and dangerously erotic essence of Tuberose. Her enchanting and alluring powers will intoxicate your senses as you inch closer to her sweet, floral aroma. She is a demanding flower, and her history is etched in complexity, yet the endless pleasure she promises is worth exploring her many seductive properties.

Essential oil of Tuberose is my queen of the night, exactly what she is known for. I use her as a perfume oil by adding a few drops to Jojoba oil and wearing her on my pulse points like my temple, behind my earlobe, on my neck, or wrist. Oh, how the essence of this oil truly captivates all the senses. I use her with caution, and only when romance is in the air, due to the dangerously seductive properties held within her lovely essence.

Why not place three drops of Tuberose in a night bath before bed to prepare yourself for a hot and steamy love session with your partner? Place about three drops in an oil diffuser in your bedroom to create a fragrant circle of this erotic flower that will stimulate your senses and surround you and your partner in the ambiance of an unforgettably passionate and romantic night of love. I'm sure the next question is: "Where do I get this exotic oil from?" No worries, I'll impart this little secret to you, but please don't share it with anyone. Promise?[94]

If you love incredible moments of mind-blowing sex or if you want to envelop all your senses with an exotic essential oil that evokes raw sensuality, then Tuberose is the essence for you. The captivating scent of this romantic and fragrant flower will surely be worth the small investment you make in owning this seductress who can captivate and allure you into her sensual world of powerful and exotic essences. Every blissful drop used during unforgettable moments of scintillating eroticism will make this essential oil a pleasure to have in your possession. Keep your lover close, and essential oil of Tuberose closer.

TEA TREE

Melaleuca alternifolia
Middle Note

Essential oil of Tea Tree has a warm, spicy, and fresh essence. She is considered a middle note in aromatherapy, and her leaves and twigs are steam distilled to produce an oil that is pale yellow in color with a thin consistency. Essential oil of Tea Tree originates in Australia.[95]

Tea Tree has astringent properties that make it great for using in nontoxic cleaners and for the skin. Its other healing properties include antibacterial, antifungal, antimicrobial, antiviral, insecticide, and stimulant. This essential oil should be diluted 50-50 before applying it on the skin.[96] Look for organically grown Tea Tree, and ensure that you place her and all other essential oils in a cool, dark place for maximum oil stability.

Tea Tree is a good support when battling colds, coughs, congestion, bronchitis, and it stimulates the immune system. This oil also helps clear acne and skin irritations, and keeps hair healthy.

When it comes to nontoxic cleaning solutions, Tea Tree has you covered. Due to its antimicrobial properties, this oil can remove unwanted bacteria that typically lurk in the kitchen or bathroom. You can make a simple cleaning spray by mixing it with distilled water and white vinegar, and voila, you have an earth friendly, multi-purpose household cleaner that may even challenge mold.[97]

Tea Tree can be used for psoriasis and eczema. You can support the treatment of these skin disorders by making a blend of Tea Tree and Lavender essential oils, along with coconut oil, and putting it directly on the skin for relief of inflammation or itchiness.

Essential oil of Tea Tree can be used as a deodorant, due to its antimicrobial properties, which eliminate body odor by destroying bacteria on the skin. You can also use Tea Tree with Lemon oil in your sneakers to make them smell fresh. Tea tree can help keep wounds, cuts, and bruises clean. After cleaning a cut with water and hydrogen peroxide, you can blend a few drops of essential oil of Tea tree and Lavender on the affected area, then bandage it, so the oils can go right to work to fight off infection.

The National Capital Poison Center says that Tea Tree is not safe for consumption and should not be used in or near the mouth. It has also caused poisoning of pets. Since pets may lick their fur, this may not be a good choice for your favorite animals.[98]

Essential oil of Tea Tree is my practical friend. I use her in my cleaning products and when I'm feeling under the weather. She helps with a variety of conditions, and having her nearby for any practical reason makes total sense to me.

All in all, Tea Tree is great to have on hand for multiple uses. Her numerous benefits and advantages are well worth the purchase. Look for organically grown Tea Tree that is 100-percent therapeutic grade, and ensure that you place her and other essential oils in a cool, dark place for maximum oil stability.

Live your true essence in mind, body, and spirit. During moments of gratitude, meditation, practicing yoga, visualizations, or affirmations, while cleaning your home, taking a long and leisurely bath, while reading, before or during bedtime, when in pain, or simply to uplift or relax your mood, you can surround yourself with essences that can trigger physical, emotional, mental, and spiritual health benefits. Adding these aromatic oils to your life will help connect you to your higher self, which in turn is a faster way toward achieving the goal of reaching your most authentic and true essence. Essential oils are a powerful way to help you feel your best. It is a secret for improving your overall health, and bringing renewed balance back into your life.

What about the ingredients used to create your own beneficial and aromatic formulations? Are all ingredients safe to use? Or are their hidden ingredients you should be aware of before you begin creating your personal recipe concoctions?

What about the ingredients in the products you already purchase? Do you know if the ingredients in that bottle are safe? Or, should you be concerned about the health risks associated with some of these ingredients? You will learn more about this in the next two chapters, so take a little respite and stretch, take a deep breath, and when you're ready, we will continue our lesson of plants and ingredients.

CHAPTER EIGHT

INGREDIENTS TO LOVE

**"When you know in your bones that your body is a
sacred gift, you move in the world with an effortless grace.
Gratitude and humility rise up spontaneously."
—Debbie Ford**

How important is your body to you? Do you give it the proper love, nourishment, and pampering it needs daily? Is it a sacred gift to you, as the quote states above? Or, do you find yourself deficient when it comes to the subject of your body?

What about the ingredients you choose to use on your body? Are you selective about which ones you prefer? Or, do you just purchase whatever suits your fancy without much thought? Do ingredients really matter?

You can choose thousands of ingredients from the market shelves. Yet, are all ingredients sold today good for you? It is in the best interest of your health to examine the ingredients contained in the personal care products, bottles and containers that you purchase for yourself and your family.

Some ingredients promise moisturized and vibrant skin, beautiful and healthy locks, and a youthful and glamorous appearance. Yes, there are wonderful and beneficial ingredients out there that you can use daily to make you feel great, ingredients that are nutrient-rich, contain loads of vitamins, and are super emollient on the skin. More than that, there are plant-derived ingredients that can penetrate through the skin and work effectively to reduce pain, soreness, irritation, and inflammation.

What are these ingredients? And what can they do for you? Why don't we start with carrier oils, shall we?

CARRIER OILS AND THEIR HEALTH BENEFITS

Carrier oils are exceptionally rich oils that come from trees, nuts, seeds, and plants. They are useful for those who suffer from excessively dry or flaky skin, and for those with skin sensitivities. Some of these oils can improve skin imbalances, such as eczema, psoriasis, and dermatitis as well as other skin problems. These disorders can cause many people to experience redness and itchy, scaly skin that may also be painful due to excessive scratching on the affected areas.

Carrier oils are emollient and penetrate the skin, allowing it to feel rejuvenated and revived. They are also helpful for skin that feels irritated or inflamed. When these carrier oils are combined with essential oils, the benefits are limitless.

There are seven processes that you should know about carrier oils prior to purchasing them to support your healing needs. Knowing these can save you time, money, and your health. You need to know if an oil is cold-pressed, expeller-pressed, solvent-extracted, unrefined, refined, partly refined, or fractionated.

"What is the difference?" you ask. It is in the creation and temperature used when making these oils. For example, cold-pressed oils are pressed in a machine that reaches no more than 110 degrees Fahrenheit. This oil is of exceptional quality and is in its most natural state. It is filled with loads of nutrients and is the best type to use for creating essential oil blends for treating innumerable health and beauty imbalances.

Expeller-pressed oils are pressed at a slightly higher temperature, starting at around 120-200 degrees Fahrenheit. They are like cold-pressed oils; however, expeller-pressed oils potentially lose their nutrients, due to the higher temperature and friction of the machine. These oils are still great for diluting essential oils or herbs; however, their quality is not as potent in its medicinal and skin-nourishing abilities as cold-pressed oils.

Solvent-extracted oils use the solvent hexane to extract the oil. This solvent is a suspected carcinogen and is usually found in the oil after extraction. These oils have no nutrients or fatty acids that benefit the body, thus would be a poor choice for creating your healthy formulations. Always look at labels to be absolutely sure that the oil you are purchasing is either cold-pressed or expeller-pressed. If there is no label that indicates this, then most likely you are getting a solvent-extracted oil, even if it says organic.

Unrefined oils are the best quality oils, since after they are pressed through the machine, a screen filters out any dust and small particles that would otherwise linger in the oil. Carrier oils are combined with other nutrient-rich ingredients and organic therapeutic essential oils, which are sold by my new company, Mariposa Essence. Their health properties remain intact, and thus are wonderful for providing balance and overall well-being to the body.

Refined, partly refined, and fractionated oils have lost most of their nutrients. Since these oils are processed using very high temperatures, freezing, deodorization, or bleaching of the oil in order for them to have a longer shelf life. These oils would not be a healthy choice for your body, since oils that are made this way lose most of their vitamins, fatty acids and nutrients, making them unsuitable for therapeutic benefits.

The best oils for use in diluting essential oils or herbs to support healing are cold-pressed and unrefined oils. Be sure to carefully read labels, so that you know that the oil you are getting is a high-quality oil that is exceptional for aromatherapy uses.

SproutingHealthyHabits is a great blog that offers more information on carrier oils. It provides an in-depth guide to help familiarize you with the benefits, uses, and healing properties found in many popular carrier oils sold today.[99]

Some carrier oils are great for food preparation. Olive, Coconut, Grapeseed, Avocado, and other fine oils are cold-pressed and can be used for cooking delicious dishes. The health benefits of using these oils daily for either food or for the skin can significantly assist in healing the body from head-to-toe.

Carrier oils are combined with other nutrient-rich ingredients and organic, therapeutic-grade essential oils which are sold in my new company, Mariposa Essence (http://mariposaessence.com). These ingredients are also incorporated in my personal daily rituals and beauty regimens to help maintain my skin, hair, mind, and spirit feeling balanced and healthy. I enjoy researching new oils that contain benefits that work effectively to reduce aches and pains, moisturize the skin, and other essential factors that contribute to healthier living. I have added many carrier oils to my repertoire of exceptional and therapeutic oils that I am blending to test their effectiveness, based on different skin types, before offering them to my customers. Many of these carrier oils have numerous beneficial properties that are perfect for massage or treatments, which I also will offer at my online store. They are combined with unique aromatherapy formulations that I create for physical, emotional, or spiritual imbalances, such as muscle pain or tension, anxiety and depression, or for spiritual rituals, such as meditation, or for working on the chakras.

Carrier oils are great for helping to improve or enhance the body's capacity to heal, as well as for uses that promote a state of optimal health and overall well-being. These wonderful oils can be blended and used for many different types of conditions, and when creating your own unique blends, you, too, will discover how valuable and beneficial they are. You will absolutely begin to appreciate and admire the world of plants and their ability to support a variety of ailments and disorders, and you will find that however you use them, you will love the results they provide.

You can start by keeping it simple, Sweetie. The best place to create your unique essential oil or herbal blends is right in your kitchen. Yes, here is where you can find oils and herbs that you already have stocked. For example, Olive and Coconut oils are usually around for food preparations for many people, so you are already set to commence your journey creating recipes that you can use on your body for pain, inflammation, skin disorders, and much more!

Begin your formulations with a few essential oils, such as Lavender, Frankincense, and Tea Tree, which are quite versatile and are great for many applications when combined with different carrier oils. You will find more information about the benefits and uses of the carrier oils below. Once you are comfortable making blends with them, you can than branch out to work with other essential and carrier oils for more benefits. The choice is yours, and however deeply you wish to dive into the world of natural health and healing of the mind, body, and spirit is completely up to you. It is a starting point that has the potential to lead you toward a path of health and wellness that will transform your life.

CHOOSE INGREDIENTS FOUND IN NATURE

Nature offers an assortment of healthy ingredients that today are found in stores and shops across the globe. They are packaged in pretty containers, jars, and bottles, and shelves are stocked full of many varieties. These ingredients provide health and overall well-being to your body from head-to-toe, and learning the benefits they contain can assist you in selecting the ones that promote true health and well-being.

These highly nourishing ingredients can support the healing of the body, inside and out. They should meet sustainability guidelines and should be natural, containing no synthetic chemicals, such as parabens, and should be cruelty free, and be effective in healing the body. Ingredients like these have worked for me since I started using them in my early twenties, and this is the reason that my skin feels soft and supple today. They have worked for me; so many of them may work wonders for you, too. However, please use caution when trying any ingredient for the first time. Ensure that when putting them on your skin, you conduct a patch test. Apply a small amount of the oil to the inside of your elbow and wait twenty-four hours to make sure that you have no reaction.

If you suffer from any allergies or are sensitive to an ingredient, such as mango, avocado, or coconut, refrain from using this ingredient. If you can't eat mangos because they cause an allergic reaction, chances are that putting mango butter on your skin will have a similar reaction, so it's best to use caution before considering applying this ingredient.

Many of these ingredients are found in shampoos, conditioners, soaps, lotions, butters, and more. You'll learn about the beneficial healing properties found in the selected ingredients I will be sharing with you in the next pages.

Some of them can be used on their own, while others are found in natural products you can easily find by shopping in places where natural and organic personal-care products are sold. Look for products that support nature and contain no fishy ingredients that can have potential side effects over time and with consistent use. Review all ingredients to ensure that you are receiving great skin care without having to resort to toxic chemicals or hazardous ingredients that do not belong on your skin, hair, or pretty much anywhere near your body.

Nature provides us with a load of ingredients that assist in nourishing, rejuvenating, softening, and moisturizing our skin and hair. Since sixty percent of all the ingredients we use penetrate the skin (which is the largest organ on our body), and enter the blood stream, it is absolutely essential that we use ingredients that promote overall balance and wellbeing—without sacrificing our health with ingredients that can cause harmful effects. More about those risk factors will be discussed in the next chapter. For now, let's focus on amazing ingredients that you should be incorporating into your collection of daily beauty care regimens and healing rituals. These super ingredients target everything you will need to feel healthy, beautiful, young, sexy, and simply fabulous.

Taking time to bring your focus to your state of well-being is important to living your true essence. When you win the battle of having a positive mindset and are feeling great on the inside, the next step is to feel great on the outside. Making the effort to use wonderful ingredients on your body is what you deserve, and staying away from cheap ingredients that many manufacturers utilize in their skin care products (which includes expensive skin care), should be eliminated from your bathroom shelves and avoided, if you can help it. Your body deserves the best possible care that in turn will enable you to live a long and healthy life. Doesn't that make better sense than allowing these personal care companies to dictate what is best for you to use in your beauty and health care practices?

Look at my favorite ingredients and the health benefits to your body they provide. The research I have conducted on these ingredients allows you to determine for yourself the difference between what nature offers, and what works to give you ultimate skin care that is good for your overall health and well-being. You can also conduct your own research on other ingredients that you may be interested in. You will find that for you to experience optimal health, you are in control of what you accept is best to put in or on your body. Doesn't that make sense?

ALOE VERA

Aloe Barbadensis

Aloe Vera is a plant that contains many healthy compounds. It has thick leaves with short stems that store water in them. The Aloe plant is native to Northern Africa and flourishes in warm and dry climates. It has often been called the miracle plant, or natural healer, because of its amazing ability to treat many illnesses.

The Aloe Vera plant grows to an average of twelve-nineteen inches in length. It is well recognized for its thick, pointed, fleshy green leaves and has many medicinal benefits. Each leaf contains a water-filled tissue that feels slimy inside of the thick leaves. This is the gel substance that we associate with Aloe products.

Aloe is widely used and extensively marketed in the food, cosmetic, and pharmaceutical industries. The annual revenue for related products is estimated to be at $13 billion globally.[100]

Found in the gel of this exceptional plant are vitamins, minerals, powerful antioxidants, and amino acids that are essential for health and nutrition. The antioxidants belong to a large family of substances known as polyphenols. These polyphenols contained in the gel of the Aloe leaves, along with several other compounds, help to inhibit the growth of certain bacteria that can cause infections in humans. In addition, the eight essential amino acids found in this gel are important to the body and cannot be manufactured or duplicated.[101]

Aloe Vera has been used for thousands of years before it became known around the world. Writings describing it go back as far as the Greek, Egyptian, and Roman eras. Aloes are even referred to in the Bible, and legend suggests that Alexander the Great used it to treat battle wounds of soldiers in his army.[102]

Aloe assists in reducing constipation. Because it is natural, it works gently within the intestinal tract to help break down food residues that have become impacted and works to easily clean out the bowel. According to Dr. Josh Axe on the benefits of Aloe Vera for the treatment of constipation, "The use of aloe latex as a laxative is well-researched; the anthraquinones present in the latex create a potent laxative that increases intestinal water content, stimulates mucus secretion and increases intestinal peristalsis, which are contractions that break down food and mix the chyme."[103]

Aloe Vera can be used topically as well as internally. It helps treat cold sores, mouth ulcers, or canker sores.[104] According to an article written by Joe Leech, a writer for *Medical News Today*, "In a 7-day study of 180 people with recurrent mouth ulcers, an Aloe Vera patch applied to the area was effective in reducing the size of the ulcers."[105]

It is known for lowering blood sugar levels in diabetics. It enhances insulin sensitivity by helping to improve blood sugar management.[106]

There are many unique therapeutic properties found in Aloe Vera. You will find that it is commonly used as an ingredient in shampoos, conditioners, soaps, lotions, and sunburn products, since it soothes, softens, and rejuvenates skin and hair. On its own, it acts as a moisturizer and hydrates the skin. It is especially affective in helping to heal various skin disorders such as psoriasis, dermatitis, and dry hair, or itchy scalp.[107]

When Aloe is absorbed into the skin, it stimulates the fibroblasts cells, causing them to quickly regenerate themselves. These are the cells that produce the collagen and elastin that make the skin get smoother and look younger.[108] Aloe accelerates the healing of burns, and studies show that it can be an effective topical treatment for first and second-degree burns.[109]

The edible parts of the Aloe plant are the seeds and the leaves. The lower leaf of the plant is used for medicinal purposes and can be directly rubbed on the skin for the healing of cuts, bruises, or burns.

Aloe plants are easy to obtain, and whether you use it on your skin, hair, or to make your own juices or smoothies, you will love and appreciate its many healing properties. You can purchase Aloe Vera pharmaceutically, however, the added chemicals and preservatives as well as using fake Aloe will significantly reduce its medicinal capabilities. According to an article in *Bloomberg*, "There's no watchdog assuring that aloe products are what they say they are. The U.S. Food and Drug Administration [FDA] doesn't approve cosmetics before they're sold and has never levied a fine for selling fake aloe."[110]

It is best to purchase Aloe from natural sources or to simply buy the plant. Whatever you do, Aloe Vera is a wonderful and inexpensive gel to have around for loads of reasons. Once you use it, I guarantee you will never want to be without its amazing healing benefits for you and your family.

COCONUT OIL

Cocos nucifera

Coconut oil has a deep, lightly intoxicating and penetrating coconut aroma. It is white in color and is a spectacular oil that contains many nutrient properties. This rich oil is extensively used around the world and is popular in the beauty and soap industry.

Coconut oil is widely known for its countless benefits to the skin, hair, body conditions, and in cooking foods. It is best when raw, virgin and unrefined, since in this cold-pressed state, Coconut oil can be used for preparing delicious meals and used in many skin applications.

It contains fatty acids, such as lauric, caprylic, linoleic, capric, myristic, and other important fats that health officials previously claimed should be avoided, due to the high content of saturated fats. However, Coconut oil has been scientifically demonstrated to provide numerous health benefits that include supporting a healthy immune system, brain, skin, heart, and thyroid imbalances.[111]

This oil also contains natural properties that make it antifungal, antiviral, antibacterial, and antiprotozoal. It is perfect as a barrier to keep bacteria and germs away from the skin. It assists in skin conditions, such as eczema, due to its ability to penetrate deep into the skin. Coconut oil also helps with some topical infections, such as athlete's foot, and offers antibacterial protection.[112]

For thousands of years, it has been used for maintaining good health and haircare. Unlike popular conditioners sold in the market today that contain loads of harsh chemicals that may soften and add shine and fill in damaged areas of the hair, research shows that these ingredients do more harm than good. They simply coat the hair with conditioning chemicals, which mimic healthy hair. These toxic chemicals may include sodium lauryl sulphate, formaldehyde (also found in baby shampoo), dioxane, propylene glycol, momoethanolamine, omoethanolamine (MEA), diethanolamine (DEA), and other dangerous ingredients that can cause numerous side effects.[113] Coconut oil. however, provides true shine and hair moisture, leaving locks feeling naturally silky soft and healthy. No need for chemicals that simply are a temporary fix with no long-term health effects.

Coconut oil is by far the number one lather-producing agent in soap. However, many soaps sold today contain lathering ingredients, such as sulfates, that strip the skin of its natural oils and can cause irritations for people with sensitive skin. Soaps made with Coconut oil naturally help moisturize and cleanse the skin, easily removing bacteria and germs without any need for chemically-based lather or bubbles.

In the cosmetic industry, most people prefer to choose products made with Coconut oil. Many body scrubs or gentle face scrubs that help exfoliate the skin contain this versatile oil. Face cleansers, moisturizers, and some face creams have Coconut oil, since it is also packed with nutrientrich vitamins and minerals to keep the skin soft and supple. Many body butters, massage oils, and hair oils have it as an essential ingredient.

On its own, Coconut oil can also be used to remove makeup, or as a face moisturizer. Use it as a lotion all over your body, or eat a teaspoon of Coconut oil each day to help trim body fat. All in all, Coconut oil deserves space in your bathroom or on your kitchen shelf. The countless benefits found in one jar of Coconut oil make this beautiful and fragrant oil worth every penny invested.

HEMP SEED OIL

Cannabis Sativa

Hemp Seed oil has been one of the world's most underappreciated oils. It is derived from the plant Cannabis sativa. When the raw seeds are pressed, it creates an oil that is rich in proteins, omega 3, omega 6, polyunsaturated fatty acids, and insoluble fiber. It was not until recently that Hemp oil re-emerged in popularity. Due to the speculation of the Marijuana plant however, this oil took a backseat in its production, thus limiting access to its numerous healing abilities. Not only does it benefit the skin, but it is also effective in healing the body from certain imbalances due to illnesses.

Do you want beautiful, young-looking skin? Good news, Hemp seed oil energizes and regenerates the protective layer of the skin. Due to the high content of omega 3 and omega 6 fatty acids, Hemp oil contains a composition that is like skin lipids, which makes it a wonderful natural emollient and moisturizer. It is especially beneficial for dry, tired, or dehydrated skin and nails. Hemp oil increases skin's elasticity and water retention capacity in tissues.

Hemp oil is also great for preventing psoriasis. Studies show that the linoleic acid present in Hemp oil slows down the aging process and fights psoriasis. The fatty acids found in Hemp oil help improve skin oxygenation and hydration. In addition, because psoriasis is a deficiency of omega-6 fatty acids in the body, by incorporating Hemp oil in your diet for two weeks, it is said that it will produce naturally moisturized skin.[114]

What about your hair? Do you want beautiful tresses that feels strong and healthy? No worries, Hemp oil has got you covered. Pure Hemp oil treats dry hair, and is often included in hair conditioners to help moisturize and bring back natural shine to hair that lacks luster. You can even use this oil as a hair masque or prior to styling, so that your locks feel soft and manageable. Yes, you can say goodbye to frizzy hair.

Hemp oil helps with ailments such as diabetes, since it contains a low carbohydrate and sugar content. The nutrients it contains can help moderate blood sugar levels. It also lowers cholesterol, because it is the only vegetable oil to contain omega-3 and omega-6 fatty acids (3:1). It can lower cholesterol levels by accelerating metabolic processes. With a metabolism that works faster, fats burn at a quicker rate, and are not deposited on the artery walls.[115] A note to remember, this oil should not be heated, since cooking Hemp oil at a high temperature can denature the unsaturated fats, converting them into saturated fats.[116]

Nutritionist Natalie Savona calls Hemp "a true superfood." "Uncooked," she says, "it contains the perfect ratio of omega fats 3, 6 and 9, which we don't produce naturally in the body but are crucial for healthy circulation, cell growth and the immune system." Hemp oil is a vegetarian alternative for fish oil, too.[117]

Hemp oil is also used for the treatment of cancer. However, due to the limits placed on Cannabis, the plant from which this oil is derived, its true healing abilities continue to be shrouded in misconceptions and misinformation that does not help an individual who is experiencing the potentially fatal effects of this disease. Blanche Levine, author and student of natural healing modalities, said, ". . . Conventional medicine and big pharmaceutical companies do NOT want to lose profits to a natural cure. You see, treatments like chemotherapy have huge profit margins and big pharma does not want any competition."[118]

Hemp oil has many healing properties and extensive benefits. Keep it around as your helper for common ailments, from skin disorders, to more complex health issues. Don't underestimate the power contained in this simple but very valuable oil. Use it, and enjoy its health advantages.

HONEY

Honey can be blended with other ingredients such as carrier oils, essential oils, oatmeal, and other nourishing ingredients to assist in cleansing, moisturizing, and boosting the skin. Raw Honey is not just for sweetening your tea or for adding as a topping to a slice of grapefruit. Although that sounds yummy, this food contains many beneficial properties that you should familiarize yourself with. For one thing, raw Honey has many uses that will keep skin happy and healthy. It has antiseptic and antimicrobial properties that can kill bacteria or fungus, making it great for clearing up acne. It moisturizes and nourishes the skin, and has a natural PH balance of 4.5, making it just right for bringing skin back to its healthy natural balance.[119]

Raw Honey contains many nutrients and minerals such as vitamin B, iron, manganese, copper, potassium, and calcium. It contains gluconic acid, which is a gentle form of alpha hydroxy acid that helps brighten complexion, leaving behind a soft glow to your skin. It evens out skin tone and can lighten scars and age spots.[120]

Another wonderful benefit of Honey is that it is great for assisting with skin problems, such as enlarged pores, rosacea, eczema, hyperpigmentation, and sensitive, mature, or dull, lifeless skin. Because it is loaded with antioxidants and healing compounds, Honey is effective in helping the skin look rejuvenated and flawless.

Honey can be used as a face mask by adding coconut oil and essential oil of Rose for removing impurities from the skin, providing long-lasting hydration. It can also be used in combination with baking soda to gently exfoliate the skin, leaving it feeling soft and supple. Make a paste of Honey and cinnamon powder and dab it on a pimple. There are so many amazing ways to use this truly essential ingredient.

Honey has been used by humans for more than 10,000 years. People have used it through the ages for things such as wrinkles and damaged skin, to healing burns and cuts. It is said that Cleopatra, the beautiful queen of Egypt, had a ritual of pampering her skin by bathing in milk and Honey to achieve a flawless complexion.[121] Luxuriate in a bath by adding two cups of milk and one-half cup of Honey, then pouring the mixture into your bath will soften and exfoliate your skin, making you smell sweet and fresh, and feeling like a queen or king when you're all done.

Honey can be blended with other ingredients such as carrier oils, essential oils, oatmeal, and other ingredients to assist in cleansing, moisturizing, and boosting the skin. Honey is also used to make hair look soft, silky, and adds shine to dull tresses. In a hot water bath or *bain marie*, melt coconut oil and add honey. This can be used as a hair masque to moisturize and bring back healthy luster to your locks.

All in all, raw Honey deserves to have a place in your cupboard. Using this multi-functional ingredient is a great way to save money while reaping the fabulous benefits of caring for your skin and hair.

JOJOBA OIL

Simmondsia chinensis

This has got to be my favorite carrier oil of all. Jojoba oil is a liquid wax. The Jojoba shrub grows in the most arid regions of the world such as Southern Arizona, Northwestern Mexico, and Southern California.[122] This plant reaches a height of approximately fifteen feet high from the desert ground. It is an odorless oil and golden in color.

Jojoba is an oil that has a satiny texture, which makes it feel like liquid silk on the skin. It has a long shelf life and does not go rancid over time like other oils. When combined with essential oils, it is readily absorbed in to the skin, providing wonderful therapeutic benefits on the mind, body, and spirit. This lovely oil is also a great preservative.

Jojoba oil contains fatty acids that are almost identical to our skin's sebum. It is a superfood for the skin. When skin imbalances occur such as:

psoriasis, eczema, acne breakouts, hair and scalp repair, inflammation, or cradle cap in infants, this oil works to return the skin back to its normal balance.[123] It glides along the skin, without leaving you feeling sticky or greasy. It is perfect for massages, since it penetrates deep into the skin and does not stain sheets.

During the '70s and '80s, Jojoba oil gained popularity. At that time, sperm whale and animal waxes were used primarily by the personal care industry to make products that moisturized the skin. However, it wasn't until whale hunting was outlawed in the U.S. that manufacturers replaced this animal oil with Jojoba oil. It was said to be superior to whale oil for cosmetics.[124] They found an oil that could help with all skin types, heal dry, cracked, or scaly skin, and could resolve other disorders that required moisturization and hydration of the skin.

Jojoba oil mixes well with other ingredients, since it has no scent and has a light composition. Studies have proven that Jojoba oil is long-lasting on the skin, providing moisture up to twenty-four hours after applying all over the body. Jojoba oil also contains anti-inflammatory properties that help ease the redness and burning from eczema.[125]

It is antimicrobial, which means that bugs will remain at bay, and it does not allow for bacteria to grow on the skin. It is nutrient-rich, since it contains vitamins and minerals that help the skin remain rejuvenated and healthy.

This is a fantastic oil for soothing the skin from sunburn, allowing it to feel calm and hydrated. It reduces the appearance of scars, even scars from acne. It also helps with stretch marks and old skin wounds. It is an excellent moisturizer, reduces the signs of aging, and can assist in the fading of fine lines.[126]

Jojoba oil is used in numerous products, such as shampoos, conditioners, lotions, creams, and sunscreens. It improves the appearance of skin and hair, leaving soft, shiny, and manageable tresses.

In addition to its external health benefits, Jojoba also works internally. It can help with inflammation, cuts, infections, and can speed up wound healing. Dab a few drops on an infected area and the oil quickly goes to work to soothe and heal the affected skin.[127]

How many uses are there in Jojoba oil? Let me count the ways. I use it as a makeup remover, face moisturizer, body or massage oil, after washing my hair, blended in essential oils for more amazing benefits, and just absolutely love and enjoy using it in my beauty and spiritual regimens. The incredible skin healing properties found in this oil will make it your new best friend. I promise you, Jojoba oil will not disappoint.

The overall benefits of Jojoba oil seem limitless. When purchasing this luxurious oil, you will find that it will hang around for years. You can always count on it to give you great looking skin, silky, soft hair, and keep you feeling young and healthy.

MARIJUANA

Cannabis

Did you know that this medicinal plant can heal many disorders or ailments in your body? It has been banned from circulation for extensive use for reasons unknown. However, this extraordinary plant provides countless healing benefits which makes it an amazing gift from the creator of nature.

Scientists have just begun to scratch the surface on the healing properties and beneficial effects found in this free-growing plant. It is evident, however, that the medical-industrial complex in the U.S. is not interested in allowing us to use the compounds that are derived from this plant, since they claim that Marijuana contains no medicinal healing benefits. Is this true?

According to an article by GreenMedInfo's founder, Sayer Ji, "In fact, as far back as 2727 B.C., cannabis was recorded in the Chinese pharmacopoeia as an effective medicine, and evidence for its use as a food, textile and presumably as a healing agent stretch back even further, to 12,000 BC." Despite marijuana's healing properties, he says, ". . . it is extremely dangerous, as far as the medical industrial complex goes, who has the FDA/FTC to enforce its mandate: anything that prevents, diagnoses, treats or cures a disease must be an FDA-approved drug by law, i.e. pharmaceutical agents which often have 75 or more adverse effects for each marketed and approved 'therapeutic' effect."[128]

"The cannabis plant may just be the future of medicine," according to Ji. It contains more than 100 proven therapeutic actions.[129] Following are just some common illnesses that can be helped through the healing properties found in this super medicinal plant.

It helps with disorders such as Multiple Sclerosis, Obsessive Compulsive Disorder (OCD), insomnia, and memory disorders. The Cannabis plant may also help to heal individuals that suffer from cancer, opiate addiction, bronchial asthma, fibromyalgia, glaucoma, and other dysfunctions in the body. It is no wonder that this plant is being thoroughly studied, and what has already been discovered is impressive.

Yet, for all the positive studies conducted on Cannabis, some contradict its medicinal benefits. For example, according to Dr. Wynne Armand, MD, this herb can impair our thinking and cause anxiety. "Physical effects may include bloodshot eyes, dry mouth, slurred speech, and increased heart rate. These sensations may last up to four hours after inhaling marijuana smoke, or up to 12 hours if consumed, though performance impairments may last for much longer."[130]

Compared to the medical drugs in the United States that contain dangerous side effects that may include death, the negative effects experienced by some users of Marijuana don't come close to the potentially serious or even fatal effects caused by many of the FDA-approved prescription drugs, or over-the-counter medications that are available and easily accessible to adults. According to federal statistics in 2017, "91 Americans die every day from an opioid overdose."[131]

These are needless deaths, yet, the Cannabis plant, which can save lives and has not been associated with fatal side effects, contains medicinal and healing properties, but is discounted as being a street drug that poses harmful effects for those using it recreationally or medically. I don't know about you, but when I do the math, Marijuana does not seem threatening. Dr. Armand admitted, "There is a lot we don't know. What is clear is that some of the long-term effects correspond to heavy use."[132]

In retrospect, what has been learned about the Cannabis plant is that it is proven to significantly reduce symptoms of many common disorders in the body, with no real known dangerous side effects. In fact, this plant's therapeutic properties contain many pharmacological actions that have assisted in improving a variety of health issues. It has been used for centuries, unlike the new and dangerous drugs made today. For example, Marijuana is well-known for its analgesic, antispasmodic, antiinflammatory, anti-depressive, bronchodilator, antioxidant, anti-platele, anti-psychotic, and vascular endothelial growth factor A inhibitor.[133] These are just some of the healing benefits found in Marijuana, which makes it a possible medicinal solution for people experiencing any of these symptoms.

For example, according to the National Institute on Drug Abuse, of the two cannabinoids of medical interest, the cannabinoid CBD doesn't make people high and "may be useful in reducing pain and inflammation, controlling epileptic seizures, and possibly even treating mental illness and addictions."[134]

In conclusion, whether Marijuana is used recreationally or as an intrinsic plant for healing, it should be allowed to be used since it is a plant, and for that reason, it deserves attention. It provides medicinal benefits, and if used responsibly, might improve your health.[135]

OLIVE OIL

Olea europaea

It smells amazing! It tastes even better. And the best part is that the beneficial properties it contains make it worth developing a close relationship with it. What am I talking about?

It's the carrier oil Olive oil, which boasts a great reputation in the United States and is mostly known as a cooking oil used for creating many healthy and delicious culinary dishes. This oil is deep olive green. It possesses a rich and characteristic odor, and has a full-body flavor. It is primarily made in countries that border the Mediterranean Sea, such as Greece, Italy, and Spain, and is pressed from fresh olives.

Olive oil contains numerous health benefits, and using this oil on a regular basis can help fight diabetes, osteoporosis, promote weight loss, and soothe ulcers. Due to the monounsaturated and polyunsaturated fats found in Olive oil, for example, the risk of developing a disease such as diabetes can be reduced almost by half. This oil contains important vitamins, is nutrient-rich, and is loaded with antioxidants that are essential for good overall health. It also has anti-inflammatory properties that helps fight inflammation, an underlying cause of diabetes.

Olive oil is also a wonderful brain food. It improves brain function by protecting it from free radical damage, maintains a good memory, slows memory loss, and even works to reduce the risk of dementia and Alzheimer's. This is partly due to the vitamins E and K that are in Olive oil that help to keep the brain sharp as we age.

Extra Virgin Olive oil has oleocanthal, which contains anti-inflammatory agents that help relieve pain. Over time and with consistent use, oleocanthal can reduce inflammation in the body. Inflammation impacts many chronic diseases, so taking advantage of the abundant inflammatory properties found in extra virgin Olive oil can help with overall balance and well-being.[136] Isn't your health worth it, especially when the oil is delicious and can be used to prepare a variety of succulent dishes? From snacks to salads, to delicious meals, incorporating Olive oil when eating a combination of nutritious foods will keep you feeling good.

Another great benefit of using Olive oil is that it helps with depression and anxiety, which research suggests is linked to heart disease. It also can help reduce the risk of a stroke. For example, researchers from the University of Bordeaux and the National Institute of Health and Medical Research in Bordeaux, France reported that Olive oil may prevent strokes in older people. The team conducting the study found that people who were sixty-five and older that regularly used olive oil for cooking and eating were estimated to have a forty-one percent lower risk of stroke, compared with their counterparts who never consumed it.[137]

Olive oil can help boost the immune system. Because of the wide range of antioxidants that are specific to this oil, it can be resistant against developing infections. It also helps to strengthen and protect the immune system, which in turn creates a healthier state of being.

What about your skin? Olive oil quenches the skin with deep moisture, due to its many nutrient-rich fatty acids. It is super beneficial for anti-aging and helps heal damaged skin. The protective coating it adds to the skin, hair, and face allows for this oil to provide hydration wherever you apply it.

On its own, Olive oil can be used as a makeup remover, nail conditioner, for dry elbows and knees, or even for cracked heels. Combine it with organic Almond and Coconut oil and you can use it as a face moisturizer, especially during cold winter months when skin tends to become dryer. Add essential oils to the mix and the health and beauty benefits increase dramatically.

Olive oil has earned a permanent place in my kitchen. I use it in many culinary recipes. From salad dressing to cooking meat dishes, the taste of Olive oil blended with my favorite meals takes my palate to another level. I mix it with organic sugar and voila, I have a great sugar scrub that I use to exfoliate my skin, and during winter for dry or chapped lips.

Overall, Olive oil can help you feel healthy inside and out. Its numerous healing benefits deserve a permanent place on your shelf. Never underestimate the powerful properties found in this oil. You will reap many rewarding benefits by making a conscious effort to add this most precious oil to everyday dishes you consume. In addition, you can make it a practice to incorporate Olive oil in your beauty regimens to help maintain healthy and beautiful skin and hair looking healthy. Why not make Olive oil your new girlfriend? The many benefits are worth the investment.

POMEGRANATE SEED OIL

Punica granatum

Pomegranate oil is another fantastic oil. It has many wonderful benefits. It is extremely nutritious and rich, and is used medicinally and as an ingredient in many skin care applications. Many personal care companies use Pomegranate Seed oil in their soaps, moisturizers, massage oils, and other beauty products, due to its regenerative properties.

Pomegranate oil assists in reinvigorating the skin. The keratinocytes, major cells which are found in the outer layer of the skin, are stimulated, helping to reverse skin damage, revive the skin, and reveal a more youthful appearance. This oil also fights against free radicals on the skin, and due to its unique polyunsaturated oil, punicic acid, an omega 5 fatty acid, it possesses strong anti-inflammatory properties. It can keep aging at bay and protect the skin against sun damage.[138]

It is great for all skin types and penetrates deep into the skin, creating long-lasting moisture with no greasy residue. It is wonderful for acne-prone skin and can control acne breakouts.[139]

Another amazing benefit of Pomegranate Seed oil is that it provides a soothing and hydrating relief for people who suffer from eczema, psoriasis, and sunburned skin. The anti-inflammatory properties found in

Pomegranate Seed oil calm irritation, redness, or inflamed skin, helping to heal wounds caused by scratching. Skin is restored to normal health from the nutrients entering directly into the cell, allowing the process of cellular regeneration and rejuvenation to accelerate on the skin.[140]

Pomegranate assists in improving skin texture for both men and women. It is used in massage oils for its soothing and moisturizing properties and it contains loads of antioxidants that help with collagen production and firm the skin. Visible signs of aging are reduced through the continuous use of Pomegranate.

I love blending this oil with Jojoba, Almond, and Vitamin E for use in massage, personal skin care, and as a stand-alone moisturizer. It makes my skin have a satiny texture and I like the slightly fruity essence. This oil can even rejuvenate the health of your hair. It helps revitalize dull or dry hair, restoring the natural beauty and shine to hair that previously lacked fullness and body. Just adding a few drops of Pomegranate oil to your palm and smoothing it through your hair will leave it soft and pleasantly scented. You can use this oil as a serum, hot oil treatment, or after washing your hair to add a bit of extra moisture before drying and styling. I purchase most of my organic carrier oils at Organic Infusions (https://www.organicinfusions.com/products/pomegranate-oil).

If you are experiencing eczema or scalp psoriasis, the anti-pruritic properties in Pomegranate Seed oil can help soothe and fight scalp bacteria, as well as work to assist with these scalp conditions. It nourishes the hair and promotes hair growth because it is a good source of Vitamin C. Pomegranate oil stimulates blood circulation in the scalp, due to its high content of vitamins and antioxidants.

According to an expert in psoriasis, use the CO_2 (carbon dioxide) extracted type. "Only this oil will be found to be very light and pleasant to use. Conventionally extracted pomegranate oil is rather pungent and sticky and does not seem to be absorbed so rapidly into the skin."[141]

Pomegranate Seed oil is worth having around, especially if you want smoother, younger-looking skin, and healthy locks. Why not experiment with it and test the results for yourself? Pomegranate Seed oil provides nutrients internally and externally, so the benefits are worth exploring. You will discover a balance in your hair and on your skin, helping to enhance your overall appearance, which I'm sure will put a glowing smile on your face.

THERAPUTIC BATH SALTS

Salts are naturally rich in minerals and have been used for centuries to cleanse the skin. There are a variety of salts that you can purchase such as Dead Sea, Himalayan Pink, and Epsom salts. Ensure that these salts are natural. Salts work to exfoliate, revitalize, and purify the skin, while helping to draw out impurities and excess oils.

Throughout history, many people have traveled large distances to bathe in salt waters, due to their therapeutic benefits, such as at the Red Sea, the Black Sea, the Dead Sea, and other salty waters around the globe. The sea minerals calcium, magnesium, potassium, sulfur, zinc, sodium, and bromide help to relax the nervous system, balance the immune system, increase circulation, energize and moisturize the body, and strengthen bones and nails. These salts are readily absorbed into the body, not only helping to promote healthy and beautiful skin, but the health properties found in bath salts will assist in supporting the healing of the body from a variety of ailments.[142]

Dead sea salts, for example, have been known to assist in alleviating even the most severe cases of dry or damaged skin, such as eczema and psoriasis. According to a Be Well Buzz article, "taking a bath in warm water containing Dead Sea Salt can provide relief from psoriasis and other common skin conditions such as acne, skin allergies, eczema, dermatitis, and seborrhea." The article later states, "both the National Psoriasis Foundation and the International Psoriasis Community recommend Dead Sea Salt as a useful alternative treatment for psoriasis."[143]

Bath salts can also help relax tired or strained muscles, release body tension, and promote cellular regeneration. They are also wonderful in improving moisture to the skin, stimulating blood circulation in the body, and helping to reduce inflammation in the joints and muscles.

Today, you don't have to travel far and wide to experience the healing benefits of mineral salts. You can enjoy a warm and relaxing bath utilizing about two cups of Dead Sea salts to help balance and detoxify the skin. When combined with organic essential oil blends, the therapeutic benefits are even greater. Essential oils will not only help relax achy or sore muscles, but these aromatic essences will also assist in rejuvenating the skin. In addition, they will tantalize your senses and their healing properties will soothe your mind, body and spirit.

I absolutely love bathing with bath salts. When it comes to bath time, I enjoy experimenting with a blend of salts and essential oils depending on my mood. For example, if I am feeling stressed and need to relax, I use Lavender, Geranium, or Chamomile. If I need a boost, I use essences like Bergamot, Orange, or Grapefruit. Typically, I blend one cup of sea salt, one-half cup Himalayan salt, and one-half cup of Epsom salt with a blend of about eight-ten drops of essential oils. You can use a single essential oil or a blend of your choice in the mix, and stir the salt thoroughly before pouring into your tub. For pregnant women or for certain medical conditions, consult a medical care practitioner prior to use.

Here's a great blend I use regularly for relaxing that I think you will like. All you need is the amount of salts stated above, five drops of essential oil of Lavender, and five drops of Chamomile for a calming bathing experience. You can also create a blend using five drops of essential oil of Orange, and five drops of Vanilla for a luxurious and uplifting bath. Have some fun experimenting with other ingredients such as powdered milk, baking soda, honey, almond oil, and take your bath time to another level. Your skin will love it, and the essences will indulge your senses as you envelop your body in the therapeutic and healing benefits of adding bath salts to your regular beauty and health regimens.

CHOOSE INGREDIENTS THAT SUPPORT HEALING

Ingredients that nature supplies are more effective in nourishing the body, and work to support healing from numerous skin disorders and problematic scalps, provide better skin care solutions, and help improve body ailments that interfere with overall body balance. Nature's ingredients are trustworthy and when used appropriately; your body will feel the difference.

Dr. Eric Zielinski, a public health researcher and Biblical Health Educator who specializes in the therapeutic use of essential oils, provides blending guidelines that can be quite helpful when beginning your journey for creating your personal formulations. He will tell you how many drops of essential oil to blend with a carrier oil (http://drericz.com/using-carrier-oils-for-double-benefits/). Follow dilution guidelines to get you started on creating your own blends for a variety of beauty, pain and inflammation, or emotional imbalances. Remember to check all safety sheets for any aromatic oils that you intend to use in your recipes.

Please keep in mind that it is very important to consult a trained aromatherapist or medical care practitioner before attempting to use any essential oil, carrier oil, or ingredient for the first time. You should conduct a patch test inside your elbow prior to putting on your skin to ensure that you do not have an allergic reaction. Pregnant women or those that may suffer from epilepsy should consult a physician before any aromatherapy regimen is started.

Natural ingredients that you choose to use on your body should be of great importance to you, due to their many beneficial properties. They are a step forward in improving your skin and your overall health, and they are better than ingredients found in loads of personal care products that may work effectively to improve the skin you're in and the hair on your head, but are sorely lacking in overall support of health and healing. Nature's ingredients, or chemical ingredients, take your pick. The choice is yours; however, before you decide, read on to learn more about the chemical ingredients you may or may not already be incorporating in your beauty regimens every day—ingredients that can potentially impact your overall health and balance. The next chapter will provide in-depth details about what those ingredients are, so that you can be well-informed and see for yourself what you're up against when considering the ingredients you choose going forward.

CHAPTER NINE

INGREDIENTS TO LOVE NOT

**"Criticism may not be agreeable, but it is necessary.
It fulfils the same function as pain in the human body.
It calls attention to an unhealthy state of things."
—Winston Churchill**

Don't we want to eat foods that nourish us and make us feel healthy ? Don't we want to use skin care products on our skin and hair that work to improve and polish our appearance?

Most of us want to look younger and make a real effort to present the best of ourselves to the world. Yet, what does that entail? Are there consequences to looking and feeling beautiful?

Some may argue that there is no real harm in using the myriad of personal care products sold on the market today that we buy and apply. Others, however, may disagree. Is there any validity to their claims?

PRODUCTS WITH QUESTIONABLE INGREDIENTS

There are tons of products sold on the market today. Go to any beauty or health store and browse the endless aisles of products, and you will find so many brands that it will make your head spin. They range from hair care to foot care and everything in between. You will always find something to help bring glim and glam to your hair and skin—everything from adding extra shine to your locks to that sorely needed pedicure you've been meaning to treat yourself to. You want to look fabulous, right? That's not necessarily a bad thing, is it?

The problem is, what are you buying? What are you being sold?

When making that crucial decision to purchase a product you feel you absolutely must try or need, do you ask yourself important questions about that product you have in your hand before you choose to purchase it?

Do you ask yourself questions like: Is this product safe? Are all the ingredients used to make this product listed on the bottle so that I know what it is I am using? You can be honest with me. I promise it will be our little secret.

Now tell me, or whisper your answer to me, do you take a little extra time to turn the bottle to the back label and read the list of ingredients on the product? Or do you leave it to the big dogs to worry about those things? After all, shouldn't they know what's best for you, since they manufacture the stuff anyway? They wouldn't make bad decisions about anything that could harm you right? Wrong . . .

News flash! Most personal care companies do not need to disclose all ingredients on their product labels. In fact, they don't even have to list certain chemicals or fragrances on their labels. They don't need to tell YOU, the consumer, the one using the product that's supposed to help solve a problem, what they added to the bottle you're about to purchase. They don't have to inform you, the consumer, exactly what makes it work the way it does if it works.[144] In other words, no, they don't know what's best for you. It's your job to find out. Doesn't that make sense?

The combination of chemicals added to many products prettily set up on store shelves, which seem attractive and harmless, can be downright dangerous to your health. Many of them contain endocrine disrupters. According to the Wikipedia Encyclopedia, endocrine disruptors are "chemicals that, at certain doses, can interfere with endocrine or hormone systems. These disruptions can cause cancerous tumors, birth defects and other developmental disorders."[145] Many of these products sold today should have your complete attention and should be seriously examined prior to purchase. Remember, this is your health we're talking about here, so it is of prime importance to consider the matter personally and conscientiously.

For example, according to a report by the Environmental Working Group, an American environmental organization that specializes in toxic chemical research and advocacy, "168 chemicals are used per day for women, 85 for men. On average, women use 12 products per day and teens use 17."[146]

Think about this for a second. 168 chemicals in twelve products you could be using during the day? Okay, I don't know about you, but I need to figure this out. I can totally see myself using twelve products or more in one day.

I get up in the morning and after my meditation, I brush my teeth. Clearly that's a good thing, right? Wrong. Not that brushing your teeth is wrong . . . but of course you knew that. I'm talking about the toothpaste.

I then jump in the shower and use my shampoo that promises to give my dull locks some shine and moisture as it cleans my hair with lots of lather, removing all traces of the gunk I used the previous day. Then goes on my conditioner that further moisturizes and detangles my hair. The soap is next, which removes impurities from my skin, leaving it cleansed and lightly scented. I grab my face-exfoliating scrub and cleanser after that, and wipe away all dirt and oil from the delicate skin on my face.

Once I'm out of the shower, I dry off and while my skin is still a little damp, I use a scented lotion that helps keep my skin moisturized and supple throughout the day. Once that's done, I take care of my face. I use toner first, eye cream second, and a light serum and moisturizer for the grand finale, with anti-aging benefits to keep my skin feeling firm and looking young and fab.

How many products is that so far? About ten? And I haven't done my hair up with hair polish, or even put on my best face yet. By the time I'm done, I can assure you that I have used over twelve products.

You may say, "So, What's wrong with that? You are trying to look beautiful. That's a great thing, isn't it?"

Indeed, but here's the punch. When you look at the ingredients you are using with these products and what they contain in them, you will think twice about putting them on your body. Trust me on this. That is why I researched the ingredients listed on the labels of each of the products I had used for quite some time. What I found disturbed me, and that is why I'm writing about it. I believe consumers deserve to know what personal care companies aren't telling you that you have the right to know before you grab a product from store shelves that can be potentially harmful to your health and overall well-being. I'm on your side here.

Did you know that according to the Environmental Working Group, "less than 20% of the chemicals in the products you use are even assessed by the industry safety panel"?[147]

Clearly, there are no strict regulations placed upon the personal care products industry, which freely allows them to use toxic and hormone-altering ingredients in beauty cosmetics that should never be anywhere near our bodies. In fact, these ingredients should not be used in great quantities or in conjunction with other dangerous chemicals that many are unaware can cause unhealthy side-effects with long-term use. Shame on these companies for not truly caring about the health and well-being of their loyal customers who may sincerely believe in the hype and massive advertising of the products being marketed.

With that being said, let's look at a few of the top toxic chemicals and ingredients found in the products you may use in your daily beauty regimens. You can judge for yourself afterward if products such as these still deserve to remain in your bath room cabinet, or worse, on your body. Don't take my word for it. But, I must warn you that you will be outraged by what you discover as you read through the list. You may even be shaking your head and asking yourself questions like, why is this even allowed to be done? Why aren't all ingredients placed on product labels? Why aren't more strict regulations imposed upon personal care companies?

Believe me, I have asked myself the same questions. The answer I came up with is that the Food and Drug Administration should get stricter with which ingredients can go into the personal care products used by millions of people, and should require full disclosure of these ingredients so that consumers know exactly what's in the products they buy. I also know that I need to be the one in charge of deciding exactly what product I put on my hair and skin. It is ultimately my decision that counts. I am the one in charge of what I put on my skin and hair, aren't I? What about you? What will YOU decide?

You may ask yourself though, "Even if I read ingredients on labels, how do I know that all the ingredients are listed? Didn't you say that personal care companies are not obligated to list them all? Besides," you may further ask, "Do I really use that many chemicals in my beauty regimens that can affect my health?"

Great questions that deserve the best answers. The beauty care industry does not have to list all ingredients on their labels as I mentioned above, however, there are natural beauty companies that care about listing the ingredients in their bottles, and even though you need to do homework to ensure that the ingredients are safe, at least you know that what you're purchasing will be healthier for you. As far as the amount of chemicals you believe you may not be using, I would advise you to simply look at your bath and beauty products and take note of how many chemicals you count as you line up all the bottles you use during the day. When you add up how many chemicals you are putting on your skin and hair, there is a strong possibility that the amount of chemicals will be staggering, and when used daily, they can potentially cause serious side effects.

IT DOES MATTER WHAT YOU PUT ON YOUR SKIN

Many desire to enjoy excellent health, however, which ingredients and fragrances you put on your skin can greatly affect this endeavor. Instead of improving your overall well-being, you may create health issues that can be avoided by taking time to read and research ingredients listed on labels before grabbing that product off the store shelves. With so many companies advertising products they claim are good for you—products and cosmetics they say you must have—it's no wonder that many people find buying the right personal care product a daunting task.

You may have heard about different beauty lines on the market that tell you that their products are the best. However, when you read their labels, you may find ingredients that are undesirable and that can be potentially harmful to your health. For example, an ingredient found in certain skin creams, beauty and antiseptic soaps, and lotions, is mercury. Yes, you heard me correctly.

What is mercury? It is a metal that can cause numerous health risks, such as: irritability, shyness, tremors, changes in vision or hearing, memory problems, muscle weakness, and skin peeling.[148] Federal health officials warn consumers against using skin care products that contain mercury. "The products are marketed as skin lighteners and anti-aging treatments that remove age spots, freckles, blemishes and wrinkles," said Gary Coody, national health fraud coordinator in the Food and Drug Administration's Office of Regulatory Affairs. He also said the young people may use these products in acne treatments, and that they had found mercury in products in seven states.[149]

That is one of the thousands of chemicals present in beauty lines around the globe today. Take a closer look at other chemicals you will probably find in personal care products you may already use, and some of the possible affects these can have on your overall health.

INGREDIENTS BEWARE

I challenge you to take a walk-through with me on the ingredients I have researched for you that are known to cause numerous health issues. Stay with me, and don't hesitate to do your own research on whichever questionable ingredients you have found in the products you currently apply to your skin and hair. I have compiled a list of common ingredients found in many brands of products and their well-known side effects, which have been evaluated and documented by the Environmental Working Group and the Environmental Protection Agency.

- **Ammonium Laureth Sulfate** is found in beauty products, such as: shampoos, body wash/cleansers, facial cleansers, personal cleansers, dandruff/scalp treatments, exfoliant/scrubs, relaxers, bubble baths, styling gel/lotions, hair colors, and bleach. Health concerns related to this chemical include a cancer hazard, reproductive developmental toxicity, harmful impurities, estrogenic chemicals, and other endocrine disrupters.[150]
- **Coal Tar Dyes** include p-phenylenediamine and colors listed as "CI" followed by a five-digit number, and are found in hair dyes, shampoos, and in other hair products. In addition, they may also be listed as "FDC Blue No. 1" or "Blue 1." Health concerns related to Coal Tar Dyes may include the potential to cause cancer and can cause heavy metal contamination with heavy metals toxicity for the brain.[151]
- **Formaldehyde-releasing Preservatives** are chemical agents that are found in a variety of cosmetics, nail polishes or nail hardeners, and in baby shampoo. They are a known human carcinogen.

Health concerns include the slow release of small amounts of formaldehyde into the air, and it can cause cancer.[152]

- **Fragrance and Parfum** are found in perfumes, colognes and deodorants, and in many other personal care products, even the marketed ones that say, "fragrance-free or unscented." Health concerns include that it may exacerbate asthma, trigger allergic reactions, and be associated with cancer. Also, evidence has shown that Phthalates, a cheap chemical used for allowing fragrances to last longer, interferes with hormone function.[153]

- **Mineral oil** is a by-product of petroleum that is used in baby oil, moisturizers, and styling gels. Health concerns include that it creates a film that impairs the skin's ability to release toxins, and it can clog the pores.[154]

- **Parabens** are used as preservatives in about seventy-five to ninety percent of beauty products,[155] and are used in fragrance ingredients. These chemical preservatives can be found in many shampoos, shaving gels, moisturizers, personal lubricants, and makeup. Health concerns related to parabens include that it may be connected to cancer; it is an endocrine disrupter; and parabens may interfere with male reproductive functions. These substances can also mimic estrogen, the primary female sex hormone, and have been detected in human breast cancer tissues, which suggests a possible connection between parabens in cosmetics and cancer.[156]

- **Sodium Lauryl Sulfate (SLS), and its close relative, Sodium Laureth Sulfate, (SLES),** were formerly used as industrial degreasers and are now used to create foam in soaps. This compound is a surfactant and is used as an emulsifying agent. You can find SLS or SLES in industrial cleaning products such as engine degreasers, floor cleaners, and in personal care products like toothpastes, bubble bath, shampoos, and shaving creams. Health concerns about these include that when they are absorbed by the body, they can irritate skin, cause direct damage to hair follicles, and can even interact with other ingredients and cause kidney or liver damage.[157]

- **Talc** may contain asbestos, and is found in baby powder, eye shadow, blush, and deodorant. Health concerns include that it may be linked to ovarian cancer and respiratory problems. It is recommended to not use talc near the groin.[158]

These are just a few ingredients that you may find listed on the bottle or container of a product you may currently use. There are many more, but it would probably take an encyclopedia to list them all. That should tell you just how many potentially dangerous or deadly ingredients can be found in a large percentage of products sold on the market today. Cosmetics are not vigorously monitored. Hopefully, this will change soon, and it would be great if more strict regulations could be put in place that would protect humans from unknowingly using harmful chemicals that they may not be aware are in the products they use every day.

OTHER POTENTIALLY HARMFUL INGREDIENTS

Intaking important nutrients through eating foods is necessary for good health, and so is acquiring nutrients through the skin, the largest organ on the body. Fragrances found in many products, such as soaps, may contain thousands of phthalates, which help fragrances last longer, but are a cocktail of harmful chemicals that are not required by the FDA to be disclosed by cosmetic companies. In many cases, synthetic and toxic chemicals that cause cancer are inconspicuously hidden under this elusive term.

What about fragrances and other ingredients that are not used on the skin, but are emitted into the air? There are many ways to create a pleasing environment at home or at the office with wonderfully aromatic essences that you can enjoy inhaling throughout the day. Essences found in candles, diffusers, air fresheners, mists, and other products are designed to permeate the air with a great variety of pleasant and beautiful scents. These aromatic essences are used to remove unwanted odors that may linger in the air. But, are these methods truly safe? Should we consider making it our business to investigate the ingredients and fragrances we use perhaps daily to scent our world?

Finding answers to these questions are important and deserve our attention if we want to live a healthier and happier lifestyle. Knowing and being aware of what we choose for ourselves and our families, as well as for our environment, can mean the difference between feeling great and alive with vibrant energy and health, or feeling tired and sick, due to unseen airborne chemicals that are making our bodies toxic. Since we are in control of what we choose to inhale in our personal space, we must learn how to find alternative solutions for the essences we decide to allow around us, and the ones we'll throw in the trash. So, let's explore the world of essence, shall we?

CANDLES

You walk into a candle shop and are immediately assailed by a plethora of scents—floral, citrus, herbaceous, rich, sweet, and everything in between. You peer at the pretty mosaic candles, the beautiful tapered candles, round candles in decorative jars in endless shapes and sizes, and so many fragrant candles. They are in light colors, dark colors, colors of the rainbow. You are dizzy with delight and excited anticipation. "Which one should I choose? They all smell so yummy!" you tell yourself.

You spot a candle in a pretty jar and take a whiff. Oh, you found the one that has an absolutely exotic floral scent you love. You glance at the label and yes, it's floral. Exactly what you like, Rose, with the sweet essence of Vanilla. You grab it and smile broadly, nodding your head yes, you will buy it! The decision has been made.

You reason, "It will look so pretty in my living room, right at the center of my coffee table." Your plan is to light it as you clean up the entire house. Yes, it will make you feel good to smell that lovely essence wafting throughout your home while you work to make everything look beautiful and inviting.

But wait. Did you check the label? Aren't you curious about the ingredients contained in this candle that you are ready to purchase? Do the ingredients matter?

Did you know that some candles are made with paraffin or soy wax? You might say, "What's the big deal if it has those waxes? Why should I worry about that? Besides, isn't soy natural?"

Today, the market shelves are stocked full of products that smell delicious, including all sorts of candles. In fact, candle sales in the U.S. were estimated at $2.3 billion dollars annually and the candle industry has grown ten percent or more each year.[159] Yet, most of the candles sold in the U.S. are made with ingredients and chemicals that are toxic to our indoor air quality and are the cause of many illnesses.

Dr. Ruhullah Massoudi, a researcher and chemistry professor in the Department of Biological and Physical Sciences at the University of Carolina, found that paraffin candles emitted undesirable chemicals in the air, such as alkanes, alkenes, and toluene. Massoudi's research showed that long-term exposure to these dangerous pollutants in the environment contributed to the development of health risks such as cancer, asthma, and common allergies.[160]

Still not convinced? According to research conducted by Lau, et al, paraffin candles contain a frightening range of carcinogenic volatile organic compounds. "Polychlorinated dibenzo-p-dioxins (PCDD), dibenzofurans (PCDF) selected chlorinated pesticides, polycyclic aromatic hydrocarbons (PAH) and some volatile organic compounds (VOC) were analyzed in the exhaust fumes of candles made from different waxes and finishing materials" (1997).[161] It is evident that surrounding yourself with these types of candles are not particularly the best choice. Wouldn't you agree?

What about soy wax candles? Many companies around the world promote their soy candles as natural, renewable, environmentally friendly, and biodegradable. Is this accurate? According to the article, "Soy vs. Beeswax Candles: The Inside Scoop," by Lauren Geertsen at Empowered Sustenance, "More than 90% of soy is genetically modified! GM [genetically modified] soy crops are heavily sprayed with toxic pesticides, causing harm to both the harvesters and the soil."[162]

There is really no such thing as a natural soy wax candle—unless it is made organically.

Yet, there is another part of the candle we haven't covered. This is the wick.

When shopping for candles, it is important to note the ingredients contained in the wicks. Some contain lead. Although they may smell delicious and are tempting to light in your home, they can have many unwanted poisonous chemicals, toxic fragrances, and waxes that can greatly affect indoor air quality and can be harmful to your health. It makes sense then to choose truly natural candles to fragrance your home that you can use safely, creating an ambiance that can calm, energize, or stimulate your mind and spirit when inhaling them. No toxic fragrances necessary, thank you very much.

I love candles too, and enjoy safely lighting and scenting my home with them, so I understand your wanting to buy them. That is why I can assure you that you don't need to worry that you won't find environmentally friendly and aromatically scented candles, even safe soy candles (if they are made organically). There are candles that smell amazing with waxes, such as honey beeswax, and you can find ones that contain essential oils instead of chemical fragrances. Some candles contain 100 percent plantbased, natural fragrances that you can use that are earth friendly for your family and even for your furry friendly companions, and you don't have to feel like you're missing out.

And do you remember that lovely essence I spoke about at the outset? The Rose with the sweet essence of Vanilla that you were absolutely crazy about? Well, you can still have it. Yes, go ahead and clap. I am happy about it too. It is Daniel Lovely's Hallowed Earth "Melana" candle, available at Etsy (http://etsy.me/2kQx4Ou). Here are seven companies that sell candles made with natural ingredients, wicks, and essential oils you can also try (www.care2.com/greenliving/7-candles-that-won t-give-you-cancer-or -make-your-kids-sick.html).

IS THERE HOPE FOR NATURAL BEAUTY AND WELL-BEING ?

Yes, absolutely! Even though there are products with questionable and health-damaging ingredients, on the flipside, there are great fragrances and quality ingredients you can choose for your home or your skin that not only exude lovely scents, but promote good health—essences that will make a noticeable difference in your life, and can relax or uplift your mind, body, and spirit.

Some personal care products make you feel beautiful, young, and sexy—without sacrificing your health.

Utilizing beauty solutions with questionable ingredients is no solution. Many of the thousands of chemicals in traditional skin care products are proven to absolutely have a negative effect on your body and can cost you your health, which I'm sure is of great value to you. You may wonder, though, "If cosmetic companies are authorizing these toxic chemicals in personal care products that we believe are good for us, then why are we even buying from these companies? They will only continue creating unhealthy products that can hurt us in the long-run, until someone intercedes to control which ingredients are allowed in these products."

You are correct. Some personal care companies are removing a few of these chemicals from their product lines. However, it is also up to us to change the way we view skin care and other products we put on our skin that we purchase. Even if actionable steps are taken today to monitor the beauty and personal care industry, we can choose healthier skin care alternatives that provide superior benefits, and which contribute to creating a more sustainable planet.

BEAUTY AND PERSONAL CARE USING ESSENTIAL OILS

Throughout this book, you have learned how essential oils, aromatherapy, and nutrient-rich ingredients can be used effectively so you can experience great health. The countless ways you can incorporate these oils from using them as a single oil, or in conjunction with other oils to enhance their healing power, is an enormous advantage for everyone. The amazing components that make essential oils support the body in a physiological, psychological, and spiritual manner should impress upon us the importance of exploring and making these little smart soldiers a major part of our lives.

As was mentioned in earlier chapters, essential oils can be blended with carrier oils for massaging on the skin for pain, muscle tension, colds, or even infections. What about in beauty and personal care? Well, here's some good news, essential oils can also be blended with carrier oils to make body oils for rejuvenating the skin. You can use them by adding distilled water and creating mists to freshen up your home or office, or simply to spray around yourself for calming the nerves, for anxiety, or for giving you a boost when you're feeling a bit tired during the day. They can be diffused in the air by adding them to diffusers with water, or they can be directly inhaled from the bottle. They can be used in candles, soaps, and other personal skin care products from shampoos, to body lotion, and beyond.

Many natural companies offer aromatic blends that are already created for you and assist with anything from skin care, to stretch marks, to firming and rejuvenating the skin from head-to-toe. Companies such as Eden's Garden, Mountain Rose Herbs, and Organic Infusions provide formulated blends that you can use to enhance your beauty. You can use a variety of carrier oils, distilled water, aloe, and other ingredients to dilute these aromatic oils so that you can use them on your skin. Always remember to conduct a patch test on the inside of your elbow to determine if these oils are safe for you.

Essential oils can be used in many beneficial ways. They can bring much comfort and well-being to you each time you use them. The variety of essences you will discover in these aromatic oils will indeed enhance your mood, which will add to the essence that makes you, you. The essential oils simply allow for a deeper connection to your own being. So much so that they can also be used during meditation, yoga, visualization, and for clearing your chakras.

In my company, Mariposa Essence (www.mariposaessence.com), we sincerely believe that when organic and natural ingredients are combined with organic and therapeutic essential oils, the result is an amazing product that works in harmony with your mind, body, and spirit. The products sold contain many health benefits that help alleviate certain symptoms, enhance the mood, and work synergistically to maintain your skin's moisture, elasticity, and overall balance. Through the active ingredients and oils found in all our personal care solutions, our intention is to provide an alternative to traditional skin care by choosing therapeutic preventative products that contain essential oils. There is no doubt that making an informed choice of great skin care and better overall health is the key to unlocking the potential to achieving optimal health and balance throughout your entire being.

When you opt to utilize products that do not contain toxic chemicals or pesticides, synthetic dyes, or fragrances, you will experience true skin care that nourishes and heals your body instead of harming it. You can have glowing skin, fabulous hair, and more, and feel balanced with products that work to provide you with the best in aromatherapy and healthy living.

So, instead of reaching for personal skin care products and ingredients that promise to keep you looking beautiful and younger, but can't guarantee that their beauty solutions are completely safe for you, wouldn't it be better to invest in personal skin care solutions that provide overall health advantages for your body? In addition, wouldn't the added benefits of essential oils that uplift, energize, stimulate, and balance your mind, body, and spirit, be a better option?

The answer is, absolutely! This is why I created Mariposa Essence, which only utilizes safe, pure, and healthy ingredients that contribute to better health and overall well-being. I felt that by using nature's ingredients, as well as aromatic essences in many of the products sold in my company, it would make a significant difference in many people's lives. Knowing the harmful effects caused by the continuous use of products that contain hazardous chemicals or toxic fragrances, I set out to develop a company that primarily focuses on the mind, body, and spirit. My goal and intention is to help people connect more easily to their higher self through aromatherapy. In addition, I want to offer customers personal care and home products, and spiritually balancing methods to enhance their ability to live by the spirit. It is my sincere belief that utilizing a variety of methods to assist in achieving our true essence is essential to experiencing great health, balance, and well-being.

Living your best means tapping into the physical, emotional, mental, and spiritual truth of who you are and living your true essence, which is, in my opinion, the best way we can use our lives. It is why I felt passionate about starting a company that expresses the embodiment of what it truly means to live your true essence, and why I decided with my partner and sister Maritza, that we would name it Mariposa Essence.

"But," you may wonder, "How did everything start for you? What motivated you to develop the idea of having your own business?"

AN BUSINESS IDEA IS BORN

When I began using essential oils for my family and me almost two decades ago, I realized the powerful impact these plant derived essences had on our lives after a short period of time. For one thing, I rarely got colds or headaches, or felt overwhelmed or anxious. I especially loved Lavender, since it helped to ease stress, relax me, and was gentle enough to use on my son's skin if he was not feeling well.

I always kept essential oils such as Roman Chamomile, Eucalyptus, and Tea Tree on hand, due to the healing and antibacterial properties contained in these wonderful oils. Not only did I use them for rubs and baths when anyone in the family felt a little under the weather, but I also used them in my cleaning solutions and personal skin care products, which I made for myself and for family as gifts.

By 2003, I was so impressed by the amazing effects of essential oils that I created a business where I could educate and provide natural alternatives to customers who didn't want to use any traditional chemical products in their homes. Many of my customers had children and pets; therefore, it was important for them to use cleaners that did not include toxic ingredients that could potentially harm their family and pets. They enjoyed a clean and aromatic home or office with products that were environmentally friendly and made with natural ingredients and organic essential oils. They were happy with the results they received, and throughout the fourteen years of my business, I felt proud to have contributed to improving the environment, one home at a time.

Yet, I wanted to do more. The amount of information and research collected from scientists and environmental organizations about essential oils and aromatherapy, as well as the major health benefits derived from plant-based ingredients, caused me to study them more. Even way back when I started my first business, I was aware of hazardous ingredients and their harmful effects on the body. I learned about the many cleaning solutions, as well as personal care products, that contained seriously harmful ingredients, which set me off on a journey to discover exactly which chemicals and ingredients they had. That is where my honest research began.

With time, I wanted to better help customers learn more about the products they bought for their home, as well as the products they put on their skin. I created another business that would not only provide home solutions that were formulated with the environment in mind, but that would also bring healthy skin and body care solutions to potential or current clients. Today, with this new business, which I started in 2016, I still have many wonderful ideas on how to offer natural and organic products that will serve to enhance the mood, assist with skin irritations, sore muscles, stress and anxiety, depression, body pain, and so much more.

My intention is to provide numerous solutions that support overall healing from a variety of physical, emotional, and spiritual imbalances.

Taking the time to conduct careful research on the advances being made today in the world of essential oils and medicinal plants is absolutely fascinating to me. It is a very passionate subject, and is a topic I could ramble on about all day. Educating ourselves on the ingredients available to us that can either hurt or heal our bodies is essential to our health and well-being. If we actively make it our business to research the ingredients we use daily on or in our bodies, we will be well on our way to experiencing optimal health. It is our responsibility to want the best for ourselves, and within our grasp, we have many resources available to us that makes it possible for us to live a health-conscious life full of energy and longevity.

YOU CAN LIVE YOUR TRUE ESSENCE IN BODY

What have you learned thus far about your mind and body? Are there changes you need to make to improve Your life in these areas? If your answer is "Yes," then I am excited for you!

When you focus on healing your mind by being honest with yourself and working on the specific areas in your life that aren't benefiting or serving you in the least, you will see positive changes in your mindset. When you focus attention on healing your body from the many toxic chemicals and potentially dangerous ingredients sold by many drug and personal care companies today, you will be well on your way to discovering what it means to absolutely live your true essence in body. Furthermore, when you incorporate therapeutic and organic essential oils, as well as natural ingredients, in your daily routines or rituals, you will feel more energized and full of vibrant health, having a sense of overall balance and vitality in your life that makes existing with purpose that much greater.

The amazing plants that were created by a higher intelligent source who obviously had a concern for our health and well-being in mind, body, and soul, make living your true essence not only possible, but achievable. It is a loving act that allows us to connect more fully with our Creator since we are at one with the earth and the universe.

When you align your entire self with the powerful Spirit that encompasses all that exists, your life will never be the same. Understanding how to tap into that spiritual awareness which you can connect to at any time, is the key to unlocking the genius that exists within you and is able to create new realities you may never have dreamed possible. Your light will shine through from within, which will be reflected in the eyes of your soul. You will become unstoppable. You will create the life that you deserve. Let's find out more of what it's all about in the following section on the spirit, shall we?

Who you are cannot be defined through thinking or mental labels or definitions, because it's beyond that. It is the very sense of being, or presence, that is there when you become conscious of the present moment. In essence, you and what we call the present moment are, at the deepest level, one.

Eckhart Tolle

PART THREE

THE SPIRIT

CHAPTER TEN

THE SPIRIT ESSENCE
THAT IS YOU

**"... Who you are cannot be defined through thinking
or mental labels or definitions, because it's beyond that. It is the
very sense of being, or presence, that is there when you become
conscious of the present moment. In essence, you and what we call
the present moment are, at the deepest level, one."
—Eckhart Tolle**

In previous chapters, we considered the mind and body, and how
important it is that each of these areas of ourselves operate and function
in a positive, balanced way. We learned that what we put in our minds can
affect our entire lives. What we put in and on our body can help us feel
healthy and alive, or weak and sick. Do you agree?

What about the spirit? How do you live the spirit essence that is you?
How essential is nourishing and caring for that spiritual part of yourself?
How can you be your true self and treasure the magnificent, spirit being
that you are?

We'll examine these questions in this chapter. Set your intention to
understanding the powerful part of yourself that goes beyond the limits
of human-based thinking to living your true essence. You will discover
three spiritually enlightening secrets and three critically fundamental spirit
qualities you must live by that can connect you more fully to that universal
energy essence that lives in you, and which is easily accessible, if you take
the time to explore how .

Spiritually Enlightening Secrets from this chapter:
- Transformation of the Spirit
- Connection to the Spirit
- Living from Your Higher Self

Critically Fundamental Spirit Qualities we'll discuss:
- Spiritual Essence of Love
- Spiritual Essence of Happiness
- Spiritual Essence of Peace

We will briefly consider the spiritually enlightening secrets of transformation, connection, and the true essence that is you, and that is right at your fingertips. In addition, we will discuss the spirit qualities of love, happiness, and peace that you must possess to express the truth of who you genuinely are. This will help you to more thoroughly experience your authentic essence when they are practiced each day. They will become part of you, just as breathing is essential to living for every one of us.

When we co-exist without these enlightening spiritual secret gems, life can be full of insecurities, anxieties, pain, and discontentment. The present can be uncertain and fear can freeze us from reaching out to do, be, and have more freedom in our lives. When we experience feelings of inadequacy, inner turmoil, or sadness, life can be a challenge. I can attest to this, especially after going through a time in my life when my spirit felt as if it was slowly extinguishing, leaving me feeling empty and lost inside. How did this happen? It was when my son, Gabriel, was around ten-yearsold and my marriage was on total hiatus.

A SPIRIT OF MOURNING

There was a time when I was clueless about who the real me was, or even that I was a powerful and divine essence. I thought my spirit would die when I did. Whatever I put in my mind was based on other people's opinions, and not the opinion that should have really counted, the one that came from me and my higher source. The life I lived during that painful time almost crushed my spirit.

Feelings overwhelmed me: not being enough, and not measuring up to the rules and regulations of my husband and a religion that promoted spirituality and holiness at a supreme level that at the time I felt was my obligation to follow. Striving to be spiritually exceptional drained my spirit.

I was expected to be perfect: a loving and submissive wife, a spiritual and exemplary mother, sister, and friend. Failure was not an option. I made sacrifices for everyone else, and left myself for last. That was what I was supposed to do, or so I thought.

Constant spiritual food, Christian literature, was the order of the day. All the information provided to us was to be followed exclusively, and any deviation from this was unacceptable. Any failure on our part to not agree with the teachings and laws set out in this faith were considered apostate thinking, and immediate action was taken to remove an individual who had a differing opinion from the one written in their literature. Was this reasonable?

What was more discouraging was that women were expected to give up being themselves to submit and please their husbands, despite disagreements or conflicts of interest. It's okay if this is what you believe. However, this level of thinking was more about mind control and not what we are, free spirit agents born as human beings. At that time, I would never have said that.

Being part of this faith made me feel like it was a man's world. A woman's opinions and ideas were of no consequence. All spiritual and theocratic decisions came from the older men in the organization. In the family, the end decision about whether the woman was in favor or not of the situation, issue, or plan, rested on the man. That is what they claimed the Bible taught, and that is what I followed because I thought it was the right course that must be taken in God's eyes.

Women cared for their children, and raised them to strictly follow the authority and guidance of their father more than their mother, since men were considered the head of the household and must follow the leadership set out by Jesus Christ. Women could serve the congregation and God by faithfully standing by her husband's side. He could have any position he wanted in the church. Women were not allowed to teach or be greater than the men. Whatever the man decided in his family or in the congregation was acceptable if it did not go against any Bible teachings.

This way of thinking was sort of like ancient times, when women had no say on pretty much anything. They were basically the property of the man. Was this the purpose for God creating woman?

My spirit was grieving, for I knew I was much more than how I was living. So many questions invaded my mind that I felt dizzy with them, but the fear of disappointing a God that I believed was outside of myself and deciding my fate, put the brakes on the choice to leave a faith that, in my opinion, was rigid and controlling. Yet, I asked myself if this was the way God meant for me to live?

Was I to blindly follow a religion based on what they believed to be true about God and the Bible, even though my opinions were at times different from what was taught? Was I created to live in a physical world, where having my own thoughts, ideas, and abilities as a woman were irrelevant? Was I a mindless robot, following the orders and commands of so-called spiritual men? Did my spirit essence matter? Was conformity about how life was supposed to be like, a way of living I had to accept and endure because these were God's words, thus they must be followed through these appointed older men of the congregation to have everlasting life?

I struggled, sometimes with tears of confusion and uncertainty. Life had to be more than this mindless repetition of strictly enforced rules and laws to remind us about how we should conduct ourselves, what type of personality we should have, and how we should speak and carry ourselves. Everyone followed the same repetitive thoughts and actions. Like I said, mindless robots. This constant barrage of what was considered the code of behavior for all members of this faith was driven into us, day in and day out.

I wept deeply for the desire of living a life that was not mine—a life where there was freedom to choose my own thoughts, beliefs, and personality. The frustration and anger I felt at how much I had to give up and conform to this way of thinking, just so that I could have God's approval, seemed unjust. Is this what a Creator who was "love," according to 1 John 4:8 in the holy book was all about? It didn't seem logical. If God is love, why did I feel imprisoned?

I asked myself, was settling for this what God wanted from me? Was standing in the shadow of my husband, where my opinion barely counted, the way I had to live the rest of my life? Regardless of my doubts, did God care about my feelings? Where was the real me in among this chaos that lived in my mind each day? What had happened to my spirit?

For years, I battled with uncertainty about life and God, becoming unhappier each moment. My spirit was deteriorating and I felt dissatisfied with my life, trapped in an existence that didn't bring true fulfillment to me. There was more to living than this, yet I remained part of a religion that led to limitations in so many ways. That way of life was full of rules and obligations that did not lighten my soul, and all because of fear of displeasing God, who had the power to bless or curse me. Boy, was I stubborn.

This way of thinking almost killed my spirit and took a major toll on the girl I once was—the joyful and loving spirit I had once possessed. My cheerful disposition, and caring and courageous spirit faded away like a flower that at one time had bloomed in its beautiful loveliness, but was now sheltered from the sun and rain, causing it to no longer show off its captivating essence.

I dissolved until I felt as though I had no personality. I became mechanical, doing the things that had to be done, following the rules that had to be followed, with no real emotion or spirit. Not only was I blindly agreeing to follow what I thought was the true path of life, but I was physically blind. The combination was horrifying indeed.

The exhaustion I felt from being emotionally and mentally abused by my husband, and the constant reminders of how perfect I had to live by following rule after rule of what was expected of me, made my spirit feel weaker and weaker. I prayed and wept to a god I no longer felt heard my pleas. I asked questions such as: "Why am I so unhappy if you are my God? Was the life you gave me created to live like this? Is this what experiencing genuine love, happiness, and peace is all about? So, if it is, why do I feel empty inside? Why do I feel as if I am never enough?"

In my heart, I believed I would probably never learn the answers to these fundamental questions. I was at such a low point during that period that I thought that anything different was going against the God I served. Yet, over time and with the opening of my eyes to what was really the truth about God, to my surprise and delight, I did receive all the answers.

However, at that moment, I moved through the motions, working a business, taking care of my son, attempting to co-exist with my husband, attending spiritual meetings, studying endless articles on what constituted spirituality and what was basically allowed as a Christian. The steep expectations left me virtually exasperated and utterly dissatisfied with this way of living.

The cream of the crop happened one day when my husband coldly spoke to me, and I knew with absolute certainty that my marriage was pretty much over. He said, "If you leave me, you will be nothing. You will come back to me on your hands and knees, begging me to take you back. Remember that once you open that door and walk out of my life, you will never come back through that door."

At this point, I had had enough of all the crap he had been dishing out on me for too long to remember. I had been attempting to reason with him on the matter of my freedom to decide who my friends should be. He hated hearing what I had to say, because it meant doing things without him.

In that instant, I thought about what I had allowed myself to be with him. I had become a shell of a person. My ideas, wants, needs, and choices were taken from me. Everything was a must. I must go to the Christian meetings; I must dress this way because it is what God and my husband wanted; I must do and say what is expected of me as a Christian. In fact, I must associate with who my husband approved. The truth of the matter was that I realized that none of it was enough for me. That I could be more and deserved more in my life than this.

I said with total conviction and while I still had all of my senses, "You will never have to worry about me coming back, Lloyd, because I don't intend, nor want to come back. I promise you that will never happen. I am not your daughter. I am your wife, and have always deserved to be treated with love and respect, something you have rarely, if ever shown toward me. Believe me, I know I won't be missing anything."

At that moment, I was set free from the captivity of my husband and a religion that was mind-controlling and unrealistic. A large bolder was removed from my heart and soul. I could breathe normally again. The need to live up to someone else's expectations was finally over. God was still on my side and in time, I would learn who I truly was and what role God, or my higher source, played in allowing me to live out the true purpose of why I came to be here. Soon, I would understand who God was in my life, and what an amazing eye-opening experience that was when I finally grasped the meaning of that.

A TRANSFORMATION OF SPIRIT

So, what changed? I knew that my spirit needed to be nourished and that it was critical that I find out what to do to live my life with purpose. I needed to understand the love that had always existed, and which will always exist. My purpose was not to unhappily pursue a way of life that did not harmonize with my spirit. I was certain this could not be what life was supposed to be like. If it was, then I could never live up to this way of thinking, and I would never enjoy peace of mind. The sacrifice would have probably crushed my spirit indefinitely, and I may have never learned the answer to the one burning question I asked myself every day.

What was that question? It was the ultimate question that set me off on a quest to search for the spirit essence that was me, the question that sent me on a new path to discover myself. I asked, "Who am I?" What was my true essence that brought me here to live as a blind woman, the real essence that would enable me to live out the true purpose I came here to complete?

Wayne Dyer said it beautifully: "The essential lesson I've learned in life is to just be yourself. Treasure the magnificent being that you are and recognize first and foremost you're not here as a human being only. You're a spiritual being having a human experience."[163]

There it was, the answers to my questions boiled down to these divine words. They opened my eyes to a new way of thinking. I could understand that I came from the invisible. The reason I came to be here was to completely accept who I was in this human body, and to help others see past their own physical, emotional, and spiritual challenges. The real purpose of my life is to find ways to encourage and stimulate others to break free from the barriers that hold them back from living from their higher self and to know how to connect to that powerful spirit that is one with each one of us, and that lives from infinity to infinity, or forever.

As Wayne Dyer said above, I was not a human having a spiritual experience. I was a spirit having a human experience. Even with my physical challenges, however I came to be here, the human experience God has allowed me to have here is temporary; thus, there are lessons to be learned, battles to be won, strengths to be discovered, and souls to be touched. Humans experience storms. In the middle of it all, we can find a moment of silence and stillness. At this level, we can feel a genuine connection with our higher source, or whatever you prefer to call this presence, that is one with the universe, the earth, all humans, animals, and nature.

Mother Teresa once said, "We need to find God, and he cannot be found in noise and restlessness. God is the friend of silence. See how nature—trees, flowers, grass—grows in silence; see the stars, the moon and the sun, how they move in silence . . . We need silence to be able to touch souls."[164]

Learning to tap into my stillness was the beginning of my true transformation. When I discovered the limitless possibilities and creative ideas that came from this elevated part of myself, I gained confidence in the ability I had to share what I know with others. It was thrilling to discover that I no longer needed to conform to a way of thinking that was outside of myself and that seemed as far away as an untouchable star from the heavens. I no longer needed to live by restrictive, same-faith expectations, which I now believe was more about control than freedom. I had opinions, thoughts, and feelings, which no longer needed to be ignored to conform or accept the opinions of others about spirituality and life.

Now, I understood that I could be my true self, despite the blindness. I could do the things I loved, living my true purpose that came from deep within my soul, and still please my Creator.

Oh yes! I finally was living the essence I came here to live. I was finally content. Now I was truly free!

With the challenges I have faced and the obstacles on the road to finding myself, I want to share with you three spiritually enlightening secrets that transformed my life, and I hope they will do the same for you. Learning the path that led me to experience the new awareness I now have in my life and in the world around me was spiritually empowering and divinely enlightening for me. This new-found clarity created a completely different person in mind, body, and spirit that I am proud to be today.

The intensive research and extensive studies I did on ancient prophets such as Jesus Christ, David, and Moses, as well as philosophers such as Aristotle, Socrates, Plato, and Lao Tzu, taught me to see a glimpse of the spiritual beings these historical figures were, and the spirit essences they left behind that continue to teach us today. The modern spiritual beings I also studied, such as Wayne Dyer, Deepak Chopra, Michael

Beckwith, Oprah Winfrey, and Eckhart Tolle, among others, showed me that they had one thing in common with their ancient counterparts. They operated from their higher selves. Their reliance was not on the physical or physically constraining barriers that could limit their capacity for spiritual growth or the fulfillment of their deepest desires, but instead, they placed their attention on that divine part of themselves that was limitless, that could shatter the glass ceiling of mediocrity and a life that lacked purpose. They ceased living from the ego which was edging God out, and lived from their higher self.

Learning the divine role these spiritually guided persons have played in history and in the modern world has inspired in me and impressed upon me the love and greatness that resided and still resides deep within all of them, and that also resides within each of us. It has allowed them to share their brilliance and spiritual gems of wisdom with all who hear them. They knew with absolute certainty that they were spirit beings living a human existence, and those that live today recognize that they are connected to that all-powerful spirit, God, or their higher source, which allows them to live and express their true essence.

Those spiritual leaders living today are aware that, even if they have a small fragment or piece of this greatness, they know that it operates deep within them, and that it is always silently present. They know with certainty who they are and live the wise words written by Lao Tzu in the *Tao Te Ching*: "Knowing others is wisdom, knowing yourself is Enlightenment."[165]

The insight into the lives of these individuals taught me that I, too, could learn new beliefs to empower, not disempower me. This also shed new light on the understanding that we all have a spirit essence that is unique to each one of us, and goes beyond thought. As the quote stated on the outset, "Who you are cannot be defined through thinking or mental labels or definitions, because it's beyond that."

You, too, can learn who you truly are inside and live from the spirit essence that is you. You, too, can operate from your eternal self.

YOUR CONNECTION TO THE SPIRIT

"I don't believe in 'thinking' old. Although I've transitioned through many bodies—a baby, toddler, child, teen, young adult, mid-life and older adult—my spirit is unchanged. I support my body with exercise, my mind with reading and writing, and my spirit with the knowing that I am part of the Divine source of all life," Wayne Dyer said.[166]

Those words were like a shining light that lifted my soul. During one of the many public talks Dr. Wayne Dyer gave, I learned that we all possess an infinitesimal fragment of this all-powerful and all-knowing spirit within us. This tiny fragment has the potential to grow into a larger piece of God as we continuously live from this place. His words resonated with me.

Who I am was no longer a mystery. I understood Wayne Dyer when in his book, *Wishes Fulfilled*, he quoted Omraam Mikhaël Aïvanhov: "The creator has planted within every creature a fragment of himself. A spark. A spirit of the same nature as himself, and thanks to this spirit, every creature can become a creator."[167]

At that moment, I realized that I was more than just a human being having a spiritual experience with something that was outside of myself or beyond my ability to understand. Within my physical self, there exists an invisible or intangible self. Deep within me, this bigger and more intelligent self that can grow and go beyond the limits of human thought and is connected to the magnificent spirit that created all things, was a part of me and I was a part of it. What an aha moment that was for me.

However, many people today rely more on the physical self. The lower self. The self that depends primarily on the ego. Why does this happen?

THE EGO TRIP

I have an ego, or in my case, I call her my shego. What does the shego do that is so challenging? Well, first, the shego's job is to stop us from living our full spirit potential. Why? Because the shego focuses on the outside of herself, instead of on the inside. The shego needs to feel like the winner. She thrives on her possessions and what she achieves or owns.

The shego fears failure, pain, and discomfort, going outside of what she knows or feels, and losing. But does that way of thinking bring true satisfaction and genuine purpose to our lives?

From personal experience, the fear I felt at one time did not bring me any happiness. I went through the motions, telling myself that I was doing the right thing. Perhaps I was thinking too much and the matter was not that serious.

"The ego is only an illusion," Wayne Dyer said, "but a very influential one. Letting the ego-illusion become your identity can prevent you from knowing your true self. Ego, the false idea of believing that you are what you have or what you do, is a backwards way of assessing and living life."[168]

The ego poses a real challenge when you are trying to find yourself. Fear of losing that divine connection I thought I had with my Creator made me remain in a place that I felt deeply inside was not where I belonged. Yet, I stayed there. The true voice within whispered warning signs, but of course, I ignored her as I had on many previous occasions. Boy, was I hard-headed.

I had dreams and aspirations of being a singer, a fiction writer, perhaps a psychologist, or teaching others in some capacity, which I put on hold because I felt it was my duty to sacrifice all that I was, and to exclusively serve God for the prize of everlasting life that I now know I have always had.

All were misconceptions driven by the ego-based thinking of others who I allowed to influence me. Due to my lack of knowledge and understanding of the ego and the divine being who is invisible and timeless, I felt confused. That is how many people may feel today.

For example, fear of losing causes many people to turn away from their dreams or true desires. They see too many obstacles to the road to success, so they push back, or give up the dream altogether. There is too much in the way. The lack of education, lack of funds, low self-esteem, pride, limiting beliefs, or lack of courage all contribute to making many people turn away from doing what they love or from being the person they wish they could be. Fulfilling that role is too difficult, or impossible, they believe.

Fear makes people lose out on great relationships, because they are afraid to trust due to past experiences. Their focus is on the other person and not on themselves. They also base their relationships on what the other person can give them. Again, their focus is not on how they can give, but on what they can get. The shego is hard at work again.

Some people stay together, despite the pain and suffering or negativity in their relationships, because they prefer drama rather than being alone. They don't want to lose the security they have or perhaps they stay for the children. In any case, the shego clings to the other person, not for love, but to feel needed or wanted. In her book, *What I Know for Sure*, Oprah Winfrey said, "What I know for sure is that a lack of intimacy is not distance from someone else; it is disregard for yourself."[169]

When you focus your attention on the other person, or your shego, you place limits on what is possible in your relationship. When you stop judging your partner and can accept him for who he is, or simply realize that perhaps the relationship will never improve because it isn't what you want anymore, or you have outgrown what you now feel for this person, then you will expand beyond the shego trip.

What about pursuing a spiritual path that seems almost impossible to follow, as was my case? You already know what that can do to your spirit. All the doubts I had were all due to the inability I had to go deep within myself to find real answers to my genuine questions. That happens to many people today, and it can have a negative impact on their lives and futures. I certainly know what that feels like.

If you can operate from the part of yourself that is timeless, that self that is a higher part of you, you will learn to create incredible change and see endless possibilities in your life.

You are an eternal being having a human experience. Your soul won't die when your physical body ceases to exist. It lives on after you complete your human experience on earth. Wow, what spiritual enlightenment that was for me, and how grateful I am to have discovered it.

Do you believe that it is possible to tap into a divine reservoir that can help you transform from living from your shego to living from your spirit essence? Do you believe that you have a connection with your higher source that is a powerful part of yourself? Do you believe that by living from this self, you can live your true essence? Oh yes. That is the answer I was waiting for. Awesome! Now, let's discover more about your higher self.

LIVING FROM YOUR HIGHER SELF

Can you see beyond what your shego wants? Can you go deeper within yourself to discover that higher being that is invisible and unchangeable, and that is connected to the supreme force that created all things? This is that invisible spirit that lives inside of you and is one with you, that small fragment which was freely given to you at birth. Philosophers and spiritual teachers call it "the higher self."

When you become familiar with the most authentic and complete expression of yourself, that divine part of you that can embrace the true essence that makes you, you, but in a higher and more powerful way, then you will have been formally introduced to your higher self. This is the part of yourself that helps you recognize that spark within you that is more powerful than the physical, which is changeable and temporary. This amazing spark is what beats your heart and makes you breathe in and out without thinking about it, and what replaces old cells with new cells every day, all without your notice. Doesn't that impress you?

This spark is but an infinitesimal part of you, yet it is located within you, and it can be the activating force that leads your life toward love, happiness, and peace. It is the gift that God, your higher source, has bestowed upon you from creation. When you live from this divine part of yourself, you take on new thinking that transcends your human aspect. The ego takes a backseat, allowing for the spiritual essence to guide you.

You see, I believe that we have two selves. The physical self depends on the ego and the human standpoint of viewing the world and yourself. It sees the things that may seem impossible or unattainable. This is the self that depends on the ego, which believes that it is defined by what it wins, achieves, or owns.

Your physical self can battle with your higher self when what you physically choose is not in harmony with what your spirit whispers in the silence to you. The ego customarily wins, and your invisible essence that is more powerful gives you signs that you are not headed in the right direction, that your choice was not very smart. That part of yourself is often ignored. I have been guilty of that many times. When I changed my beliefs about where my own thoughts had brought me, I transformed my way of thinking. Then, I forced myself to take a closer look at the reflection I had of myself. Not a really happy place, that's for sure.

Many times, I contemplated the deep things of life, the visible and the invisible. I asked myself the fundamental question of "Who am I?" but also, "What is the real meaning of life? What happens when I leave this world? How can I live my true essence while I am still present?"

The higher self transcends beyond the sensory aspects of yourself. You can connect to the higher being that is always present and all-knowing, or omniscient.

What is so amazing and extraordinary about this part of myself? How is this related to living my true essence?

Once you understand that you are not the physical or lower self that most people operate from, and not the part of yourself that only sees the physical aspects of solving problems, not even the mental part of yourself that sees the limits of what is possible for you—and most definitely not the self that believes that if you can't achieve your goals or accept the opinions of others who believe they know what is best for you, then you are a big fat zero—then, you escape the ego. The ego. Oh, that damn ego again. Horrible, isn't it?

The higher self is unchangeable, unlike the changing human body. It is not outside of you, but is inside of you. It is infinite and timeless, like the universe, like God—not separate or away from, but at one with everything.

Who am I? Who are you? You and I are changeless, birthless, and deathless. We are spirit beings living a human experience. Thus, we are an expression of God's love. The diverse traits and abilities we have, and the variety of good qualities we possess, can be seen throughout the universe and in all creation. This understanding helps us see that we are one with this all-powerful spirit that is God. It is not the name that is most important, but knowing how powerfully your higher source can positively affect your entire life. For example, the word "water" does not denote any power. It's just the name. You can't touch it or know it. However, when you experience water, that is when you understand its true power. This is what I mean by the name not being as significant as what extraordinary strength and ability comes from what that name represents.

When we realize that we are all one with this all-powerful spirit being, we can see ourselves in others. Why not go out today and study a person? See if there is something in them that you have seen in yourself. The experience will absolutely enlighten you.

All of us have felt aggravation, betrayal, resentment, pain, or jealousy. We have also felt love, happiness, and peace.

Understanding this means that there is the possibility and capacity to live our true essence in mind, body, and spirit. When we realize that we are spirit beings, divinely created, then we know that there is nothing impossible from the standpoint of God and our higher self, according to Matthew 19:26. That leaves nothing out. There is no longer any reason to rely on our shego for the answers. We can go align ourselves with the eternal spirit that knows everything and is everywhere, and can do anything.

You may wonder though, "What are those spiritually enlightening qualities that can help us live our true essence?" And how can I transform my life into a more authentic expression of this spirit essence that created me?

All great questions. Let's find out what these essential qualities are.

THE SPIRITUAL ESSENCE OF LOVE

"The real you is loving, joyful, and free. The real you is just like a flower, just like the wind, just like the ocean, just like the sun."
—Don Miguel Ruiz[170]

The very essence of love is God. This is evident from the creation of the universe to a planet filled with everything we need that is perfect. For example, love is seen in nature in all its splendor and abundance, from watching a shooting star, to listening to the sweet song of a nightingale, to feeling the warmth of the sun on your face. Miracles we witness each day make it evident that love is the essence of the divine source that lives in us.

The fact that we are connected to this all-loving, spirit being should enable us to express love in all we do. For instance, you can express love in a smile that can brighten someone's day, or a word of encouragement that can help someone feel better about a situation they are going through. It can be by sharing a meal with a friend, cheering someone up, helping a stranger, or by going the extra mile to comfort someone.

When we unselfishly give love, the universe unselfishly gives us love. There is more happiness in giving than there is in receiving, says the good book in Acts 20:35. Therefore, we should love all that we are, and embrace the love that is you. Share that love with everyone, even if it seems difficult. Love never fails.

Love helps us care for everyone that crosses our path. It helps us diffuse an argument with our significant other. It helps us forgive when we have been wronged. An Indiana child who was blind once said, "Forgiveness is the fragrance the violet sheds on the heel that has crushed it."[171]

When we learn to see past the shego that only sees the pride or resentment, then we will feel free from the chains of hatred, as stated in Proverbs 10:12: "Hatred stirreth up strifes: but love covereth all sins." Living from the spirit of love allows us to let go, and let God.

Comparing the practices and spiritual rituals I had faithfully followed for years with the spiritual freedom and grace I now experience, I have concluded that love means knowing that I am a spirit being that is free to feel and be—to live each moment and be aware of that conscious presence within. I learned that it's not just "knowing about God," but it is "knowing God" that makes all the difference.

For instance, if you know about swimming because you saw someone do it, that is not the same as knowing how to swim. Knowing is when you get in the water and start swimming. It's the conscious contact that allows you to know. It is the same with connecting to your higher spirit being. It is the conscious contact you make with it, not simply hearing about it that is the knowing.

You, too, can connect with your spirit and know that you are one in love with all that exists. Unlocking the divine power of love that you have inside will create the most authentic and true person you want to embody. Living your true essence means becoming consciously aware that you are more than your shego, and that love is the activating force that moves through you and out of you.

THE SPIRITUAL ESSENCE OF HAPPINESS

"Happiness cannot be traveled to, owned, earned, worn or consumed. Happiness is the spiritual experience of living every minute with love, grace, and gratitude."
—Denis Waitley[172]

When you come from a place of love, every emotion flows with ease. You live each day from the present. Your past is gone, and your future is uncertain. What you have is the now.

So, what do you do with the now? Appreciate and love each moment.

When you are presented with situations that cause negative emotions, such as sadness, unhappiness, or disappointment, you can flip the switch and reframe these emotions with positive ones such as excitement, joy, and elation. It's okay to feel negative emotions, for they are part of life. However, when you pack them away like luggage and take them with you wherever you travel, happiness becomes an illusion—never within your reach.

Look for loads of reasons to be happy. I find it in the simplest things, such as when my beautiful two-year-old granddaughter, Olivia-Rose, wants to dance and sing songs with her Mema. That's what she calls me. When I give her a bubble bath and she splashes water everywhere, including on me, and thinks it's a big joke. How she laughs that devious little laugh. I am so happy. When I am ready to take my service dog, Chikita out for a walk, she runs to get my black Labrador retriever's leash and tries to put it on her. She says with that enthusiasm and cuteness I absolutely adore, "Oli (her nickname for Olivia) help Mema." That adorable voice fills me with so much love and joy, just to see that she has such a naturally giving spirit. She melts my heart.

You have so many reasons to find pleasure and satisfaction in your life. Even when a bitter moment rears its ugly head, or when the angry winds of turmoil and unhappiness blow relentlessly around you, attempting with fierce determination to tear you down, you can find reasons to be happy.

The graceful, slender palm tree can weather any storm. It maintains its ground and "has three distinctive features that help them survive the punishing conditions of hurricane and cyclones, and even tsunamis," according to the article, "How do palm trees survive hurricanes?" by Melissa Breyer.[173]

The palm tree's rambling roots, wiry trunk, and clever leaves work together to give it storm-resistant strength. While a storm rages, the palm tree can "bend over forty or fifty degrees without snapping," Breyer said.[174] The palm tree is an example of strength and courage when enduring a difficult situation or big challenge in your life. Happiness doesn't depend on possessions or the things that you have, it comes from the spirit of tenacity and resilience to weather problems or crises in your life, as the palm tree does with a severe tempest.

Not everything is peaches and cream always. However, you have the capability to stop the bad thoughts from invading your mind or crushing your spirit. You can reframe your thoughts to find something positive, while sloshing through all the mud and mire that life presents. You don't have to dwell on the dark clouds of misery that may hover over your head. You have the power to turn your attention to the lightening sky on the other side. Isn't that better than strolling about with a complaining spirit that will only make you feel worse, if that's possible?

Jim Rohn said, "Happiness is not something you postpone for the future; it is something you design for the present." Every moment is important and has meaning. Even when you experience negative emotions such as sadness, they teach you to know happiness. Life may bring you challenges, but know that you can go deep within yourself to find that unifying connection with your higher source that will enable you to remain flexible in mind and free in spirit. You possess the ability to transform from living on a weak foundation that is easily torn down by a passing storm, to living on a foundation that is solid and can withstand disaster. As author, motivational speaker, and consultant Denis Waitley said above, "Happiness is the spiritual experience of living every minute with love, grace, and gratitude."

THE SPIRITUAL ESSENCE OF PEACE

"Through allowing the isness of all things, a deeper dimension underneath the play of opposites reveals itself to you as an abiding presence, an unchanging deep stillness, an uncaused joy beyond good and bad. This is the joy of Being. The peace of God."
—Eckhart Tolle, *The Power of Now: A* *Guide to Spiritual Enlightenment*

In this world and in the universe, there exist cycles of good and bad. There is growth and disillusion. Empires rise and fall. Wars come and go. Creation and destruction occur; births and deaths happen; nations rise and fall; flowers bloom, and then wither away; trees grow, flourish, then die; stars are born and destroyed.

Growth is good. However, if everything in nature and the universe continues to grow on and on, then it becomes monstrous, and would be destructive. In the cycle of an individual's life, there is also growth and disillusionment. There are cycles of gain and loss, joy and pain, achievement and failure. The cycles around us continue to change, and all of them have an opposite.

Many people believe that if their life is filled with stuff, they will feel happy and at peace with all their attachments. Without these attachments, they may feel as if they have failed; thus now, they are unhappy.

Others may climb the ladder of success, yet feel empty inside. They have all the stuff they can possibly want, yet peace and happiness elude them. They confuse life with life situations.

Your life attachments may come and go; however, the real YOU that is infinite remains the same. Pain is an inevitable part of life, yet when disillusionment comes knocking, an opportunity presents itself to either grow or remain attached to what is gone. If we remain attached, transformation cannot take place. The potential for new growth becomes stagnant. Pain and suffering ensue.

For some, letting go is not an option. Perhaps, the love of your life you believed would always be there for you is no longer by your side. Or, an accident caused a disability that you refuse to accept and you cling desperately to what used to be before the tragedy changed your entire life. Maybe the loss of a child caused you to mourn and suffer the pain and loss of that child, and now life is too grievous to find anything worth fighting for. Perhaps your beauty is fading away with time, and life cannot be beautiful unless you are.

There are endless cycles that we may or may not have control over. Yet, every cycle can be a chance to experience new growth. When disillusionment occurs, it can be the beginning of something new, a lesson that can help you move forward with new possibilities. The situation can change you for the better, or keep you locked in an interminable cycle.

Life situations can be quite difficult for a time. Yet, when you understand that you are powerful and eternal, an unchangeable spirit being, you can learn to view life situations as temporary. Cycles change in the physical world. Nothing remains the same. It is this way with the earth, the universe, and you. Cycles come and go, but eternity lasts forever.

Let's dissect the examples of life problems from above. For example, what if the person you loved dearly has gone. How do you feel? Crappy, you say? That's understandable. You probably feel lost and alone. Perhaps there is sadness or tears. The pain of an undesirable situation is unpleasant when the wound is raw.

Yet, think about this: is there a lesson that can be learned in this life situation? Can you please leave your shego out of this? Contemplate this situation. Can you eventually forgive the other person? Can you search deep within your spirit to send love to this person?

To find inner peace, you don't necessarily have to be happy. When you move beyond the physical world and beyond what's good or bad, you can view your circumstances differently. You can either stubbornly cling to what was, or find it within yourself to continue moving or flowing forward with the constantly changing universe.

What if an accident has caused a disability that you now must live with for the rest of your life? From one day to the next, your life has done a 180. What now? Pity and anger sweep over you. Life has new meaning—or becomes meaningless. Questions flood your mind.

"What am I going to do? How will I live? What things do I have to give up now? Why did this happen to me? Why did God allow this to happen? What did I do to deserve this? Life is unfair."

You may feel sadness, anger, frustration, and pain. Yet, in time, you must accept what is, or resist what has happened and become consumed by your unhappiness and lack of inner peace. Although there have been changes in your physical or mental self, inside, you are still the same person. The challenges you face may be grueling at times, but when you see past the disability and realize that there are many opportunities for growth and new ways of doing the same things you did before, this situation can be a blessing in disguise. You can find joy and inner peace again.

What about when you lose a child? Life can feel like an open void ready to swallow you up. The inexplicable pain can be unbearable and inconsolable. It can feel as if someone has taken a piece of your soul away from you. Death can never be a pleasant experience when love is present. The emptiness you feel can rob you of joy and peace.

With time, can you learn to accept that death is a part of the cycle of life. Due to circumstances you cannot control, this inevitable time may unexpectedly arrive. No one can determine when death, this enemy of the physical realm, makes its presence.

In *The Power of Now*, Eckhart Tolle said, "The cyclical nature of the universe is mostly linked with the impermanence of all things and situations."[175] Those words ring true when you examine life's cycles and how they continue to change, even without our notice. They are impermanent, or have an end.

There is no happiness with death. When you exist from the standpoint of your eternal self, there is a difference with death—you accept life's physical cycles and despite the unhappiness, you feel a deep sense of inner peace. You don't resist or cling to what no longer is. You can recline on the source that created all life cycles and knows loss.

What about feeling and looking beautiful? For most women, beauty is very important and oftentimes, when it comes to their appearance, it is at the top of their list. Yet, when beauty fades, some women panic and think that all is lost. Age creeps up on you and the once beautiful and flawless skin you had loses its elasticity and firmness. This can be tragic for many women.

However, beauty is only skin deep. Haven't you heard that saying? Well, do you believe that? Consider your inner beauty, the timeless, beautiful spirit that lies within you. This inner beauty can shine right through and allow you to feel and look ageless, even on the outside.

Today, we can do many things to have a gorgeous appearance, no matter what our age. And no, I am not talking about plastic surgery. By properly caring for yourself and eating well, naturally caring for your skin and hair, and by wearing clothes that suit your body, you can look fabulous, no matter how old you claim to be. This can help you feel happy and at peace with your appearance, and with yourself.

No matter the cycles that come and go in our lives, we can decide the outcome of how we will grow from these difficult, or even complex situations. We can either resist and cling to what no longer is, ignore the present moment and refuse to move forward, or we can find lessons that will teach us to grow and create real joy and rediscover true inner peace. Remember, though, when we refuse to accept what is, we can cause pain or suffering to ourselves, or even to our loved ones around us.

Also, keep in mind that the shego is good at remaining separate from your spiritual self. Many times, suffering comes from the shego. She can refuse to accept a change in circumstances or cling to what she can no longer control. When operating from your higher self however, you can allow all the noise and negativity to simply pass right through you and choose to see past the temporary annoyances or disturbances that may arise.

When you let go, stop resisting, forgive, and love when it may be challenging, then you will know that you are not living from the shego, but from your spirit essence. You will be living from your own power and not dependent upon someone else's. Your mind no longer can obsess over what you possess or don't possess, what you win or lose, what you gain or have failed in. Your spirit essence will be the driving force that remains the same.

When you stop looking externally for answers and turn inward to where all the answers lie, when you live from the present moment and become consciously aware of yourself, reasons for attempting to win an argument, or staying angry at someone for something they did that hurt you will lose its significance and pass right through you. When you no longer allow resistance, and accept things for what they are, you can then learn to live from the essence of your spirit.

More than that, and I must say, much more exciting than that, you will discover that you can create magic in your life. Yes, by living from your higher essence, you can utilize the power you hold within to manifest your desires. This may seem unrealistic to many, but considering what we have discussed in this chapter, magic comes from the collaboration between you and your higher source. It is very possible, and we will discuss more on this subject in the next chapter.

CHAPTER 11

STEP INTO YOUR
TRUE ESSENCE

**"When we are able to look beyond appearances and
to behold that which we truly are, we recognize that
our essence is interwoven with the divine and that
we exist as one of its expressions."**
—Alexandra Katehakis

Throughout this book you have learned about how your mind, body, and spirit work as one to become the best and most authentic expression of yourself. You learned that your mind should be filled with positive thoughts that uplift your spirit. You also learned that your body should be balanced and healthy, and what you give to it should matter significantly. As for your spirit, you learned that it is eternal and connected with your higher source, and that by living from this higher and more powerful part of yourself, nothing will be impossible for you to create.

In this chapter, you will learn three powerful, secret tools that can more fully connect you to the source that is already within your reach. These fundamental tools will help you get from where you are at this present moment, to stepping into the true essence that is you. "But," you may ask, "how can I do this, though?" Great question, up ahead, we will consider what they are, and how they can work to create new realities in your life, allowing you to live from the part of you that is endless, unchangeable and eternal.

Your transformation from caterpillar to butterfly will surprise and delight you, and as you continue working on yourself each day, you will see changes that will motivate and inspire you to keep practicing these critical tools. What's more, you will attract people, places, and things that are not coincidences, but synchronicities which you create with your thoughts and imagination. What are they? They are meditation, affirmations, and creative visualizations.

Learning to meditate, speak affirmations, and visualize my life was exciting for me when I first heard about it. I am confident it will be for you too. Now, let's start with my favorite practice.

MEDITATION

What is meditation? What benefits are derived from meditating? Why should this daily practice be incorporated into your life?

Meditation is the avenue that connects you to the source of thought, pure consciousness awareness. It is where the field of possibility, synchronicity, and creativity lies. It is a place of silence.

Dr. Wayne Dyer, explained the meaning of meditation for the holidays on his blog. He said, "Everything that's created comes out of silence. Your thoughts emerge from the nothingness of silence. Your words come out of this void. Your very essence emerged from emptiness. All creativity requires some stillness."[176]

Meditation means meeting the source that created you. It makes you aware of that infinite presence and expresses genuine gratitude for being a part of this incredible force. It is part of you, and you are part of it. You can speak words of gratitude for all that you have, such as: love, peace, harmony, beauty, and opulence. This is what Lao Tzu, a Chinese philosopher and author of the *Tao Te Ching*, and other spiritual beings believed could bring any manifestation into your world. The silence brings the deep connection with the highest spirit essence that can usher true fulfillment into your life.

When you are going to meditate, find a quiet place. If there are noise or disturbances around you, this will not allow you to completely focus on your meditation, thus your time for deep contemplation will not be as effective. It requires quiet and stillness on your part to transcend your thoughts to that higher plane where you can experience oneness with the powerful source that is everything and everywhere, and in you.

If practicing meditation is difficult at home, why not go out to nature? Surround yourself with the beauty and creation that is also at one with you. If you live in a mountainous region, stand where your eyes can see far and wide into the distance and recognize the privilege to experience the awesome site before you that is also at one with you.

The ocean is a wonderful place for intense contemplation. As a blind woman, I too, appreciate beauty and nature, but in a different way. I love to breathe in the salty air when I am near the ocean. I enjoy touching the soft sand, allowing it to slip through my fingers. It is fascinating to me to listen to the seagulls as they fly overhead from branch to branch, or soaring high above the sea. They captivate me as they sing their joyful song.

I laugh with glee when I am frolicking in the waves as they rise and fall around me. I am in awe when I lift my face up to the blue sky and feel the brilliant sun as it warms my skin. There is such a deep sense of connection with my Creator. I am at one with the earth and my spirit is at one with this powerful source that commands the ocean, bending to its will, and allowing it to move in perfect precision.

Here, I become still. Here, I feel the immense power and magnificence of God, or my higher source. I feel surrounded by that presence and know with absolute conviction that when I connect to this higher power, all things are possible.

There are psychological and physiological benefits to meditating, according to thousands of studies conducted in the past fifty years. Meditation can bring calmness, help you sleep better, balance immune system functionality, lower blood pressure, and improve overall health. Meditating consistently can also awaken long-dormant potentiality that becomes a renewed possibility. You become more creative and the conditioning thoughts and patterns that once ruled over you will lessen. You learn to make better decisions, see your goals more clearly. You are better aligned with the universe, since you are made from the same forces and elements. You can create magic.

Meditation allows you to become abundant. Money is a part of life and having it can help you use it to do good. When you utilize the skills and talents you possess, you will manifest abundance, and through the practice of meditation, these abilities will become more pronounced in your life. You will have more energy to do more, which in turn will bring you abundance.

When you meditate regularly, you will be freed from the repetitive patterns that can sometimes be difficult to break. You will experience synchronicity and transcend beyond conditioning, and move into the field of infinite possibility. What you thought or believed was impossible, becomes possible when you state your intention. You become a co-creator with the universe.

The more connected you are to this conscious awareness, the more you can express the divine essence that you are. You will be able to more fully express divine qualities or attitudes such as: love, joy, kindness, peace, goodness, self-control, and patience. Your true essence will shine through and your shego will no longer be in charge. The shego that clings to what she possesses, or who she can compete against to be the winner, will cease to be the driving force in your life.

Why would you not want to meditate when there are countless benefits? Some people may feel intimidated to be in union with such a powerful force. However, when you begin meditating, you will realize that what you will feel is an inner sense of love and peace. All you should do is relax, breathe deeply, and try to control your thoughts. Begin meditating for 10 minutes and gradually, as you feel more comfortable, have longer periods of stillness. There is no set amount of time to be silent; however, the more you meditate and contemplate, the more connected you will be with this powerful spirit essence.

If you feel that it is difficult to focus while meditating, find online meditations. You can go to YouTube and find plenty of guided meditation videos from experts like Deepak Chopra, Lisa Nichols, Wayne Dyer, Michael Bernard Beckwith, or Vishen Lakhiani. If you prefer to do your meditations with music and no words, you can find them on YouTube or Spotify. Search for meditation music.

There are a variety of sounds you can use during meditation. There is music, but there are also sounds of nature, such as ocean waves, rain storms, and forest sounds. There are also meditation sounds such as dolphins singing for healing strength, Tibetan bowls, chakra balancing, Tai Chi, and yoga music. Whatever helps you focus more easily, you can try until you find what best works for you. Consider meditation as an important part of your daily practice. When it becomes a habit, within one to three months, you will notice great changes in your life and inner spirit. You will be motivated to continue practicing meditation for a lifetime.

AFFIRMATIONS

What are affirmations? What benefit is there to this practice? Why should you practice affirmations each day?

Neville Goddard, who was known for many years as a supremely influential teacher in the new thought field, provided in my opinion the best definition of what affirmations are. He said, "Disregard appearances, conditions, in fact all evidence of your senses that deny the fulfillment of your desire. Rest in the assumption that you are already what you want to be, for, in that determined assumption you and your Infinite Being are merged in creative unity, and with your Infinite Being (God) all things are possible."[177]

To manifest anything in your life you must become aware of what that is for you. What are your hopes? What are your dreams? What essence do you wish to live?

If you already believe that you are there, then you will take actionable steps to be what it is you desire to become right now. You will act as if you already are that person. The words you speak aloud or affirm with conviction affect your conscious and unconscious mind, which in turn brings images to your mind that motivate or inspire you. You will attract people who can assist you with reaching your desired vision.

Today, many people operate in their unconscious mind. At times, the images they see in their mind's eye are developed by their environment, education, parents, siblings, peers, or society. Affirmations on how their life should be are decided by these things. Some are advantageous; however, some are not and must be relearned.

The conscious mind has provided instructions to the subconscious mind that works on autopilot. For example, when you brush your teeth, get dressed, make a meal, start your car, go to the gym, or work on the computer, you don't need to determine how to do these things. You already know from repeated actions what needs to be done. Your conscious mind has been trained and now the unconscious mind is influenced; thus, you don't need to learn the same things repeatedly, as if learned for the first time.

A case in point: have you ever prepared a meal and were lost in thought, yet your food was cooked, and you didn't burn it? Why was that? Your unconscious mind acts without you paying much attention. You don't need to solve this process because you already know how to cook.

Some of my friends have told me that while they drive to work, their thoughts are on other things, yet they somehow make it to work. Why is that? Your subconscious mind knows what to do. You don't have to think about how to move the steering wheel, press the breaks, or accelerate. If that were the case, how many more accidents would there be on the road?

Yet, when my friends first learned how to drive a car, the idea of using the gear shift, steering wheel, and gas simultaneously were probably difficult. With time and experience, driving a car became automatic. There was no thought given to shifting gears, turning the steering wheel, or hitting the brakes. It became so normal that they could think of anything and still arrive at their desired destination. The conscious mind taught the unconscious mind, and with practice, the unconscious mind took over.

What you see, hear, smell, touch, or taste repeatedly eventually becomes normal and is accepted by your unconscious mind. This is how habits, behaviors, actions, and reactions are formed. It starts with exposure to these things that eventually becomes an integral part of your daily routines. Why not create new habits, such as reading self-development books or writing down the goals you wish to achieve? You can repeat affirmations that motivate and inspire you to obtain your desires. Whatever the dream or fantasy you want to bring into your physical world, when you practice daily affirmations, they will become part of your subconscious mind and will be as automatic as riding a bike or driving a car.

How exactly is this done? First off, you must repeat the same positive statements every day. Do this anywhere. It can be while you're taking a shower, on your way to work or school, as soon as you wake up, or before bed. Whatever is your preference, repeating affirmation statements and feeling as if the goal has been achieved will influence the subconscious mind and change the previous behaviors and thoughts you had that did not help you to reach your true potential.

When in doubt, affirmations will not work. If you believe or are uncertain about the goal you think you want, affirmations will not come to fruition because your doubts and disbeliefs are in the way. You must have love and faith, and believe that what you want is as good as accomplished. You must feel the way you would feel if that goal had already been achieved. Become the persona you would be if that dream had come true. It is in your power to do this.

As Neville Goddard quoted above, you must "disregard appearances, conditions . . . all evidence of your senses that deny the fulfillment of your desire." Remember that you are not alone. You are working with an infinite power that has your back. No matter what your circumstances, life situations, or environment, as an infinite being yourself, you and your higher source can create and manifest what it is that you want to appear in your inner and outer worlds.

The most effective affirmations, I believe, come from the spirit essence we came from. My daily affirmations always begin with the words "I AM." Why? It is partly due to the words I read from the *I AM Discourses*, which were written during the early 1930's by Guy Ballard, and were based on his encounters with Saint Germain, an ascended master. Ballard wrote, "When you say and feel 'I AM,' you release the spring of Eternal, Everlasting Life to flow on Its way unmolested. In other words, you open wide the door to Its natural flow. When you say, 'I AM not,' you shut the door in the face of this Mighty Energy."[178]

That mighty energy is God, or the name you wish to call this infinite Being. The name He calls Himself is "I AM THAT I AM." You can find the only place this name is stated, which is in the earliest written words of the Torah.

In the book of Exodus, Chapter Three, and verses 13,14, it states:

> And Moses said unto God, 'Behold, when I come unto the children of Israel, and shall say unto them, The God of your fathers hath sent me unto you; and they shall say to me, what is his name? what shall I say unto them?'

> And God said unto Moses, 'I AM THAT I AM:' and he said, 'Thus shalt thou say unto the children of Israel, I AM hath sent me unto you.'

The words "I AM" are the full activity of God. So, when I speak affirmations, such as, "I am healthy. I am balanced. I am abundant. I am successful at what I love to do. I am a cheerful giver. I am happy," these words are being spoken through me.

These affirmations empower and motivate me to act on what I affirm. Every day, I repeat them and am elated when I see people and circumstances come into my life that help me to reach the desired goals I have placed in front of me.

When I started writing this book, for instance, I spoke the affirmation, "I am a bestselling author." Shortly after, I attracted people in my life who are helping me write a book that will succeed. I connected with other authors and learned from them how I could organize my book and received ideas on how to market and promote it. I also found an excellent editor who is helping me to create a great book that I believe will help so many people.

Day by day, I feel good and believe that what I affirm will become a reality. I am not worried about not accomplishing this goal. As Dr. Wayne Dyer said, "When you dance, your purpose is not to get to a certain place on the floor. It's to enjoy each step along the way."[179]

In my mind, I am already a bestselling author. On my desk, I have a book that I hold each day and tell myself that it is mine. I feel excitement and joy that I have written an inspiring book that can transform many people's lives.

You, too, can repeat daily affirmations that will eventually show up in your life. Be patient and happy as you work toward manifesting them. Add this tool to your arsenal of secrets for a life filled with all that you wish to have.

Obliterate discouraging or disempowering affirmations. Sometimes, we inadvertently repeat destructive words. For example, you may repeat negative statements, such as: "I am not enough. I am so unattractive. I am too fat. I am not smart like other people. I am never going to succeed at anything. I am too old. I am disabled, so how can I be of help to others?"

None of these statements empower or motivate. They weaken your mind, body, and spirit.

In the *I AM Discourses*, Master Saint Germain said, "When you say, 'I AM not,' you shut the door in the face of this Mighty Energy."[180] You throttle the name of God.

Words have the power to hurt or to heal. Therefore, speak words that uplift, encourage, and make you feel good about yourself. Your words are energy; therefore, attract the good that will come to you if you persist and never give up on manifesting your deepest desires.

You can try reversing those statements to ones that bring love, joy, and peace to your soul. Look at all the great things in your life, even if nine things are wrong and one thing is right. Reframe your negative affirmations to positive ones, and then take actionable steps to become the true essence you wish to live right now.

"I am enough." Believe it without doubting. People will knock at your door to assure you that you are more than enough. "I am attractive." You will begin to feel very beautiful, for you are. "I am successful." Success will be there sooner than you expect. "I am youthful." Reasons to feel youthful will appear, putting a smile on your face. "I am very capable." Opportunities to help others will be on their way.

Believe with all your heart and soul that all the affirmations you repeat each day will inevitably present themselves in your life. Know with absolute certainty that, as you think, so shall you be. Feel the emotions that sweep through you when you affirm each statement. Act as if you are already living the wish fulfilled. This positive mindset will get you from where you are, to where you want to be.

THE POWER OF CREATIVE VISUALIZATION

You might wonder, what is creative visualization? What am I supposed to visualize? Why should I practice creative visualization? What's the point of learning how to do this?

The point? Well, let me enlighten you. Let's begin with, what is visualization?

Visualization is a technique involving focusing on positive mental images to achieve a goal. You can visualize about anything you wish to achieve. For example, you can take a few minutes each day to visualize the future you want to create. If you want more positive and happy outcomes in your life, imagine what those are and set aside time to practice creative visualization.

Perhaps you want to start a new career, become an entrepreneur, travel, discover love and romance, improve your family life, create wealth and abundance, or want to grow spiritually. Using creative visualization techniques each day helps you attain those goals faster and can also be fun as you begin imagining all the possibilities that can happen in your life. You will come to realize just what a powerful tool creative visualization really is.

"The journey of a thousand miles begins with one step," Lao Tzu said. This journey begins with your imagination. When you can imagine what your life could be like, what you consistently think about will expand and you will see people, circumstances, and situations move you toward the fulfillment of what you have imagined.

Children have the most creative and active imaginations. Girls may imagine themselves as a princess living in a beautiful castle with her strong and handsome prince who loyally and faithfully stands by her side. Boys may imagine themselves as a powerful king that rules his kingdom and subjects with strength and courage. He may imagine finding his beloved queen, but cannot marry her because she has been kidnapped by ruffians, and he now must rescue her before she is taken away from him forever. Children imagine being the heroine or hero of their fantasies, all without realizing it. It's normal for them.

Why should our imagination cease when we grow up? It comes easily to us as children, yet when we grow older, the reality of our circumstances and disempowering beliefs sets in and we forget this amazing ability that we all possess. We can, at any time, activate pictures or movies in our mind's eye. I consider it like a magic switch we turn on when we want to create miracles.

The external world we live in reflects what we believe inside ourselves. The subconscious mind is where all our thoughts lie and if our thoughts are negative, pessimistic, or scarce, then the results in our outer world will be exactly that. What we think about most is what we become.

Begin using your imagination again to create new possibilities for yourself. Like a child, you can dream of all the things you want to come true. Your imagination has no limitations or impossibilities. You can do, be, and have anything you want that will bring you more love, joy, and peace. Pretend you're watching a movie. The screen of your life is right in front of you. Now all you must do is create what that movie looks like to you.

Do you read fairy tales to your children? Continue reading them.

Fairy tales activate the imagination that makes the impossible, possible. As adults, we stop using this effective tool to create magic.

Dr. Wayne Dyer said, ". . . Initiate a practice of filling your creative thoughts to overflow with ideas and wishes that you fully intend to manifest. Honor your imaginings regardless of others seeing them as crazy or impossible."[181]

According to a post in *Psychology Today*, in his study on everyday people, Guang Yue, an exercise psychologist from Cleveland Clinic Foundation in Ohio, compared "people who went to the gym with people who carried out virtual workouts in their heads." He found a 30 percent muscle increase in the group who went to the gym. The participants who conducted mental exercises of the weight training increased muscle strength by almost half as much (13.5 percent). This average remained the same for three months.[182]

What does that tell you? Your mind can create whatever it wants. Without budging a finger, you can rehearse in your head goals, ideas, and mental practices you wish to come true. Do you want to climb Mount Kilimanjaro? Do you dream of acting in a Broadway show? Dancing in a ballet? Getting your body fit? Or preparing for the life you deserve? Whatever it is, you can create it.

Some creative visualization techniques can help you use your imagination more effectively. To make the best of your time spent practicing and learning creative visualization techniques, feel that what you imagine is real, which will create the desired outcome. You can immediately reap the benefits of tapping into your imagination and allowing for your mind to conjure up a vivid story of what you want by taking advantage of proven useful techniques. The magnificent vision you hold has the potential to emerge if you believe that the scenes in your mind's eye can absolutely become a physical reality.

For example, if your dream is to have your own thriving business where you experience major success and prosperity, then imagine what that would look and feel like. Think what it would be like to be ensconced in your immense office overlooking the ocean. You are surrounded by a dream team of people you trust and that are thrivers, just like you. You are dressed impeccably and exude confidence as you prepare to meet with a prospective client who can create a new source of revenue in your company.

Imagine how you would feel when the account is yours. The excitement and joy of achieving the goals you have set out for this awesome company you have created. Now you travel and find new and innovative products that can help solve a need that would benefit many people. Your amazing products make a huge impact in their lives. What emotions swirl inside of you? Do you feel proud? Are you happy that you created real change in many lives?

That is the power of creative visualization! When you envision your desired future, and you feel the emotions you would have if this vision were real, you exist in a field of pure potentiality and unlimited possibility that will eventually show themselves in your outer world. If you persist and act on what you imagine, the universe will conspire with you to bring to you what you hold in your mind and heart. It will bring to fruition all that you want, as you harmonize your thoughts with the actions you take to actualize your mission and purpose.

Plug into the power residing in your imagination. Be the driving force that reprograms your mind to go after the absolute possibilities within your grasp. To do it, visualize it.

Find a technique that best suits you. Access some of the many creative visualization free videos and audios on YouTube to help you practice your daily sessions. Online courses from Mindvalley.com or Neurogym.com will assist you with doing this more effectively. You can also take ten minutes a day, several times a day, to relax and be quiet so you can properly imagine what you would like your life to resemble. Remember to act as if this is your life at this moment. Now, you are ready to step into the true essence that is you, and that you deserve to live each day.

LIVE YOUR TRUE ESSENCE

Will You Decide Right Now to Live Your True Essence?

Can you live your true essence? Is it possible? What do you think?

Well, that depends on you. What do you think of yourself? Will you be ordinary or extraordinary? Will you begin today to live your purpose?

Are you ready to work on having a positive mindset? Are you grateful for where you are right now, despite your current circumstances? Will you be aware of the power you hold within yourself and use it to create magic in your life? Will you care about what you put in your mind and on your body each day? Will you change your thoughts, which can bring you closer to your desired destiny? Are you determined to live from your spirit essence?

If your answers were in the affirmative, then I congratulate you. You will live your true essence. You will live an extraordinary life.

On the other hand, if you are content with going to school, getting a secure job, paying your taxes, filling out forms, and living each day going through the motions with no direction or set intention in your life, can you be extraordinary? If you are wrapped around your life situations and allow them to rule your life, are you capable of transformation? Or, if you prefer to walk through this world believing that everything should come to you with no real effort on your part, and then you perish, have you lived your true essence?

Well, you know the answer. Living your most authentic essence would just be a pipe dream. There will always be troublesome waters. Fear will stop you from fulfilling your true purpose. You will always have a reason for pain and resentment. A complaining spirit will be the master of your life. You will never feel contentment, which is no way to live in a world that could otherwise be quite fulfilling.

To me, that is less than ordinary. Life can be so much more than that. Ordinary is not living your best. Why settle for ordinary? I am not attempting to put down this life view; however, as for me, when I realized that I was more than what I gave myself credit for, everything changed. I decided to be extraordinary!

Extraordinary means getting out of your comfort zone and changing the thoughts and patterns that have held you captive, to those that empower you. It means going above and beyond to do, be, have, and give the best of yourself by living your truest purpose and authentic essence. You will have a purpose-driven life to pursue because you know that this is the essence you're supposed to live in until your last breath on this earth.

The expectations that I previously believed about myself no longer remained latched onto my mind or spirit. I learned to let go and expect better opportunities and relationships and happier moments by living in the now instead of the past or the future. My new beliefs carry real meaning.

In my view, if you expect anything, it should be a life of love, joy, peace, health and balance, abundance, and great relationships where you are enough. You should live with contentment and grace, knowing that you can weather any storm. Even if the winds of turmoil blow in your direction, setbacks momentarily slap you about, or if you experience a tumble in the dirt, you should know with certainty that the incredible strength you possess comes from your inner spirit, and this strength helps you move forward with confidence, knowing that you will prevail.

When problems strike, get up, dust yourself off, and move toward being the person you desire to become. You are no longer living from your shego. You are now embracing your spirit essence. Isn't that better than believing that situations are too difficult or complicated? Step into the essence that fills your heart with love and peace, by allowing yourself to be guided by that powerful force that is greater than yourself, and that knows all things.

However, maybe you are satisfied with living a mundane, mediocre, limited, and easy existence, where you settle for being the passenger who is driven wherever without a real direction to unknown places, so you must deal with dark, dreary, and undesired circumstances. Does this way of thinking sound reasonable?

To think or believe that you shouldn't be the driver in your life and accept a bland existence with no higher thoughts or with no inner power that can propel you to do extraordinary things is not living. To have no purpose is like a man that walks through the rain forest, thirsting for water, but settling for drinking a few drops, even though water surrounds him.

The divine Source represents that water, and this powerful Source is everywhere. You have free access to it at any time. So, why settle for just a few drops?

The beliefs we grew up with, which many times came from our teachers, parents, peers, and the environment we were raised in have contributed to this way of thinking. The thoughts that we have about ourselves and the world around us can be developed by these factors.

An example of the influence others can have on our thoughts can begin as early as infancy. The words children hear parents speak, if positive or negative, help form the thoughts in a child's head, and the attitudes witnessed by a child will create lifelong memories and thoughts, whether good or bad.

When children begin school, they are taught skills that may find them a secure job. However, educational institutions fail to teach them about finances or money, which would have helped many to avoid falling into the trap of spending, instead of saving or investing for an early retirement. They may have learned at home that it is difficult to find money, so they develop an idea that money is scarce, creating a concept in their little minds that there is not enough.

What about their peers? They may tell them that life is full of problems and everybody is out for themselves, thus creating limiting beliefs that we are isolated from others, and that we should fight our own battles. When marriage comes, they believe that life will be different, perhaps better, but then realize that they have attracted a person with the same limiting beliefs they have.

Yet, it is possible to reverse this old way of thinking. You can change your thoughts and live your true essence. Your thoughts expand and that is what you attract. It's important to face your current beliefs and ask yourself: are my beliefs making my life better or worse? Am I repeating the same patterns with the same negative results? Is it time to change my current beliefs to new ones that will transform my life?

If your beliefs aren't improving your situation, then put a pause on the thoughts that have gotten you this far, and think positive and empowering things. Ask fundamental questions. Find the answers to your questions in a book like this one, through an inspiring talk you hear, while traveling, or through an overheard conversation. Whatever it is, the answers are close. Pay attention to the signs and intentionally look for them. Remember to ask, ask, and ask again.

We all came packaged with a purpose, yet many of us wander through the rain forest barely tasting what our existence could be like if we only knew without a doubt what that fulfilling purpose was. We may have an inkling, but we ignore it because too many obstacles inhibit us from getting there faster. We act in the same manner as that thirsty man who is not aware that water is all around him. He believes there isn't enough.

He thinks there is a limited supply, when in fact, free water is in unlimited abundance.

Once you truly wish to transform and renew your mind, according to Neville Goddard, a brilliant metaphysical teacher from the last century, and you crave a different life and intend to fulfill that purpose, then you can change yourself.

"By desiring to be other than what you are, you can create an ideal of the person you want to be and assume that you are already that person. If this assumption is persisted in until it becomes your dominant feeling, the attainment of your ideal is inevitable," Goddard said.[183]

When you make the conscious choice to not allow the obstacles, bumps on the road, hiccups in your life, or whatever temporarily blocks your path to inhibit you from living your true essence, believe that nothing is impossible for God. Therefore, transformation is not impossible for you, either. Learn to look at obstacles, bumps in the road, and hiccups as lessons, opportunities, or new growth that will get you closer to your dreams and desires.

If you want to become your true essence, then you must change your thoughts to reflect the YOU that you want to observe in the mirror or feel in your mind each day. You must get out of your comfort zone, walk into that giant building you aspire to enter, walk into the elevator, and press the button to the limit, and move toward the essence that will break through the glass ceiling of what's possible for you.

Do not settle for an unfulfilling existence, where at the end of your journey here, you regret wishing you would had ever allowed fear, resentment, low self-esteem, a complaining spirit, or procrastination to block your true purpose. May that never be.

Can you change your way of thinking? Absolutely! You can go from mediocre to successful, from being in a state of low, to moving in a state of flow. You can go from drab to fab, and go from feeling out-of-spirits, to feeling healthy and balanced. It all starts with your thoughts. What you think about expands, so think about all the wishes you want to fulfill in a lifetime, and get cracking on doing it.

A caterpillar doesn't know that it will change into a butterfly. Before metamorphosis, it crawls and looks creepy. Yet, when that transformation takes place, the caterpillar becomes a beautiful butterfly that soars high above, unrecognizable even unto itself.

What about you? You have the power to transform from ordinary to extraordinary. You can go from simply living alongside the shego to living intertwined with your spirit essence.

The time has come to reprogram the way you think and see the world. If you look at it through a small lens, then you will see or experience a tiny fraction of it. However, if you look at it through a wide lens, you will see it for its endless possibilities.

By changing your thoughts, not looking on the outside of yourself to find the answers, but by looking on the inside, you will discover that within you lies the secret to owning your true essence. Once you understand how to seek for the answers deep within, you can change the negative talk you have spoken to yourself for years, to positive talk that can transform your life. You can soar high with wings of new hopes and desires that you will bring to fruition because you choose to live extraordinarily.

Don't allow your shego to take control. You have learned in the previous chapter how the shego seeks to win at all costs. She needs the approval of others to feel good. She does not accept failure. She seeks to glorify herself. She believes that she is never enough.

However, the shego is great at edging God out. The higher self and the shego are sometimes at odds with each other, as if there are two selves: the higher self and the shego. Which one wins the battle? You choose.

DECIDE NOW TO LIVE YOUR TRUE ESSENCE

When you operate from your higher self, this part of you is unchangeable, limitless, content. You can express more love, joy and peace when you come from this aspect of yourself. This is the divine part of you, the Thinker behind your thoughts that realizes that striving and struggling to obtain the things that perish is futile. When they are obtained, we get bored and set out to acquire more things. What is more valuable is seeking the invisible things that bring true happiness and peace, and becoming love, just as your Maker is love.

Set yourself up for accepting the truth of who and what you are now. Determine to do, be, have, and give all to step into the essence that makes you, YOU. Be consciously aware that you are love, peace, and joy, and that you come from a powerful and undeniable Force that is love, and that being one with this spirit will transform your life and create magic in your world. You will know and understand that this spirit essence will always walk beside you and is a part of you. You will be able to say with conviction that you are now living your true essence in mind, body and spirit.

You and I are a part of a great cosmic Force that will sustain us through all our endeavors. We are not alone. We have the support, guidance, and love from a powerful spirit that is greater than ourselves, and will be there to help us fulfill the purpose we have come to this life to complete. Stand firm, be bold, face your fears, and do it anyway.

Now that you are equipped with the twelve powerful secrets and more to live your true essence, go and create magic in your life. Drink the water that is free and operate from that place of love that transcends all thought. Like the wise words spoken from the ancient philosopher, Lao Tzu, "Mastering others is strength. Mastering yourself is true power."

Live your true essence now, tomorrow, and forever.

ENDNOTES

1   "Robin Williams," IMDb, accessed on October 20, 2017, http://www.imdb.com/name/nm0000245/awards.

2   Deepak Chopra, M.D., AZQuotes.com, Wind and Fly LTD, accessed on October 20, 2017, http://www.azquotes.com/quote/835707.

3   Wayne W. Dyer, *Wishes Fulfilled: Mastering the Art of Manifesting* (Carlsbad, California: Hay House, Inc., 2012), 39.

4   James Allen, *As A Man Thinketh*, as appears in the book, Aaron Kennard, *Affirm Your Truth A 30 Day Mental Transformation from Stressed, Anxious, or Depressed to Happy, Hopeful, and Full of Peace* (United States: Truly Amazing Life, Inc., 2015).

5   Wallace D. Wattles, *The Science of Getting Rich* (New Delhi: General Press, 2016).

6   "Thesaurus—Meditation," The Free Dictionary by Farlex, accessed on October 20, 2017, https://www.thefreedictionary.com/meditation.

7   Deepak Chopra, M.D., *The Spontaneous Fulfillment of Desire* (New York: Harmony Books, 2003), 167.

8   Joel Osteen, *You are Not Damaged Goods*, Joel Osteen Videos, accessed on October 20, 2017, http://jovideo.sermon-video.com/archives/1091.

9   Napoleon Hill, *Think and Grow Rich: A Black Choice,* as quoted on Goodreads, Inc., accessed on October 20, 2017, https://www.goodreads.com/quotes/77253-whatever-the-mind-can-conceive-and-believe-it-can-achieve.

10 "2 Corinthians 9:6," Biblehub, accessed on October 20, 2017, http://biblehub.com/2 corinthians/9-6.htm.

11 Michael Stewart (book) Irvin Brecher (screenplay), *Bye Bye Birdie*, "Bye Bye Birdie (1963)," IMDb, accessed on October 20, 2017, https://www.imdb.com/title/tt0056891/.

12   Neville Goddard. AZQuotes.com, Wind and Fly LTD, 2017, accessed October 20, 2017, http://www.azquotes.com/quote/669147.

13   Dr. Robert C. Worstell and Earl Nightingale, *How to Completely Change Your Life in 30 Seconds--Part V, Part 5*, containing notes transcribed from recordings of Earl Nightingale (Missouri: Midwest Journal Press, 2017), 106.

14   Jack Canfield, "@jackcanfieldfan, Facebook, accessed on October 21, 2017, https://www.facebook.com/JackCanfieldFan/posts.

15   Dr. Mark Waldman, "How to Eliminate Stress and Anxiety," The Energy Blueprint, accessed on October 26, 2017, https://www.theenergyblueprint.com/eliminate-stress/.

16   Andrew Newberg, M.D., and Dr. Mark Robert Waldman, "The Most Dangerous Word in the World," Psychology Today, Sussex Directories, Inc., accessed on October 26, 2017, https://www.psychologytoday.com/blog/words-can-change-your-brain/201208/the-most-dangerous-word-in-the-world.

17   Daniel G. Amen, MD, "How to Develop Your Own Internal Anteater to Eradicate Automatic Negative Thoughts," American Holistic Health Association, accessed on October 26, 2017, https://ahha.org/selfhelp-articles/ant-therapy/.

18   Ron Breazeale, Ph.D., "The Power of 'Automatic' Positive Thinking," Psychology Today, accessed on October 26, 2017, https:// www.psychologytoday.com/blog/in-the-face-adversity/201303/the-power-automatic-positive-thinking.

19   Tony Robbins, "Where Focus Goes, Energy Flows," Tony Robbins, accessed on October 26, 2017, https://www.tonyrobbins.com/career-business/where-focus-goes-energy-flows/.

20   Tony Robbins, Facebook, posted on April 5, 2015, accessed on October 27, 2017, https://www.facebook.com/TonyRobbins/posts/.

21   Tony Robbins, BrainyQuote, accessed on October 27, 2017, www.brainyquote.com/quotes/quotes/t/tonyrobbin176913.html.

22   Napoleon Hill, "Page 136," *Think and Grow Rich*, Success Learned, accessed on October 27, 2017, www.successlearned.com/napoleon-hill- think-grow-rich/files/basic-html/page136.html.

23   Emily Nowak, "Incredible: What Trump Just Did for Our Veterans," Before It's News, June 5, 2017, accessed on October 27, 2017, http://

beforeitsnews.com/prophecy/2017/06/incredible-what-trump-just-did-for-our-veterans-video-2491680.html.

24 "VoiceOver Overview," *VoiceOver Getting Started Guide*, Apple Inc., accessed on October 27, 2017, https://help.apple.com/voiceover/info/guide/10.12/#/vo2681

25 "16 Examples of Steve Jobs Being a Huge Jerk," Business Insider, accessed on October 27, 2017, http://www.businessinsider.com/steve-jobs-jerk-2011-10#.

26 "Oprah Winfrey," *Biography*, A&E Television Networks, LLC., accessed on October 27, 2017, https://www.biography.com/people/oprah-winfrey-9534419.

27 Ibid.

28 Ibid.

29 "What Oprah Knows for Sure about Finding the Courage to Follow Your Dreams," Oprah.com, accessed on October 27, 2017, http://www.oprah.com/spirit/what-oprah-knows-for-sure-about-finding-your-dreams.

30 "Henry Ford Biography," Engineering and Technology History Wiki, accessed on October 27, 2017, https://ethw.org/Henry_Ford.

31 "Dale Carnegie," *Biography*, A&E Television Networks, LLC., accessed on October 27, 2017, https://www.biography.com/people/dale-carnegie-9238769.

32 "About Us," Dale Carnegie Training, accessed on October 27, 2017, https://www.dalecarnegie.com/about-us/.

33 Tony Robbins, "Where Focus Goes, Energy Flows," posted by Team Tony, Tony Robbins, accessed on October 27, 2017, https://www.tonyrobbins.com/career-business/where-focus-goes-energy-flows/.

34 Oprah Winfrey, "Commencement Address at Stanford University," American Rhetoric, delivered 15 June 2008, accessed October 28, 2017, http://www.americanrhetoric.com/speeches/oprahwinfreystanfordcommencement.htm.

35 Dr. Wayne D. Dyer, *Everyday Wisdom* (Carlsbad, California: Hay House, Inc., 2005), 4.

36 D.H. Lawrence, "D.H. Lawrence Quotes," Goodreads, accessed October 28, 2017, https://www.goodreads.com/quotes/316416-those-that-go-searching-for-love-only-make-manifest-their.

37   "Statistics on OTC Use," Consumer Healthcare Products Association, accessed on November 3, 2017, www.chpa.org/StatsNR.aspx.

38   "Prescription and Over-the-Counter Medications," National Institute on Drug Abuse; National Institutes of Health; U.S. Department of Health and Human Services, accessed on November 3, 2017, https://www.drugabuse.gov/publications/drugfacts/ prescription-over-counter-medications.

39   Ibid.

40   "What is Holistic Medicine?" WebMD, accessed on November 3, 2017, www.webmd.com/balance/guide/what-is-holistic-medicine#1.

41   Dr. Eric Lartey, *Matters of LIFE Magazine*, Facebook, posted on March 20, 2014, accessed on November 3, 2017, https://www. facebook.com/permalink.php?story_fbid=732927320072010 &id=695248373839905 "Stress Facts," Global Organization for Stress, accessed on November 3, 2017, www.gostress.com/stress-facts/.

43   "Exploring Aromatherapy," National Association for Holistic Aromatherapy, accessed on November 3, 2017, https://naha.org/ explore-aromatherapy/about-aromatherapy/what-is-aromatherapy

44   Lea Harris, CCA, "Essential Oils and Children," Using Essential Oils Safely, accessed on November 3, 2017, http://www.usingeossafely. com/essential-oils-and-children/.

45   Ibid.

46   Dana Scott, "Essential Oils for Dogs," *Dogs Naturally Magazine*, accessed on November 3, 2017, www.dogsnaturallymagazine.com/ essential-oils-for-dogs/.

47   Katie, "Risks and Use of Essential Oils," Wellness Mama, accessed on November 3, 2017, https://wellnessmama.com/26519/ essential-oils-risks/.

48   Dr. Josh Axe, *The King's Medicine Cabinet*, accessed on November 3, 2017, http://s3.amazonaws.com/PDFs Draxe/Freebies/The-Kings-Medicine-Cabinet.pdf.

49   Dr. Ashley Mayer, "What are Essential Oils?" Dr. Green Mom, accessed on November 3, 2017, www.drgreenmom.com/get-well-soon/ essential-oils/

50 ABC NEWS, "Beauty Secrets from the Dead Sea," ABC NEWS, November 21, 2005, accessed on November 3, 2017, http://abcnews. go.com/GMA/BeautySecrets/story?id=1333102.

51 Kac Young, Ph.D., *The Healing Art of Essential Oils: A Guide to 50 Oils for Remedy, Ritual, and Everyday Use* (Woodbury, MN: Llewellyn Worldwide, 2017).

52 Dr. Josh Axe, "What is Frankincense Good For? 8 Essential Oil Uses," Dr. Axe, accessed on November 3, 2017, https://draxe.com/ what-is-frankincense.

53 H.K. Lin, Ph.D., "Can Frankincense Oil Kill Cancer and Boost Immunity?" Dr. EricZ.com, LLC, http://drericz.com/ frankincense- oil-cancer-immunity.

54 Ibid.

55 "Frankincense Effective in Killing Ovarian Cancer Cells, Study" University Herald, December 20, 2013, accessed on November 3, 2017, https://www.universityherald.com/articles/6350/20131220/ frankincense-christmas-gift-ovarian-cancer-cells-leicester-university-gum.htm.

56 Dr. Josh Axe, "15 Geranium Essential Oil Benefits for Healthy Skin and Much More," Dr. Axe, accessed on November 3, 2017, https:// draxe.com/10-geranium-oils-benefits-healthy-skin-much/.

57 "13 Incredible Benefits of Geranium Essential Oil," Organic Facts, accessed on November 3, 2017, https://www.organicfacts.net/ healthbenefits/essential-oils/health-benefits-of-geranium-essential-oil.html.

58 Dr. Josh Axe, "13 Grapefruit Essential Oil Benefits — Starting with Weight Loss," Dr. Axe, accessed on November 3, 2017, https://draxe. com/grapefruit-essential-oil/.

59 Rachel, "6 Essential Oil Safety Tips for Cat Owners," Meow Lifestyle, February 15, 2016, accessed on November 3, 2017, http:// meowlifestyle.com/6-essential-oil-safety-tips-for-cat-owners/.

60 "10 Wonderful Benefits of Grapefruit Essential Oil," Organic Facts, accessed on November 3, 2017, https://www.organicfacts.net/ healthbenefits/essential-/oils/grapefruit-essential-oil.html.

61 "Reap the Antioxidant Benefits of This Citrus Essential Oil, Dr. Joseph Mercola, December 29, 2016, accessed on November 3, 2017, https://articles.mercola.com/herbal-oils/grapefruit-oil.aspx.

62 Lea Harris Jacobson, CCA, "Phototoxic Essential Oils – how to stay safe in the sun," Using Eos Safely, April 22, 2015, accessed on November 3, 2017, http://www.usingeossafely.com/phototoxic-essential-oils-how-to-stay-safe-in-the-sun/.

63 Mind Body Soul Health and Wellness Blog, December 20, 2015, accessed on November 3, 2017, https://healthyhappyandskinnyblog.wordpress.com/tag/healthy/

64 "Love Lavender? Try Lavender Oil," Dr. Joseph Mercola, July 21, 2016, accessed on November 3, 2017, https://articles.mercola.com/herbal-oils/lavender-oil.aspx.

65 Chad Pegura, "Using Essential Oils around Your Pets," Organic Aromas, February 15, 2017, accessed on November 3, 2017, https://organicaromas.com/blogs/aromatherapy-and-essential-oils/using-essential-oils-around-your-pets-1

66 Dr. Tina Wismer DVM, DABVT, DABT, "Do Essential Oils Pose a Risk to Pets?" Vet Street, May 26, 2016, accessed on November 3, 2017, http://www.vetstreet.com/our-pet-experts/do-essential-oils-pose-a-risk-to-pets.

67 "Essential Oils for Spirituality," Aroma Web, accessed on November 3, 2017, https://www.aromaweb.com/aromatherapyspirituality/spiritualityessentialoils.asp.

68 Dr. Josh Axe, "Top 10 Lemon Essential Oil Uses and Benefits," Dr. Axe, accessed on November 3, 2017, https://draxe.com/lemon-essential-oil-uses-benefits/.

69 "Lemon Oil Uses: A Citrus Delight with a Powerful Bite," Organixx, accessed on November 3, 2017, https://organixx.com/lemon-oil-uses/.

70 Admin, "Lemongrass," Herbalpedia, September 24, 2010, accessed on November 3, 2017, www.herbalpedia.com/blog/?p=73.

71 "25 Surprising Benefits of Lemongrass," Organic Facts, accessed on November 3, 2017, https://www.organicfacts.net/health-benefits/herbs-and-spices/health-benefits-of-lemongrass.html.

72 Dr. Josh Axe, "10 Proven Myrrh Oil Benefits and Uses," Dr. Axe, accessed on November 3, 2017, https://draxe.com/myrrh-oil/.

73   Dr. Joseph Mercola, "Myrrh Oil: Benefits of this Holy Oil," Dr. Joseph Mercola, accessed on November 3, 2017, https://articles.mercola.com/herbal-oils/myrrh-oil.aspx.

74   Dr. Josh Axe, "10 Proven Myrrh Oil Benefits and Uses," https://draxe.com/myrrh-oil/.

75   Dr. Josh Axe, "Top 25 Peppermint Oil Uses and Benefits," Dr. Axe, accessed on November 3, https://draxe.com/peppermint-oil-uses- benefits/.

76   Ibid. 77 Ibid.

78   "15 Amazing Benefits of Patchouli Essential Oil," Organic Facts, accessed on November 3, https://www.organicfacts.net/healthbenefits/essential-oils/health-benefits-of-patchouli-essential-oil.html.

79   Ibid.

80   Beverley Gray, Alive Publishing Group, April 24, 2015, accessed on November 3, http://www.alive.com/health/essential-oils- for-meditation/.

81   Dr. Joseph Mercola, "What Benefits Can You Derive from Patchouli Oil?" Dr. Joseph Mercola, April 13, 2017, accessed on November 3, 2017, https://articles.mercola.com/herbal-oils/patchouli-oil.aspx.

82   Jayne Leonard, "21 Magical Benefits & Uses of Rosemary Essential Oil," Natural Living Ideas, October 13, 2015, accessed on November 3, 2017, http://www.naturallivingideas.com/rosemary-essential-oil-benefitsuses/. *and* "11 Amazing Benefits of Rosemary Oil," Organic Facts, accessed on November 3, 2017, https://www.organicfacts.net/healthbenefits/essential-oils/health-benefits-of-rosemary-oil.html.

83   "Bridal Lore and Customs," Novareinna, accessed on November 3, 2017, http://www.novareinna.com/festive/bridal.html. *and* "Rosemary, That's for Remembrance," Monterey Bay Spice Company, accessed on November 3, 2017, http://www.herbco.com/t-rosemary-article.aspx.

84   Dr. Josh Axe, "Rosemary Oil Uses and Benefits," Dr. Axe, accessed on November 3, 2017, https://draxe.com/rosemary-oil-uses-benefits/.

85   Ibid.

86   Ameya C, "7 Amazing Benefits of Tuberose Essential Oil," Stylecraze, November 1, 2017, accessed on November 3, 2017, http://www.stylecraze.com/articles/benefits-of-tuberose-essential-oil/#gref.

87   Ibid.

88   "5 Best Benefits of Tuberose Essential Oil," Organic Facts, accessed on November 3, 2017, www.organicfacts.net/tuberose-essential-oil.html.

89   "Tuberose Absolute Oil," Greener Life Club, September 14, 2017, accessed on November 3, 2017, http://ayurvedicoils.com/tag/natural- aphrodisiac/page/2.

90   Ibid.

91   "CaFleureBon: Tuberose in Perfumery + Dangerous Pleasure (10 Fragrant Prizes) Draw," ÇaFleureBon, March 15, 2012, accessed on November 3, 2017, www.cafleurebon.com/cafleurebontuberose-in-perfumery-dangerous-pleasure-10-fragrant-prizes-draw/.

92   Sergey Borisov, "Tuberose: Flower, Scent, History and Perfume," Fragrantica, January 17, 2014, accessed on November 3, 2017, www.fragrantica.com/news/Tuberose-Flower-Scent-History-and-Perfume-5041.html.

93   "CaFleureBon: Tuberose in Perfumery + Dangerous Pleasure (10 Fragrant Prizes) Draw," ÇaFleureBon, www.cafleurebon.com/cafleurebontuberose-in-perfumery-dangerous-pleasure-10-fragrant-prizes-draw/.

94   "Tuberose Absolute," Organic Infusions Inc., accessed on November 3, 2017, www.organicinfusions.com/products/tuberose-absolute.

95   "13 Amazing Tea Tree Oil Benefits," Organic Facts, accessed on November 3, 2017, https://www.organicfacts.net/health-benefits/essential-oils/health-benefits-of-tea-tree-essential-oil.html.

96   "Top 10 Tea Tree Oil Benefits and Uses," Dr. Josh Axe, Dr. Axe, accessed on November 3, 2017, https://draxe.com/tea-tree-oil-uses-benefits/.

97   Sierra Bright, "13 Uses for Tea Tree Oil that will Change Your Life," Natural Living Ideas, April 5, 2017, accessed on November 3, 2017, http://www.naturallivingideas.com/tea-tree-oil-uses/.

98   "Tea Tree Oil," Poison Control National Capital Poison Control Center, accessed on November 3, 2017, www.poison.org/articles/2010- dec/tea-tree-oil.

99 "Carrier Oils," SproutingHealthHabits.com, accessed on November 12, 2017, http://www.sproutinghealthyhabits.com/carrier-oils/.

100 Joe Leech, "Eight evidence-based health benefits of aloe vera," Medical News Today, last reviewed May 28, 2017, accessed on November 12, 2017, https://www.medicalnewstoday.com/articles/318591.php.

101 Ibid.

102 Amar Surjushe, Resham Vasani, and D G Saple, "Aloe Vera: A Short Review," PubMed.gov, U.S. National Library of Medicine National Institutes of Health, sharing from the Indian Journal of Dermatology, accessed on November 12, 2017, https://www.ncbi.nlm.nih.gov/pmc/articles/PMC2763764/.

103 Dr. Joshua Axe, "Aloe Vera Benefits: Heal Skin, Constipation & Immune System," Dr. Axe, accessed on November 12, 2017, https://draxe.com/aloe-vera-benefits/.

104 Bhalang K1, Thunyakitpisal P, Rungsirisatean N., "Acemannan, a polysaccharide extracted from Aloe vera, is effective in the treatment of oral aphthous ulceration," PubMed.gov, U.S. National Library of Medicine National Institutes of Health, accessed on November 12, 2017, https://www.ncbi.nlm.nih.gov/pubmed/23240939. 105 Joe Leech, ""Eight evidence-based health benefits . . ."

106 Ibid.

107 Dr. Joshua Axe, "Aloe Vera Benefits . . ."

108 "Aloe Vera from Vitality Unlimited," The Tortoise Shell Life Science Puzzle, accessed on November 12, 2017, http://customers.hbci.com/~wenonah/new/aloevera.htm.

109 Maenthaisong R1, Chaiyakunapruk N, Niruntraporn S, Kongkaew C., "The efficacy of aloe vera used for burn wound healing: a systematic review," PubMed.gov, U.S. National Library of Medicine National Institutes of Health, accessed on November 12, 2017, https://www.ncbi.nlm.nih.gov/pubmed/17499928.

110 Lydia Mulvaney and Zeke Faux, "No Evidence of Aloe Vera Found in the Aloe Vera at Wal-Mart, CVS," Bloomberg, accessed on November 12, 2017, https://www.bloomberg.com/news/articles/2016-11-22/no-evidence-of-aloe-vera-found-in-the-aloe-vera-at-wal-mart-cvs.

111 Dr. Joshua Axe, "20 Coconut Oil Benefits & Side Effects," Dr. Axe, accessed on November 12, 2017, https://draxe.com/coconut-oil-benefits/.

112 "11 Surprising Benefits & Uses of Coconut Oil," Organic Facts, updated October 25, 2017, accessed on November 12, 2017, https://www.organicfacts.net/health-benefits/oils/health-benefits-of-coconut-oil.html.

113 "The 10 Most Unwanted Ingredients in Personal Care & Beauty Products," Natural Health Way, accessed on November 12, 2017, http://naturalhealthway.com/articles/chemicals.html.

114 Z Living Editors, "9 Health Benefits Of Hemp Oil That You Should Know," Z Living Network, February 16, 2016, accessed on November 12, 2017, http://www.zliving.com/wellness/natural-remedies/9-health-benefits-of-hemp-oil-that-you-should-know.

115 Delilah Butterfield, "10 Incredible Benefits of Hemp Oil," HERB, October 17, 2016, accessed on November 12, 2017, http://herb.co/2016/10/17/incredible-benefits-hemp-oil/.

116 Karissa, "How to Cook with Hemp Seed Oil (+ Recipes!)," Karissa's Vegan Kitchen, September 16, 2015, accessed on November 12, 2017, http://www.karissasvegankitchen.com/how-to-cook-with-hemp-oil/.

117 Louise France, "Devon's oil boom," The Guardian, November 7, 2004, accessed on November 12, 2017, https://www.theguardian.com/lifeandstyle/2004/nov/07/foodanddrink.features9.

118 Blanche Levine, "Stop Cancer Naturally" NaturalHealth365, September 28, 2012, accessed on November 12, 2017, https://www.naturalhealth365.com/hemp-oil.html/.

119 "Raw Honey for the Skin," Forever Healthy and Young, accessed on November 12, 2017, http://foreverhealthy.blogspot.com/2012/05/raw-honey-for-skin.html.

120 Ibid.

121 "Beauty Secrets of Cleopatra," Beauty & tips Magazine, accessed on November 12, 2017, https://www.beautyandtips.com/beauty-2/beauty-secrets-of-cleopatra/.

122 "Jojoba oil," Wikipedia, accessed on November 12, 2017, https://en.wikipedia.org/wiki/Jojoba_oil.

123 Dr. Joshua Axe, "Jojoba Oil — Skin & Hair Healer and Moisturizer," Dr. Axe, accessed on November 12, 2017, https://draxe.com/jojoba-oil/.

124 "Jojoba oil," https://en.wikipedia.org/wiki/Jojoba oil.

125 Laura Sumner, "Is Jojoba Oil a Carrier Oil? Another Beauty Elixir for All Skin Types?" Essential Bazaar, March 21, 2016, November 12, 2017, https://www.essentialbazaar.com/is-jojoba-oil-a-carrier-oil-elixir-for-all-skin-types/.

126 Dr. Joshua Axe, "Jojoba Oil . . ." 127 Ibid.

128 Sayer Ji, "Why Cannabis is the Future of Medicine," GreenMedInfo, LLC, September 1, 2014, accessed on November 12, 2017, http://www.greenmedinfo.com/blog/why-cannnabis-future-medicine.

129 Ibid.

130 Wynne Armand, MD, "Marijuana: Health effects of recreational and medical use" Harvard Health Publishing, Harvard University, updated August 21, 2016, accessed on November 12, 2017, https://www.health.harvard.edu/blog/the-health-effects-of-marijuanafrom-recreational-and-medical-use-2016081910180.

131 "Understanding the Epidemic," Centers for Disease Control and Prevention, updated August 30, 2017, accessed on November 12, 2017, https://www.cdc.gov/drugoverdose/epidemic/index.html.

132 Wynne Armand, MD, "Marijuana . . ."

133 Sayer Ji, "Why Cannabis is the Future . . ."

134 "What is Medical Marijuana?" National Institute on Drug Abuse, revised April 2017, accessed on November 12, 2017, https://www.drugabuse.gov/publications/drugfacts/marijuana-medicine.

135 "Medicinal Cannabis and Its Effect on Human Health," Top Documentary Films, James Schmachtenberger (Executive Producer), Lindsey Ward (Director/Producer), Troy Brajkovich (Director of Photography), accessed on November 12, 2017, https://topdocumentaryfilms.com/medicinal-cannabis/.

136 Andrew Weil, MD, "Olive Oil for Pain Relief? Is it true that olive oil can help relieve pain?" Andrew Weil, MD, January 10, 2006, accessed November 12, 2017, https://www.drweil.com/health-wellness/ balanced-living/healthy-living/olive-oil-for-pain-relief/.

137 Nathan Gray, "Olive oil slashes risk of stroke: Study," June 16, 2011, accessed November 12, 2017, http://www.nutraingredients.com/ Research/Olive-oil-slashes-risk-of-stroke-Study.

138 Vineetha, "17 Amazing Benefits and Uses of Pomegranate Seed Oil," Health Beckon, January 17, 2014, accessed November 12, 2017, https://www.healthbeckon.com/pomegranate-seed-oil-benefits/.

139 Ibid.140 Ibid. 141 Eric Bakker N.D., "Pomegranate Oil," The Psoriasis Program, accessed November 12, 2017, http://www. thepsoriasisprogram.com/ pomegranate-oil/.

142 Sharon, "The Healing Benefits of Bath Salts," Natural Health Ezine, April 3, 2016, accessed November 12, 2017, http://naturalhealthezine. com/healing-benefits-of-bath-salts/.

143 Be Well Buzz staff, "The 5 Medicinal Salt Benefits for Body & Mind," Be Well Buzz, accessed November 12, 2017, https://www. bewellbuzz.com/wellness-buzz/medicinal-benefits-salt/.

144 "Test your knowledge of cosmetics safety: 8 myths debunked," Environmental Working Group, July 23, 2010, accessed November 13, 2017, https://www.ewg.org/enviroblog/2010/07/test-your-knowledg e-cosmetics-safety-8-myths-debunked#.WgoypXZrxLM.

145 "Endocrine Disruptor," Wikipedia, accessed November 13, 2017, https://en.wikipedia.org/wiki/Endocrine disruptor.

146 Sydney Lupkin, "Women Put an Average of 168 Chemicals on Their Bodies Each Day, Consumer Group Says," ABCNEWS, April 27, 2015, accessed November 13, 2017, http://abcnews.go.com/ Health/women-put-average-168-chemicals-bodies-day-consumer/ story?id=30615324.

147 "Test your knowledge . . ."

148 "Mercury Poisoning," Wikipedia, accessed November 13, 2017, https://en.wikipedia.org/wiki/Mercury poisoning.

149 "FDA warns consumers not to use skin products with mercury," FOX News Health, March 7, 2012, accessed November 13, 2017, http:// www.foxnews.com/health/2012/03/07/fda-warns-consumers-not-t o-use-skin-products-with-mercury.html.

150 "Ammonium Laureth Sulfate," EWG's Skin Deep® Cosmetics Database, Environmental Working Group, accessed November

13, 2017, https://www.ewg.org/skindeep/ingredient/700373/
AMMONIUM LAURETH SULFATE/#.Wgo5k3ZrxLM.

151 "The Dirty Dozen: Coal Tar Dyes," David Suzuki Foundation, accessed November 13, 2017, https://davidsuzuki.org/queen-of-green/ the-dirty-dozen-coal-tar-dyes/.

152 "The Dirty Dozen: Formaldehyde-releasing preservatives," David Suzuki Foundation, accessed on November 13, 2017, https://davidsuzuki.org/queen-of-green/dirty-dozen-formaldehyd e-releasing-preservatives/.

153 "The Dirty Dozen: Parfum (a.k.a. fragrance)," David Suzuki Foundation, accessed November 13, 2017, https://davidsuzuki.org/ queen-of-green/dirty-dozen-parfum-fragrance/.

154 Britta Aragon, "3 Key Reasons to Avoid Mineral Oil," April 28, 2014, accessed November 13, 2017, https://www.bewell.com/blog/ 3-key-reasons-to-avoid-mineral-oil/.

155 "The Dirty Dozen: Parabens," David Suzuki Foundation, accessed November 13, 2017, http://davidsuzuki.org/issues/health/science/ toxics/chemicals-in-your-cosmetics---parabens/.

156 Vanessa Cunningham, "10 Toxic Beauty Ingredients to Avoid," HuffPost, updated Jan 23, 2014, accessed November 13, 2017, https:// www.huffpost.com/entry/dangerous-beauty-products_b_4168587.

157 Vanessa Cunningham, "10 Toxic Beauty Ingredients . . ."

158 "Talc," Campaign for Safe Cosmetics, accessed November 13, 2017, http://www.safecosmetics.org/get-the-facts/chemicals-of-concern/ talc/.

159 Terry White, "How Big Is the Candle Industry?" Chron, Hearst Newspapers, LLC, accessed November 13, 2017, http://smallbusiness. chron.com/big-candle-industry-69541.html.

160 Emily Main, "Study: Candle Chemicals Pollute Indoor Air New study finds candles may muck up your indoor air quality," Rodale Wellness, August 25, 2009, accessed November 13, 2017, https:// www.rodalewellness.com/living-well/candles-and-indoor-air-quality.

161 C. Lau, H. Fiedler, O. Hutzinger, K.H. Schwind, J. Hosseinpour, "Levels of selected organic compounds in materials for candle production and human exposure to candle emissions (1997)," National Center for Biotechnology Information, U.S. National Library of

Medicine, National Institutes of Health, accessed November 13, 2017, www.ncbi.nlm.nih.gov/pubmed/9134692.

162 September 14, 2012, accessed November 13, 2017, https:// empoweredsustenance.com/soy-vs-beeswax-candles/.

163 "Wayne Dyer Quotes," BrainyQuote, accessed November 13, 2017, www.brainyquote.com/quotes/quotes/w/waynedyer718093.html.

164 "The Wisdom of Mother Teresa," Beliefnet Inc., accessed November 13, 2017, http://www.beliefnet.com/prayables/quote-galleries/ mother-teresa-quotes.aspx?p=3.

165 "Lao Tzu quotes," Thinkexist.com, accessed November 13, 2017, http://thinkexist.com/quotation/knowing others is wisdomknowing yourself is/148363.html.

166 LetusQuote.com, accessed November 13, 2017, https://www. brainyquote.com/quotes/wayne_dyer_718026.

167 Lisa Hill DiFusco, "The Spark Within," The Lightheart Institute, April 18, 2013, accessed November 13, 2017, www.lightheart.com/ the-spark-within/.

168 Joshua Boorman, "The Best Life Advice Ever," Place of Persistence, accessed November 13, 2017, http://placeofpersistence.com/ the-best- life-advice/.

169 Oprah Winfrey, "What I Know for Sure," Oprah.com, accessed November 13, 2017, www.oprah.com/omagazine/ what-i-know-for- sure-oprah-winfrey/all.

170 Aimeelovesyou, "Don Miguel Ruiz: The Real You," Sunday Is For Lovers by Aimeelovesyou, April 23, 2017, accessed November 13, 2017, https://sundayisforlovers.wordpress.com/tag/ don-miguel-ruiz-quotes/.

171 Garson O'Toole, "Forgiveness Is the Fragrance the Violet Sheds on the Heel That Has Crushed It," Quote Investigator, accessed November 13,2017, https://quoteinvestigator.com/about/.

172 Denis Waitly, DailyGood, accessed November 13, 2017, www. dailygood.org/search/quote/happiness/.

173 Treehugger, October 6, 2016, accessed November 13, 2017, https:// www.treehugger.com/natural-sciences/how-do-palm-trees-survive- hurricanes.html.

174 Ibid.

175 Eckhart Tolle, The Power of Now A Guide to SPIRITUAL ENLIGHTENMENT, accessed November 13, 2017, https://brahmstalks.files.wordpress.com/2016/05/the-power-of-now.pdf.

176 Dr. Wayne Dyer, "Embracing Silence," Dr. Wayne D. Dyer, accessed on November 15, 2017, www.drwaynedyer.com/blog/embracing-silence.

177 Neville Goddard, The Power of Awareness, accessed on November 15, 2017, http://www.thepowerofawareness.org/chapter-seventeen.

178 Guy Ballard, "I AM: The Full Activity of God (Psychic and Spiritual Protection)," Return of the Saviors, YouTube, February 28, 2017, accessed on November 15, 2017, https://www.youtube.com/watch?v=KYE2p7LKi8k.

179 Dr. Wayne Dyer, Dr. Wayne W. Dyer, Facebook, September 28, 2010, accessed on November 15, 2017, https://www.facebook.com/drwaynedyer/posts/164245320256828.

180 Master Saint Germain through Godfre Ray King, "I AM Discourses," Healing Energy Tools, accessed on November 15, 2017, www.healingenergytools.com/iam/.

181 Dr. Wayne D. Dyer, Dr. Wayne D. Dyer, Facebook, May 21, 2014, accessed on November 15, 2017, www.facebook.com/drwaynedyer/posts/10152414279206030.

182 AJ Adams, MAPP, "Seeing Is Believing: The Power of Visualization," Psychology Today, December 3, 2009, accessed on November 15, 2017, https://www.psychologytoday.com/blog/flourish/200912/seeing-is-believing-the-power-visualization.

183 Neville Goddard, "Neville Goddard on Manifesting Now," Apply the Law of Attraction, accessed on November 15, 2017, www.applythelawofattraction.com/neville-goddard-quotes-manifesting-now/.

CPSIA information can be obtained
at www.ICGtesting.com
Printed in the USA
BVHW032319140119
537850BV00001B/91/P